ERSTWHILE

Untold Tales from the Brothers Grimm

Adapted by

Gina Biggs, Louisa Roy, Elle Skinner

ErstwhileTales.com

First printing: September 2012

Published by Strawberry Comics LLC

ISBN: 978-0-9856195-0-3

Printed in Canada

Maid Maleen

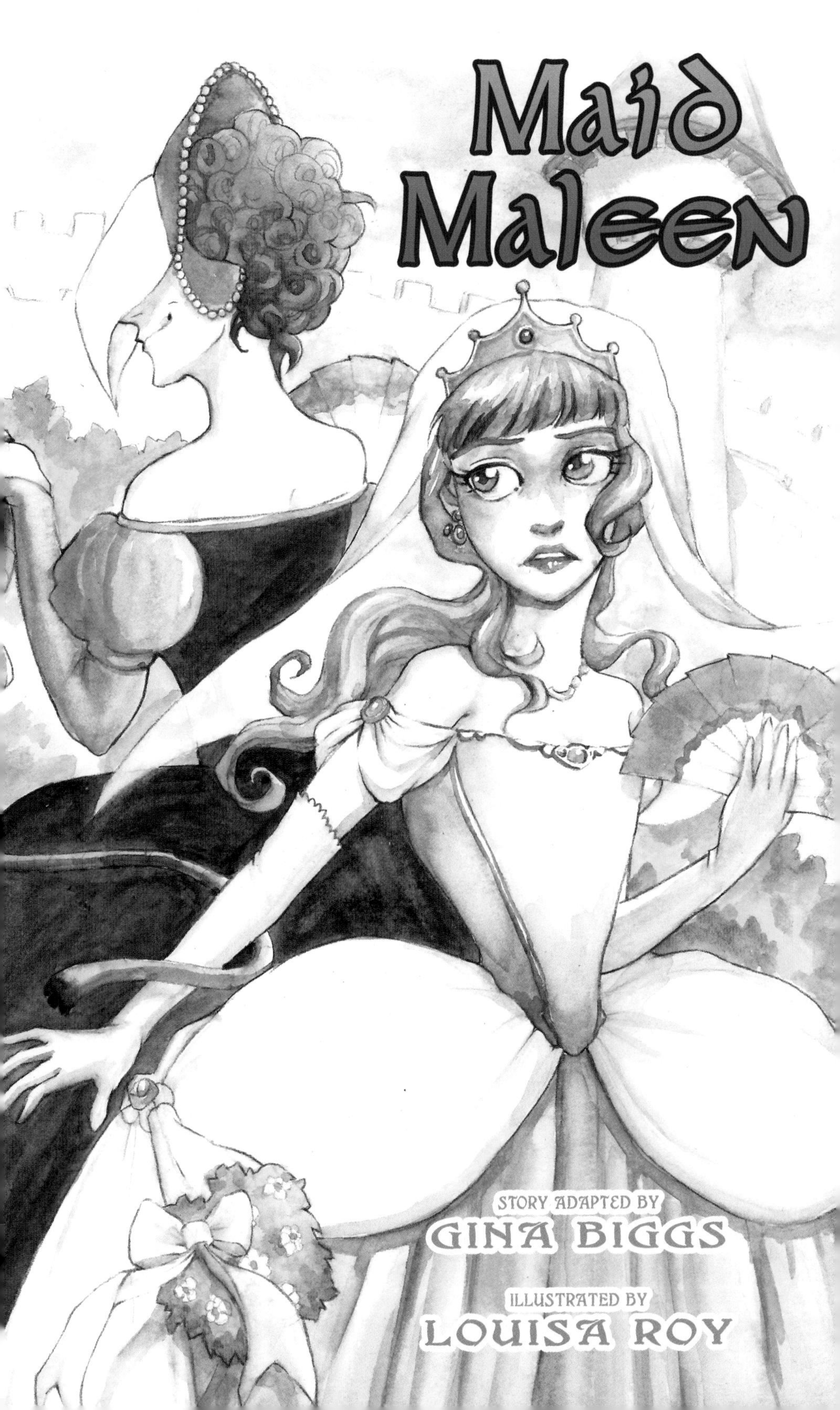

STORY ADAPTED BY
GINA BIGGS

ILLUSTRATED BY
LOUISA ROY

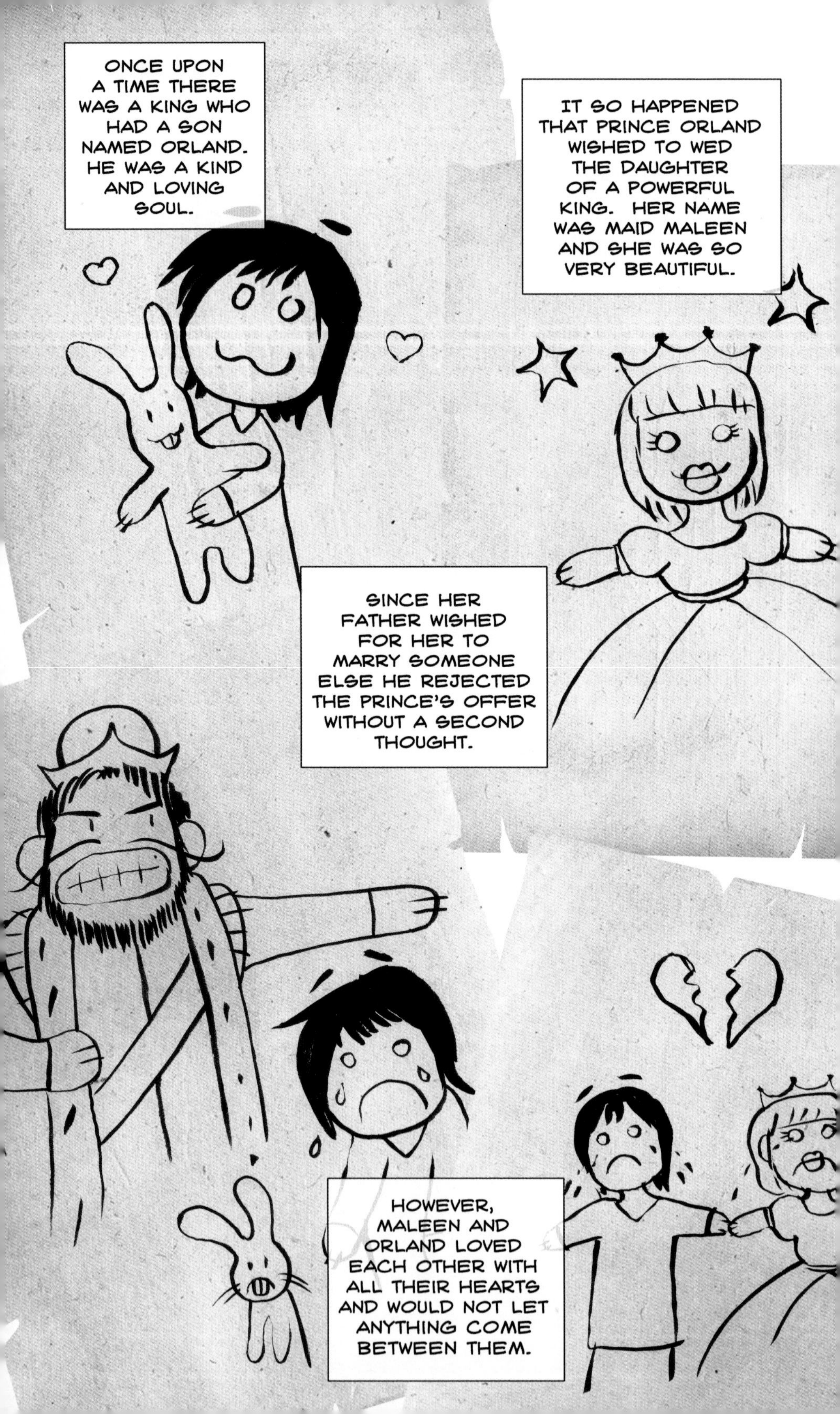
ONCE UPON A TIME THERE WAS A KING WHO HAD A SON NAMED ORLAND. HE WAS A KIND AND LOVING SOUL.
IT SO HAPPENED THAT PRINCE ORLAND WISHED TO WED THE DAUGHTER OF A POWERFUL KING. HER NAME WAS MAID MALEEN AND SHE WAS SO VERY BEAUTIFUL.
SINCE HER FATHER WISHED FOR HER TO MARRY SOMEONE ELSE HE REJECTED THE PRINCE'S OFFER WITHOUT A SECOND THOUGHT.
HOWEVER, MALEEN AND ORLAND LOVED EACH OTHER WITH ALL THEIR HEARTS AND WOULD NOT LET ANYTHING COME BETWEEN THEM.

ERSTWHILE

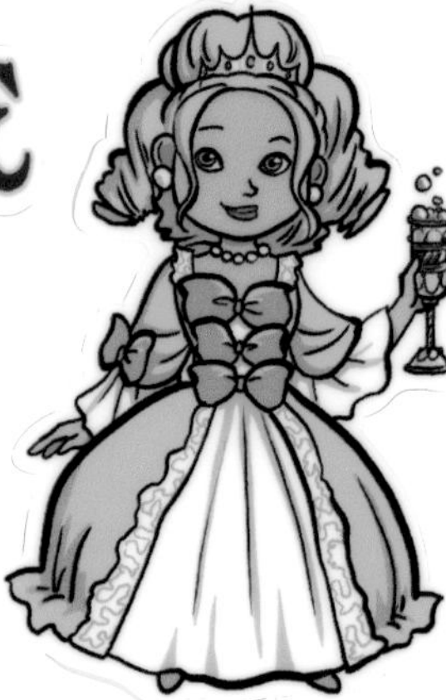

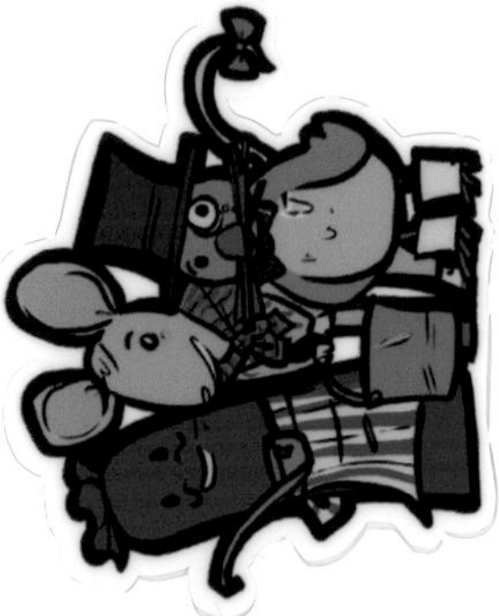

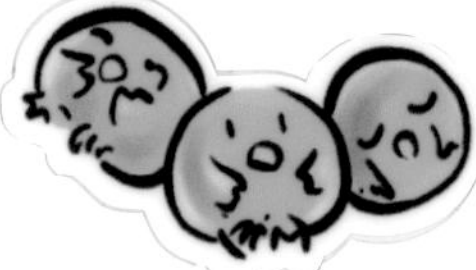

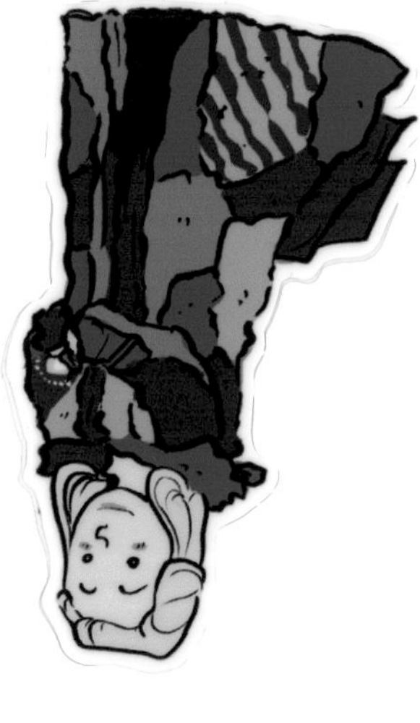

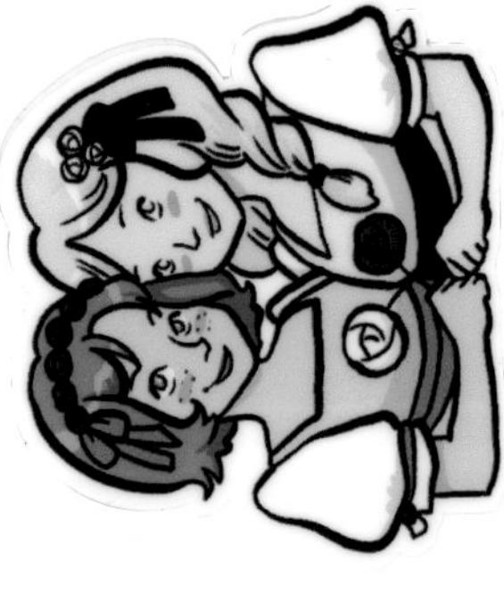

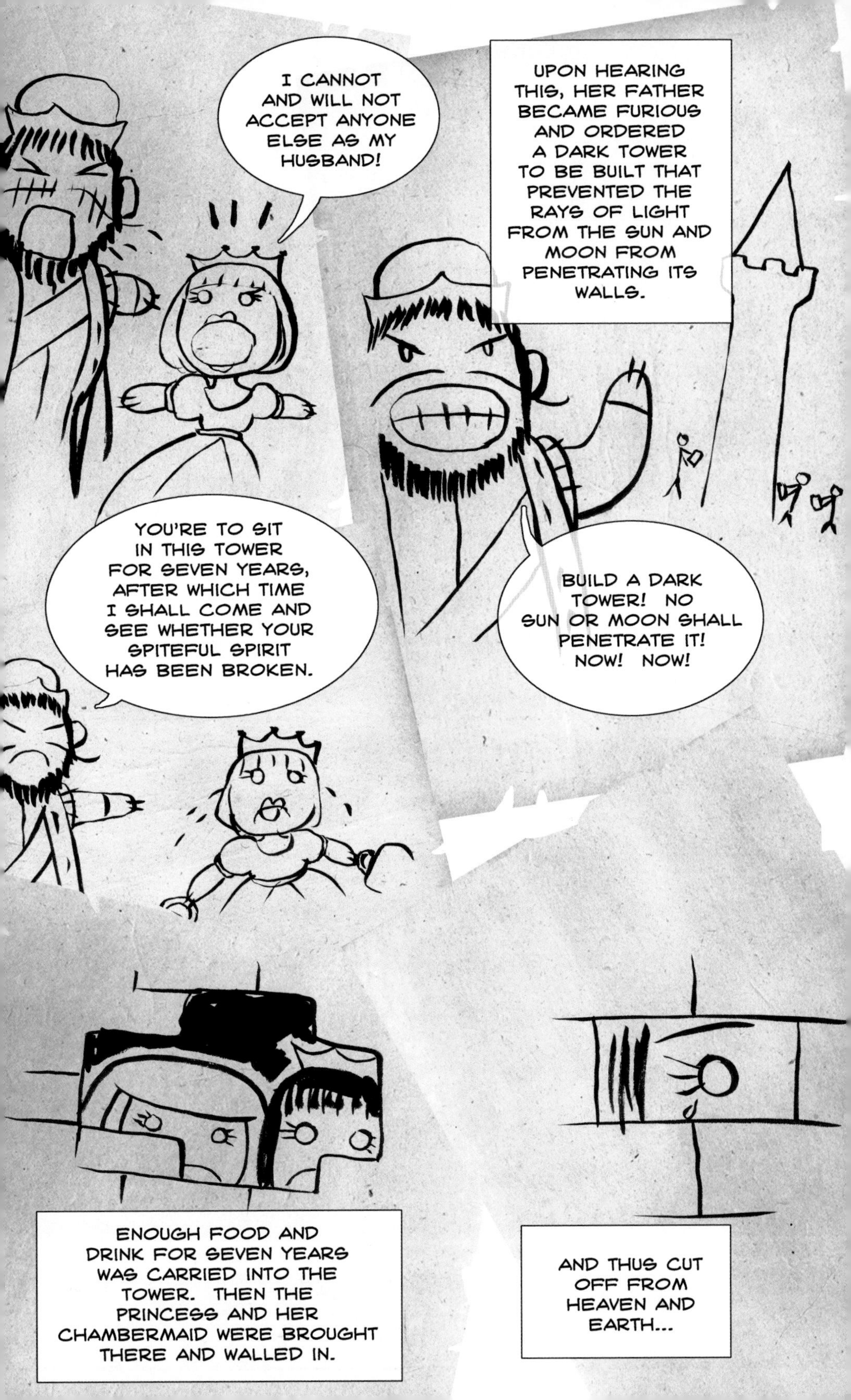
I CANNOT AND WILL NOT ACCEPT ANYONE ELSE AS MY HUSBAND!
UPON HEARING THIS, HER FATHER BECAME FURIOUS AND ORDERED A DARK TOWER TO BE BUILT THAT PREVENTED THE RAYS OF LIGHT FROM THE SUN AND MOON FROM PENETRATING ITS WALLS.
BUILD A DARK TOWER! NO SUN OR MOON SHALL PENETRATE IT! NOW! NOW!
YOU'RE TO SIT IN THIS TOWER FOR SEVEN YEARS, AFTER WHICH TIME I SHALL COME AND SEE WHETHER YOUR SPITEFUL SPIRIT HAS BEEN BROKEN.
ENOUGH FOOD AND DRINK FOR SEVEN YEARS WAS CARRIED INTO THE TOWER. THEN THE PRINCESS AND HER CHAMBERMAID WERE BROUGHT THERE AND WALLED IN.
AND THUS CUT OFF FROM HEAVEN AND EARTH...

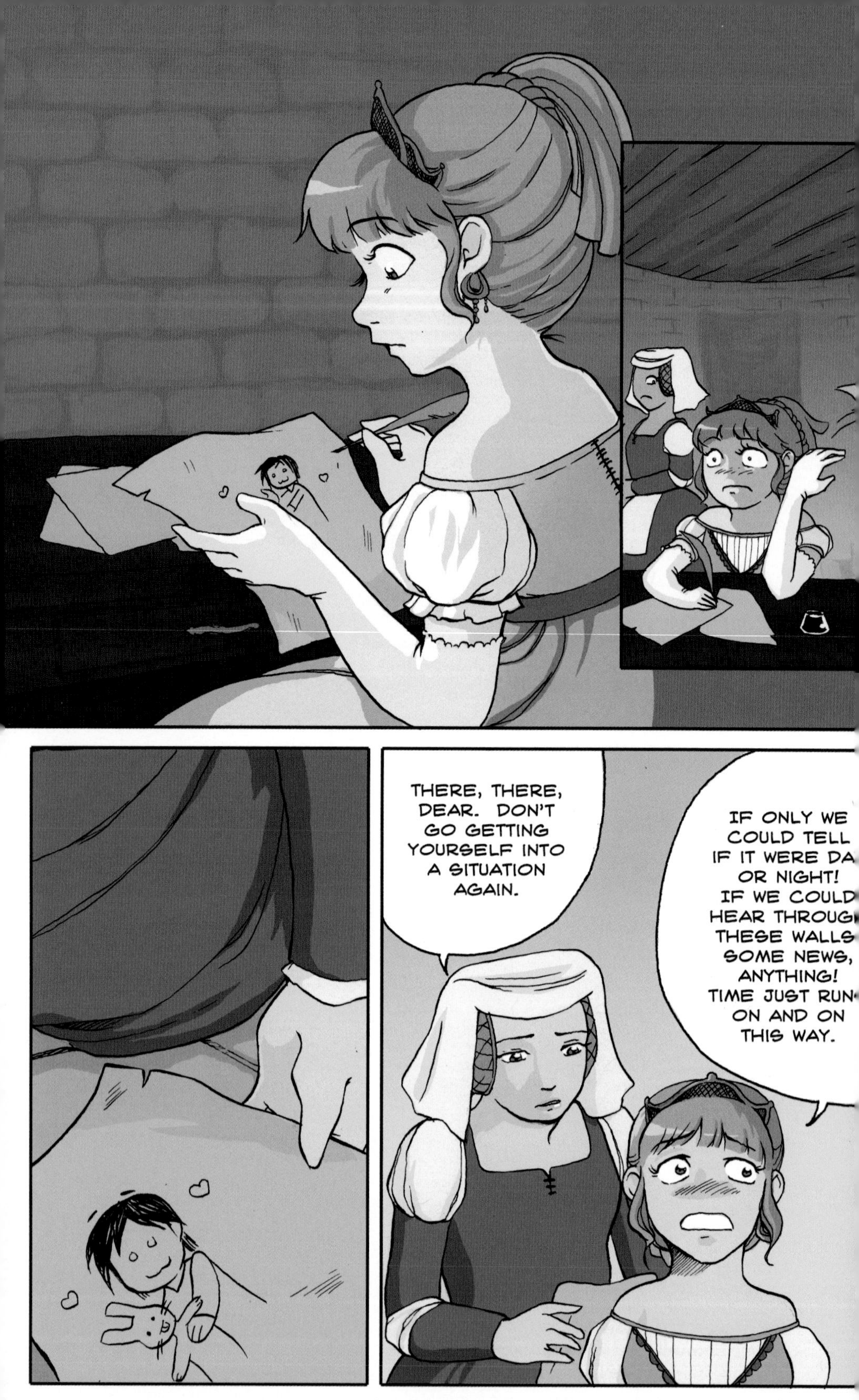

THERE, THERE, DEAR. DON'T GO GETTING YOURSELF INTO A SITUATION AGAIN.
IF ONLY WE COULD TELL IF IT WERE DA OR NIGHT! IF WE COULD HEAR THROUG THESE WALLS SOME NEWS, ANYTHING! TIME JUST RUN ON AND ON THIS WAY.

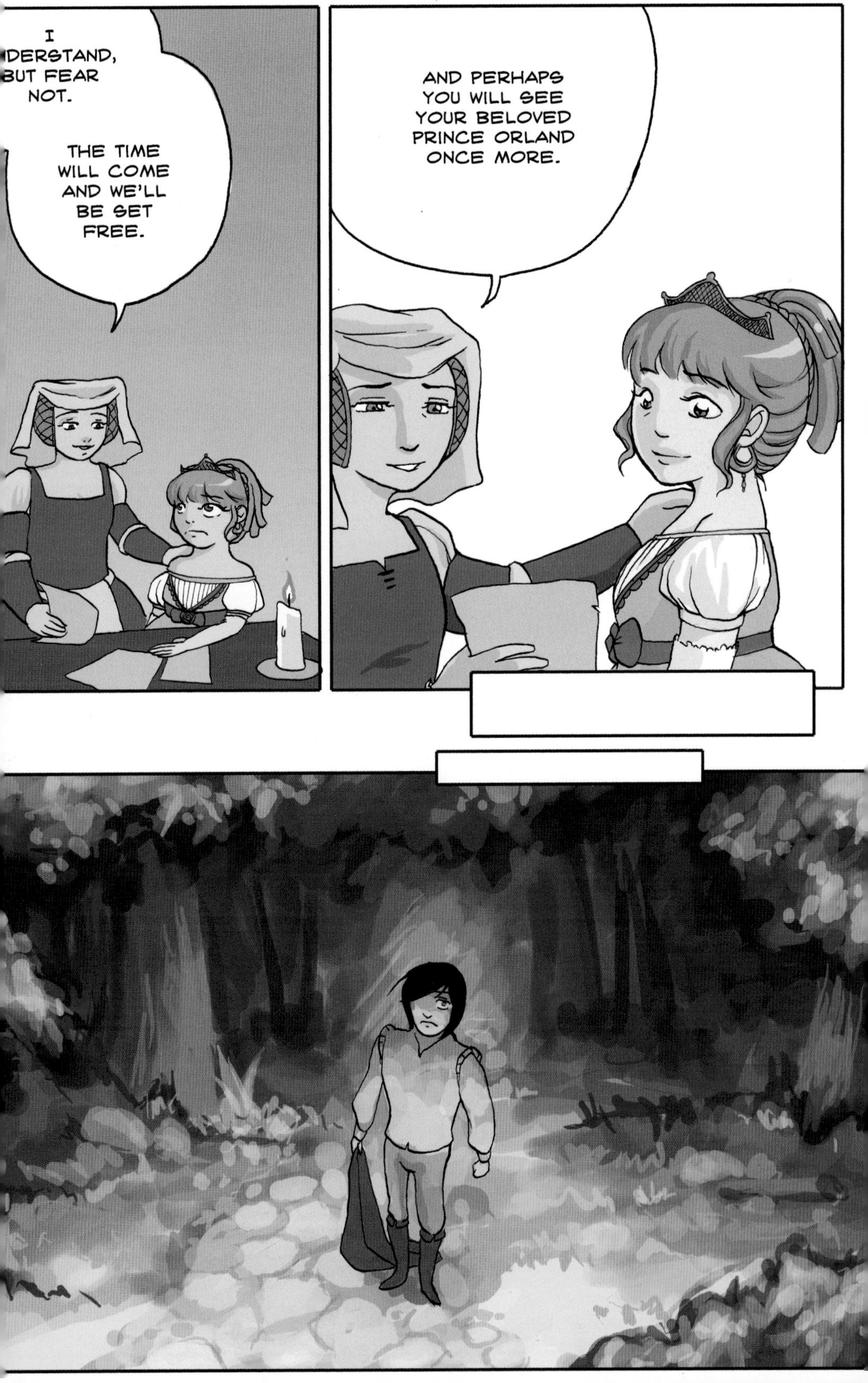
I DERSTAND, BUT FEAR NOT.
THE TIME WILL COME AND WE'LL BE SET FREE.
AND PERHAPS YOU WILL SEE YOUR BELOVED PRINCE ORLAND ONCE MORE.

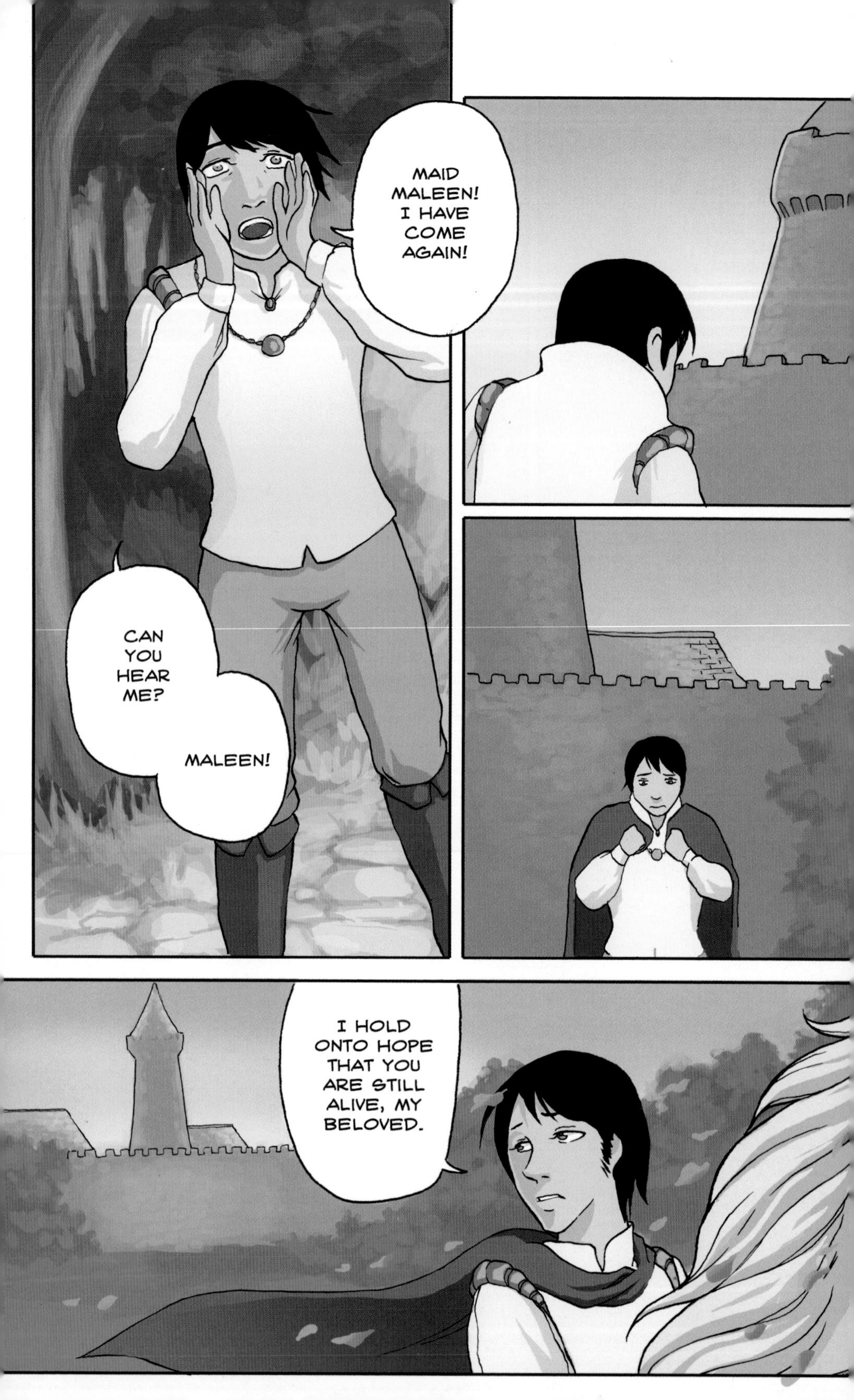
MAID MALEEN! I HAVE COME AGAIN!
CAN YOU HEAR ME?
MALEEN!
I HOLD ONTO HOPE THAT YOU ARE STILL ALIVE, MY BELOVED.

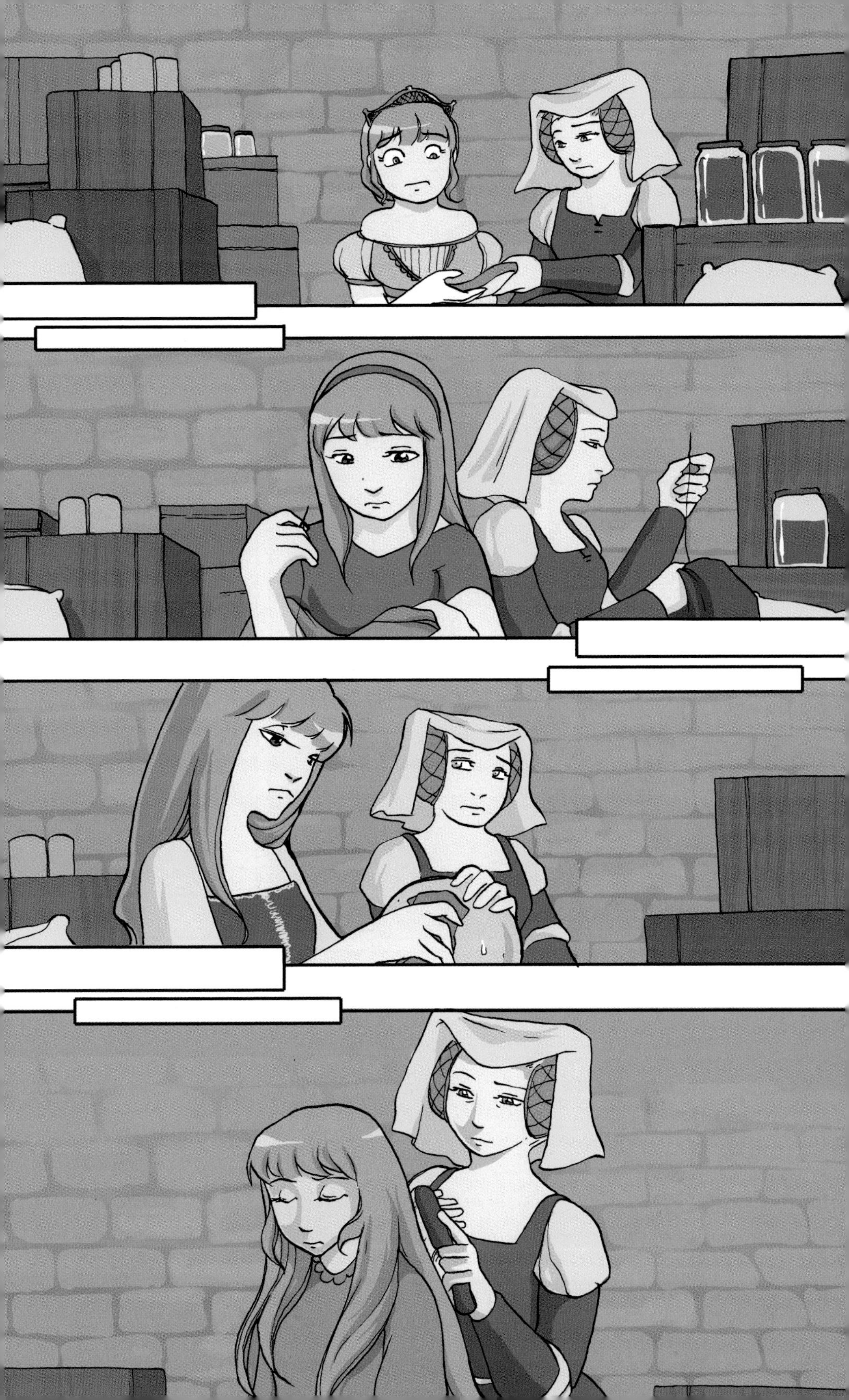

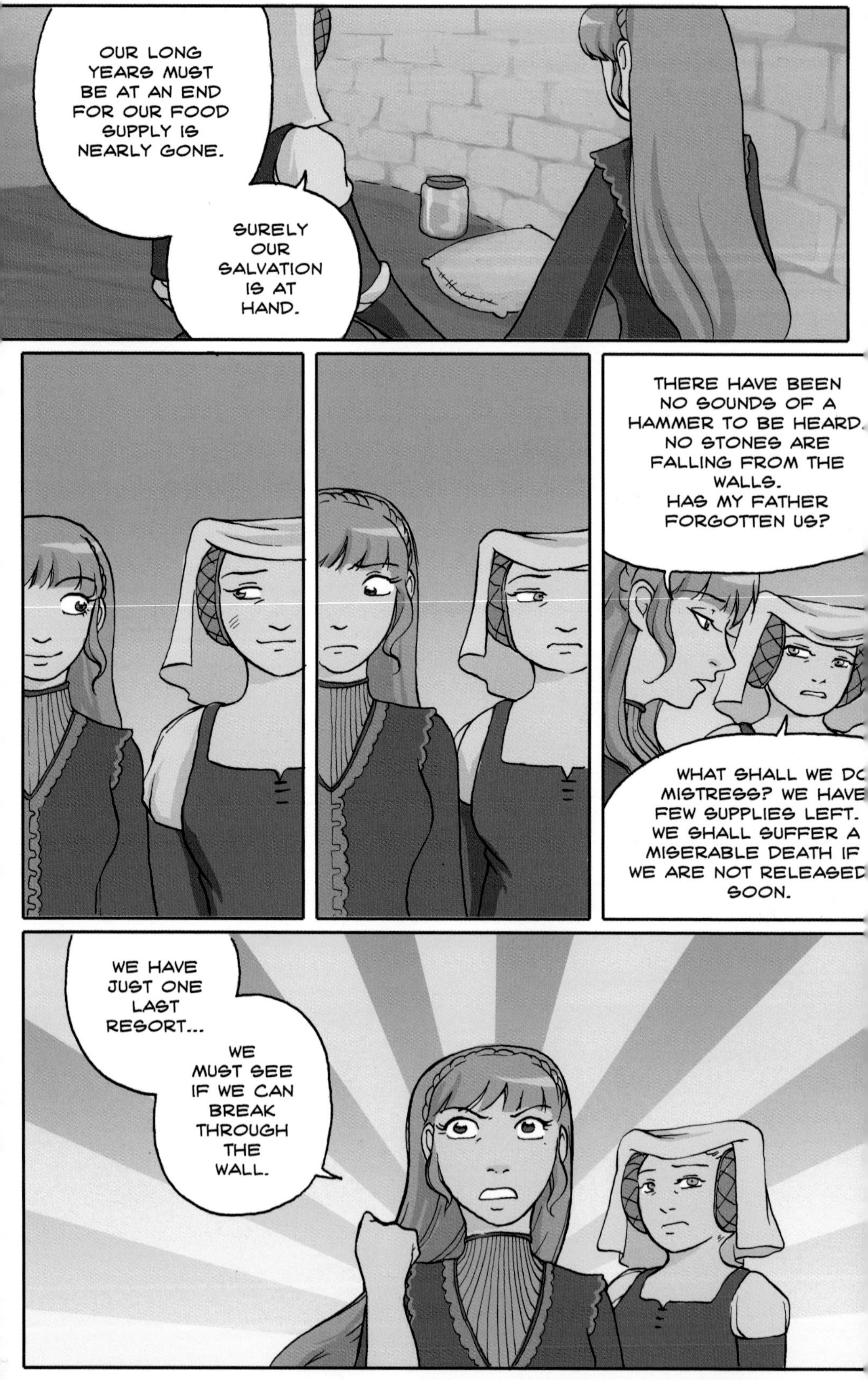

OUR LONG YEARS MUST BE AT AN END FOR OUR FOOD SUPPLY IS NEARLY GONE.
SURELY OUR SALVATION IS AT HAND.
THERE HAVE BEEN NO SOUNDS OF A HAMMER TO BE HEARD. NO STONES ARE FALLING FROM THE WALLS. HAS MY FATHER FORGOTTEN US?
WHAT SHALL WE DO MISTRESS? WE HAVE FEW SUPPLIES LEFT. WE SHALL SUFFER A MISERABLE DEATH IF WE ARE NOT RELEASED SOON.
WE HAVE JUST ONE LAST RESORT...
WE MUST SEE IF WE CAN BREAK THROUGH THE WALL.

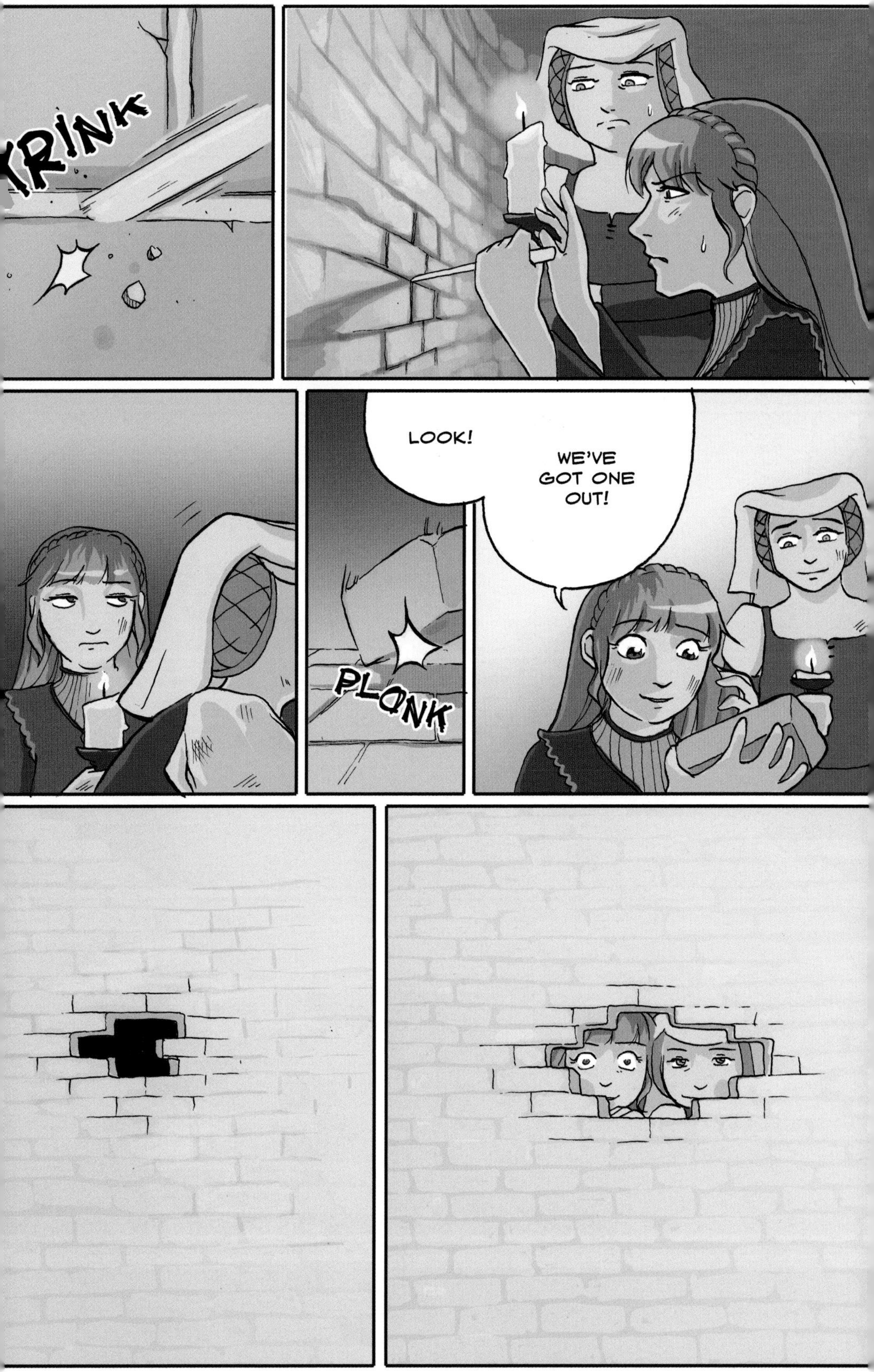

TRINK
LOOK!
WE'VE GOT ONE OUT!
PLONK

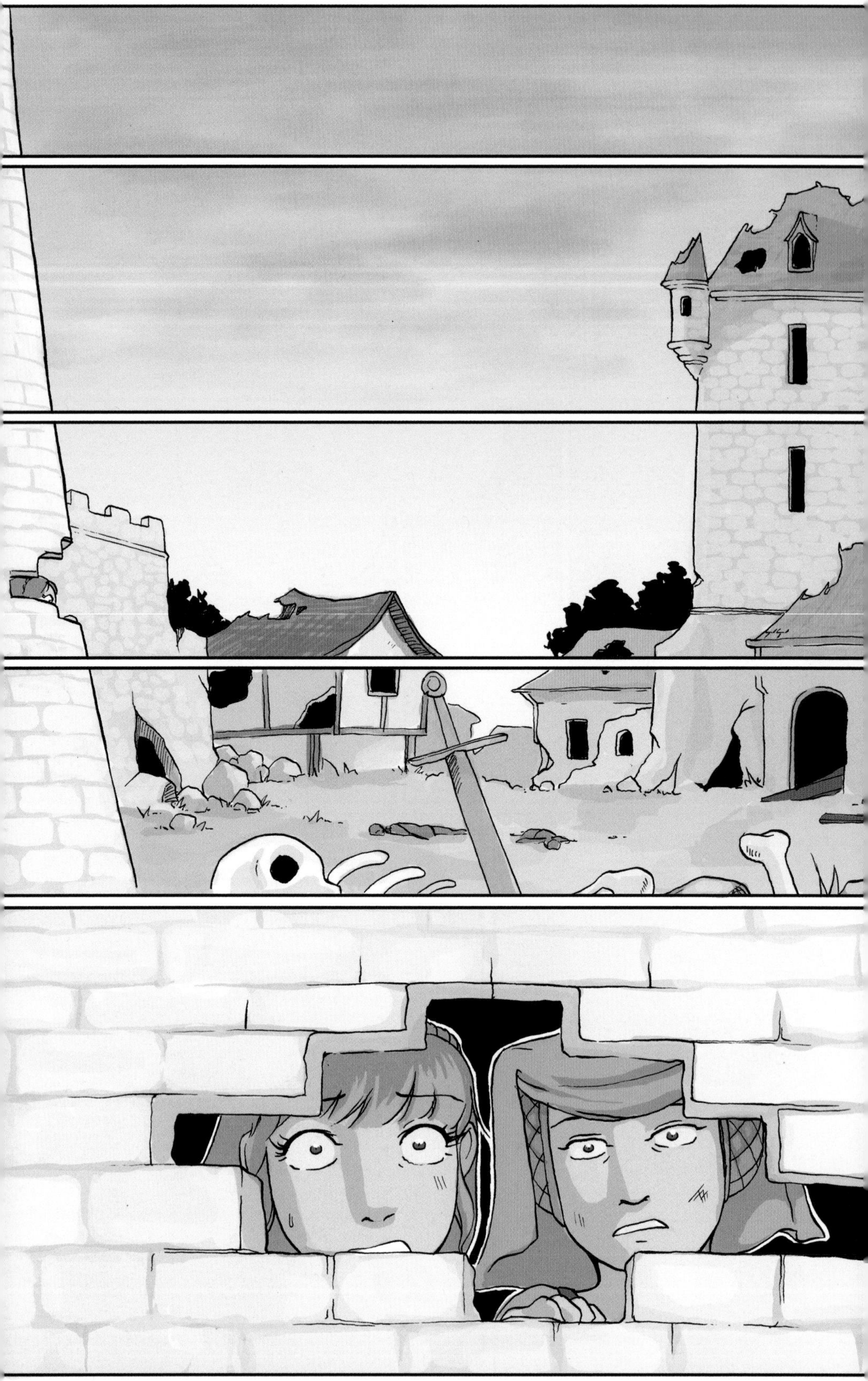

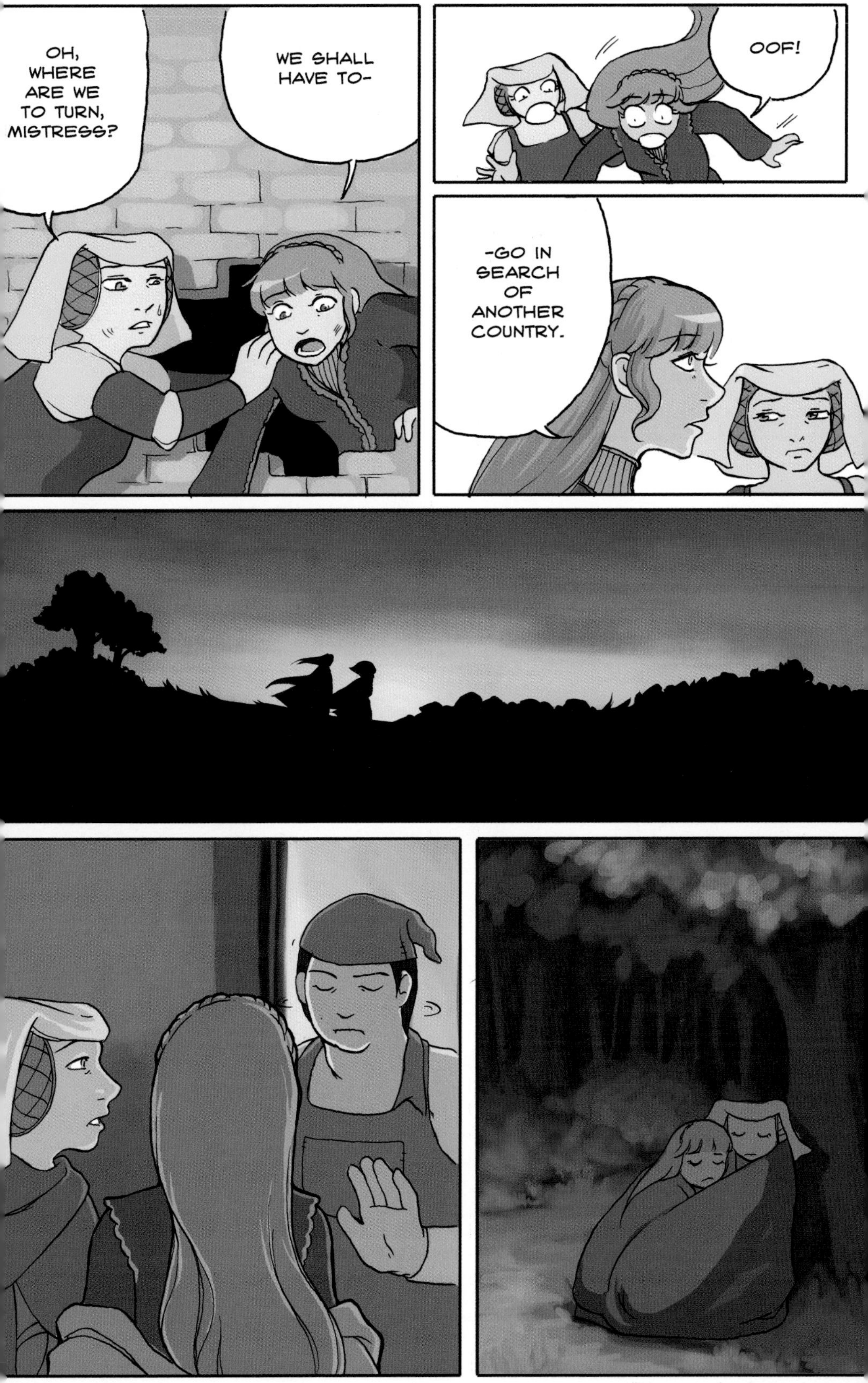
OH, WHERE ARE WE TO TURN, MISTRESS?
WE SHALL HAVE TO-
OOF!
-GO IN SEARCH OF ANOTHER COUNTRY.

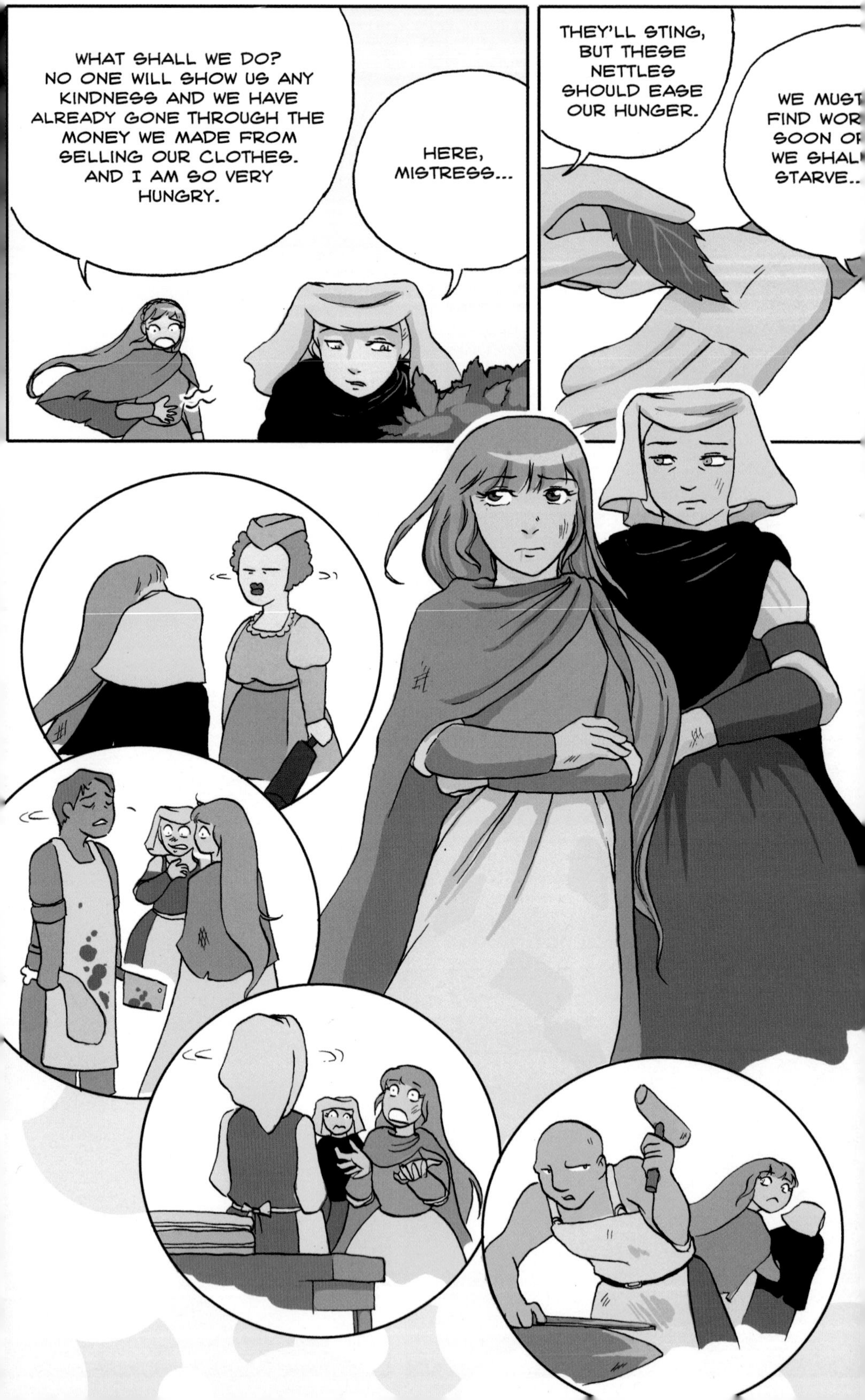
WHAT SHALL WE DO? NO ONE WILL SHOW US ANY KINDNESS AND WE HAVE ALREADY GONE THROUGH THE MONEY WE MADE FROM SELLING OUR CLOTHES. AND I AM SO VERY HUNGRY.
HERE, MISTRESS...
THEY'LL STING, BUT THESE NETTLES SHOULD EASE OUR HUNGER.
WE MUST FIND WOR SOON OF WE SHAL STARVE..

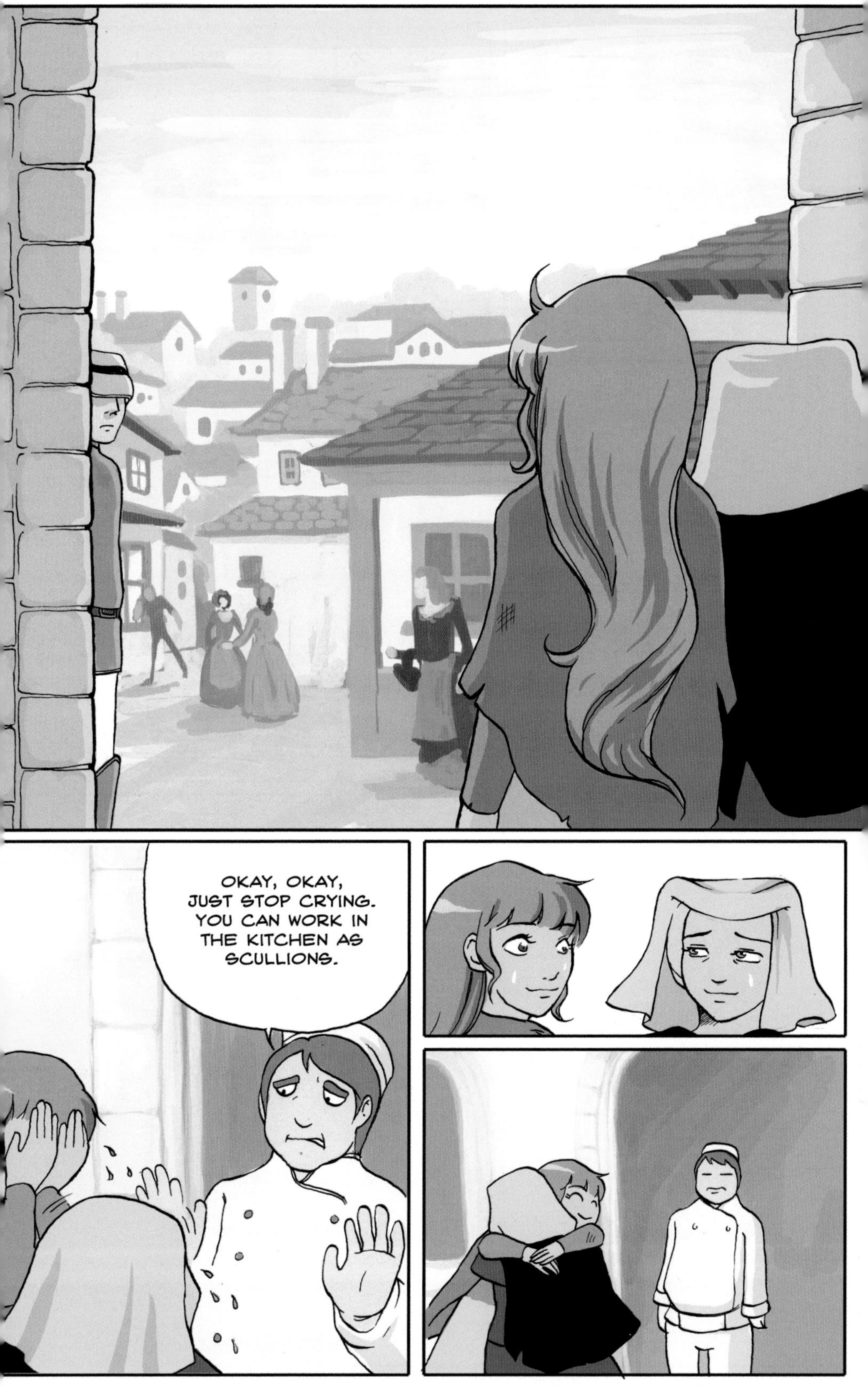
OKAY, OKAY, JUST STOP CRYING. YOU CAN WORK IN THE KITCHEN AS SCULLIONS.

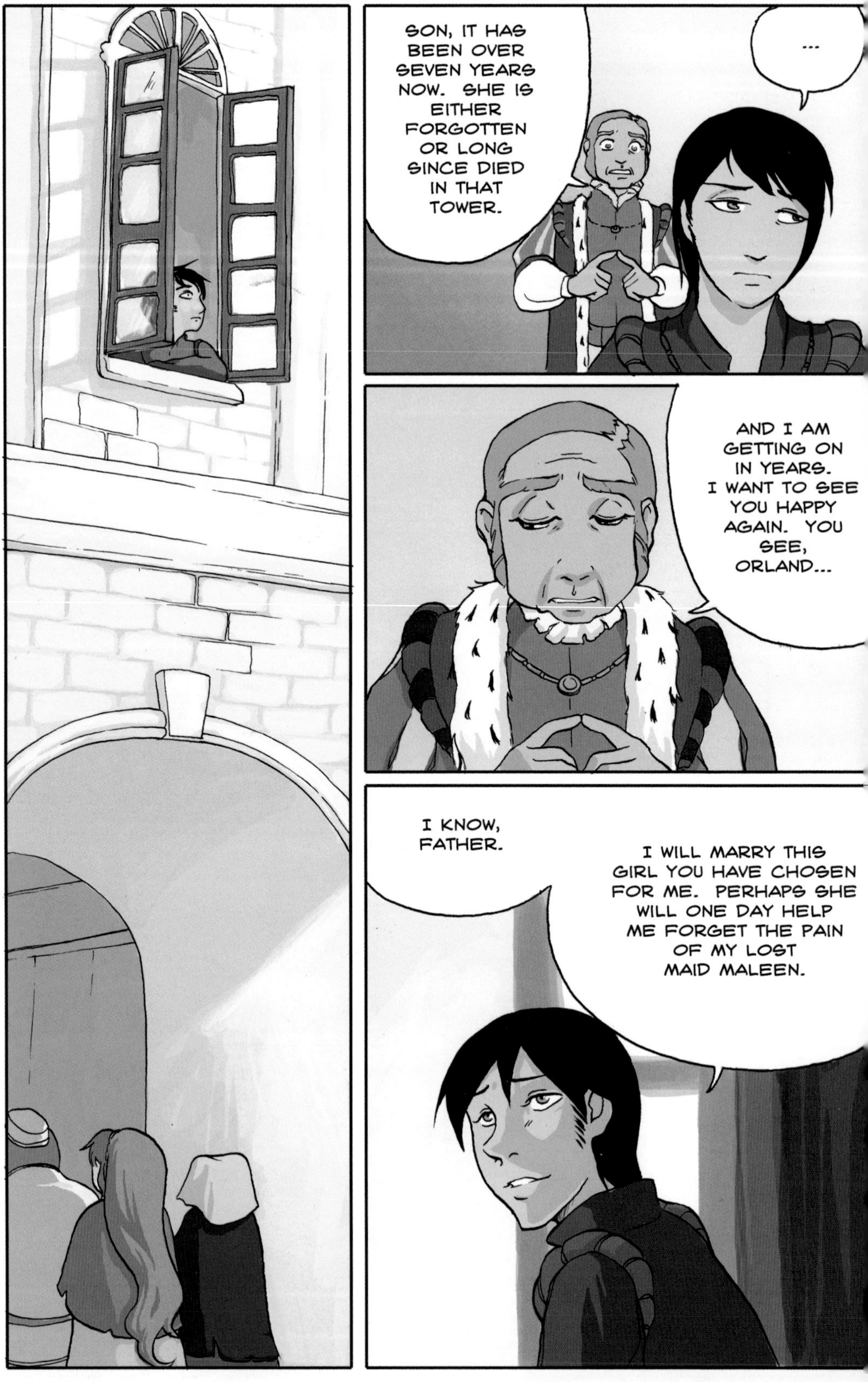
SON, IT HAS BEEN OVER SEVEN YEARS NOW. SHE IS EITHER FORGOTTEN OR LONG SINCE DIED IN THAT TOWER.
...
AND I AM GETTING ON IN YEARS. I WANT TO SEE YOU HAPPY AGAIN. YOU SEE, ORLAND...
I KNOW, FATHER.
I WILL MARRY THIS GIRL YOU HAVE CHOSEN FOR ME. PERHAPS SHE WILL ONE DAY HELP ME FORGET THE PAIN OF MY LOST MAID MALEEN.

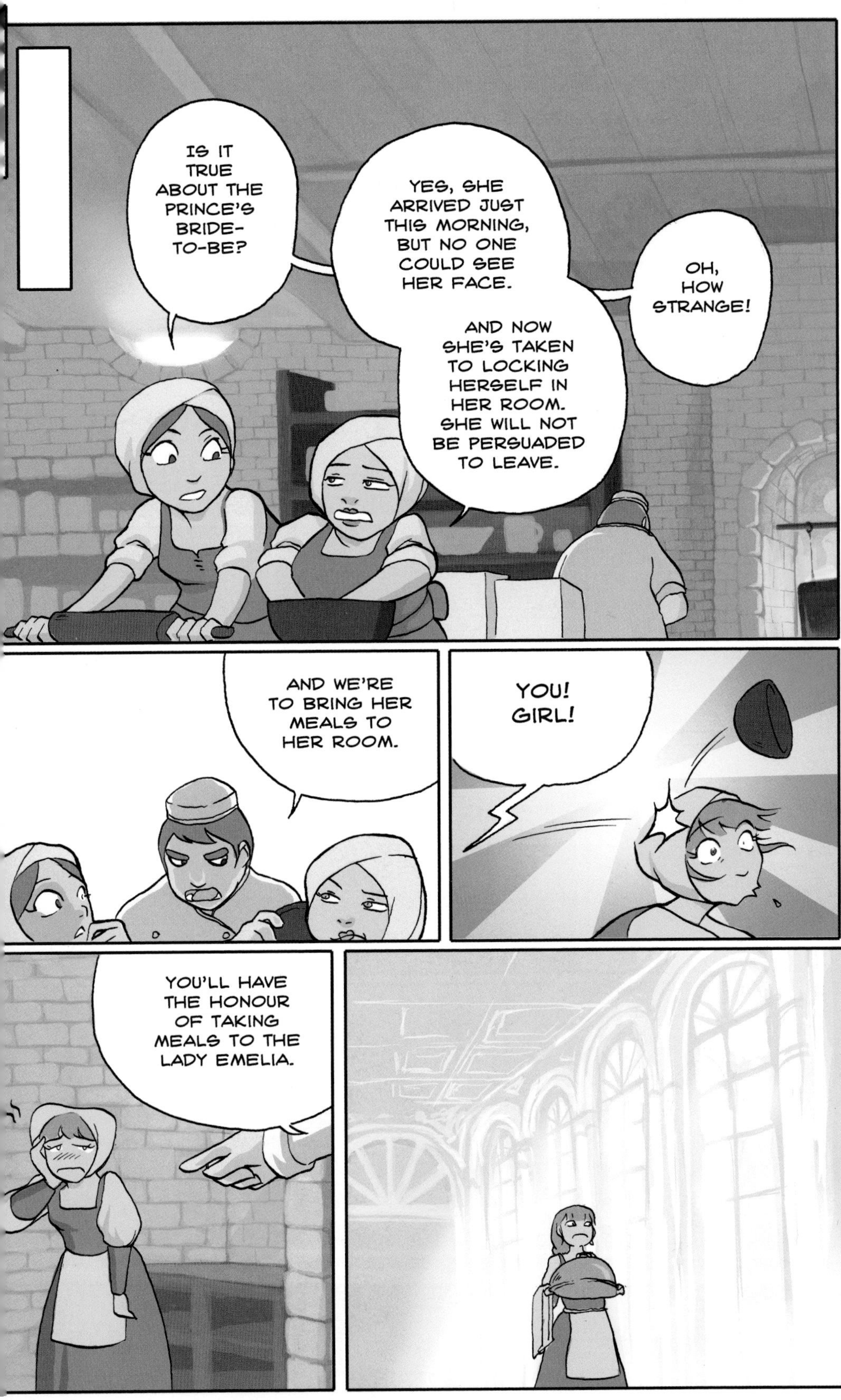
IS IT TRUE ABOUT THE PRINCE'S BRIDE-TO-BE?
YES, SHE ARRIVED JUST THIS MORNING, BUT NO ONE COULD SEE HER FACE.
AND NOW SHE'S TAKEN TO LOCKING HERSELF IN HER ROOM. SHE WILL NOT BE PERSUADED TO LEAVE.
OH, HOW STRANGE!
AND WE'RE TO BRING HER MEALS TO HER ROOM.
YOU! GIRL!
YOU'LL HAVE THE HONOUR OF TAKING MEALS TO THE LADY EMELIA.

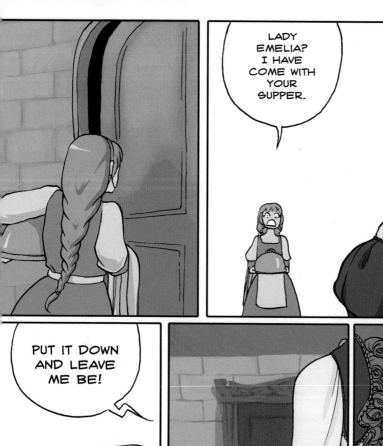

LADY EMELIA? I HAVE COME WITH YOUR SUPPER.

PUT IT DOWN AND LEAVE ME BE!

WHEW...

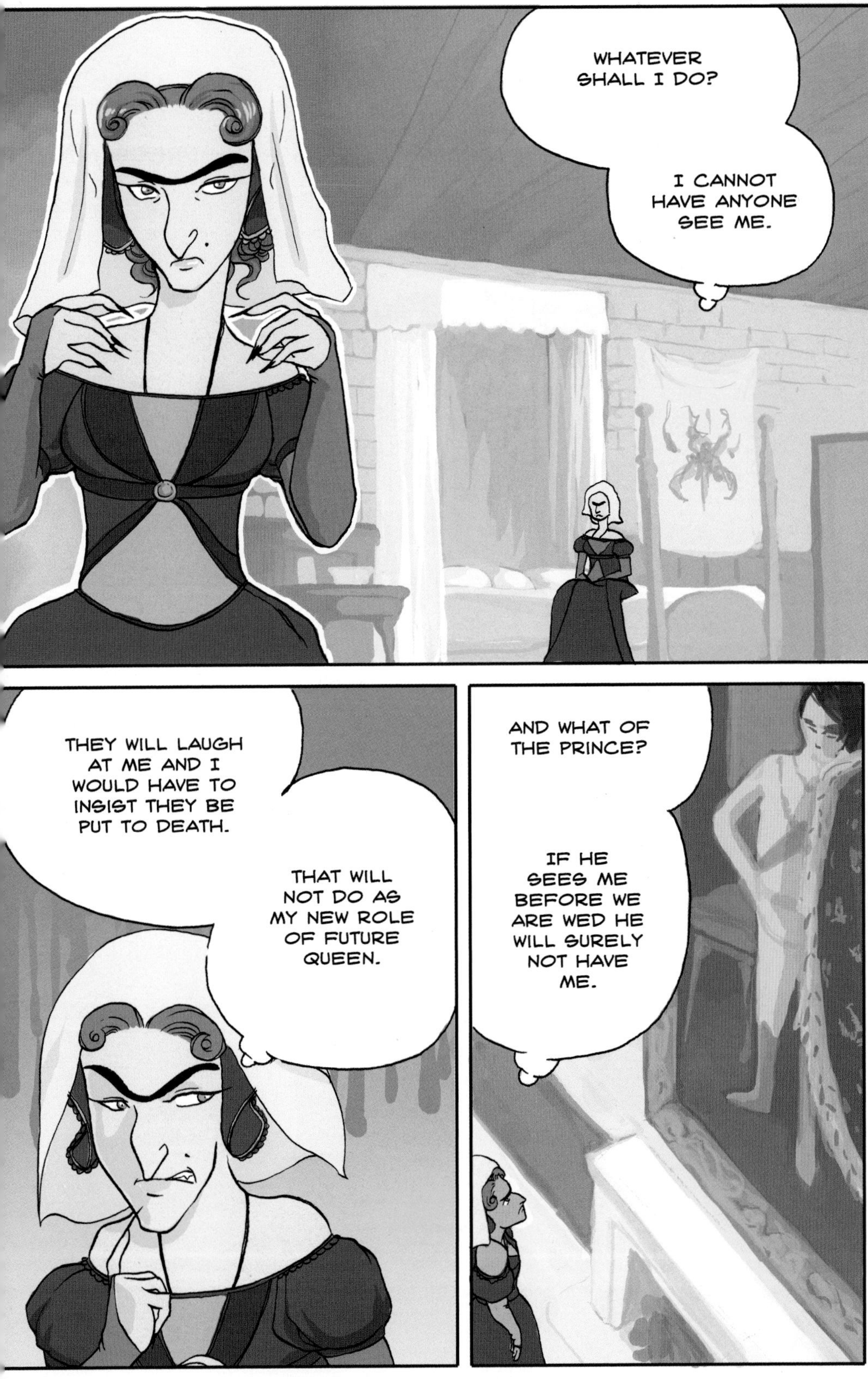
WHATEVER SHALL I DO?
I CANNOT HAVE ANYONE SEE ME.
THEY WILL LAUGH AT ME AND I WOULD HAVE TO INSIST THEY BE PUT TO DEATH.
THAT WILL NOT DO AS MY NEW ROLE OF FUTURE QUEEN.
AND WHAT OF THE PRINCE?
IF HE SEES ME BEFORE WE ARE WED HE WILL SURELY NOT HAVE ME.

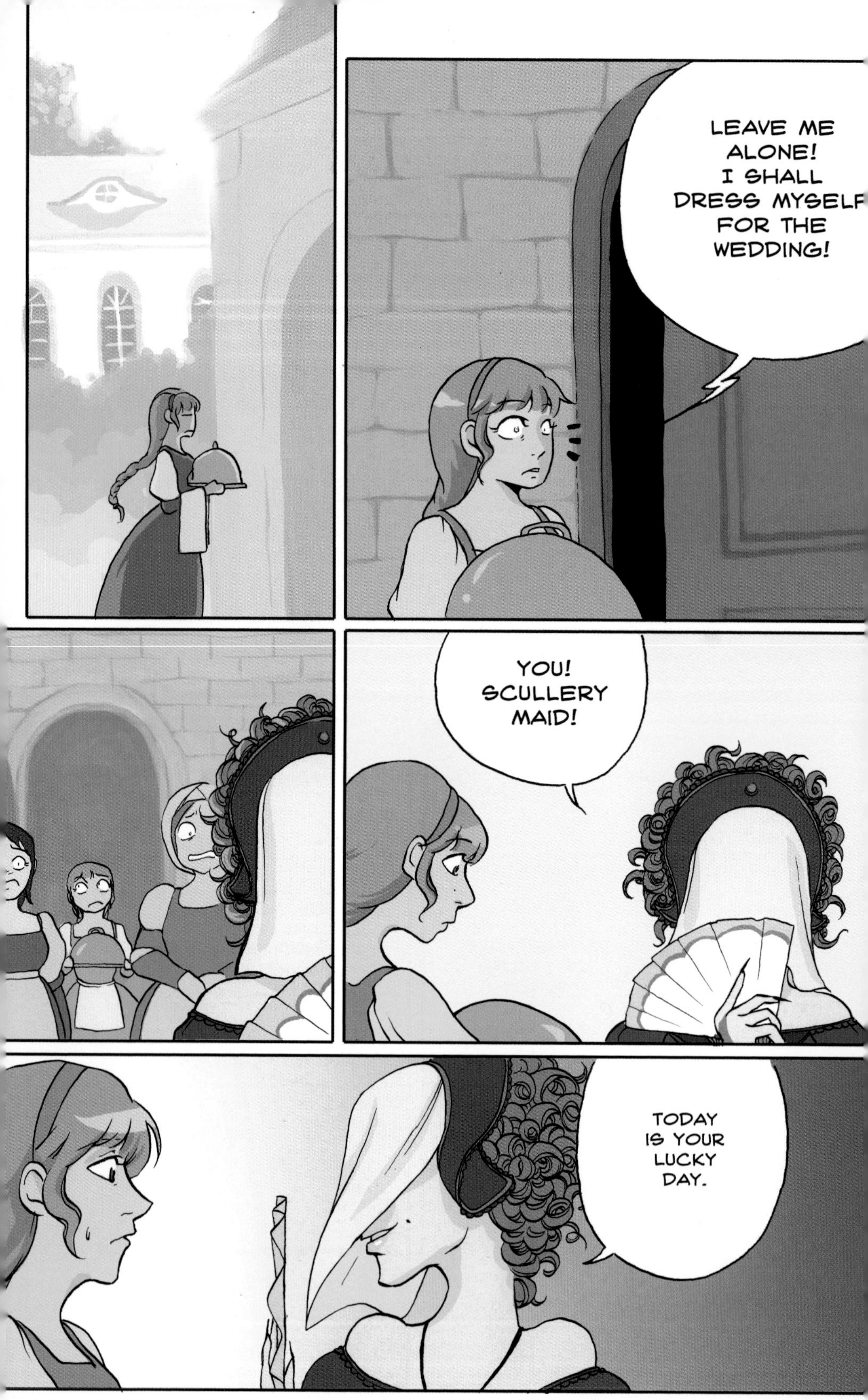
LEAVE ME ALONE! I SHALL DRESS MYSELF FOR THE WEDDING!
YOU! SCULLERY MAID!
TODAY IS YOUR LUCKY DAY.

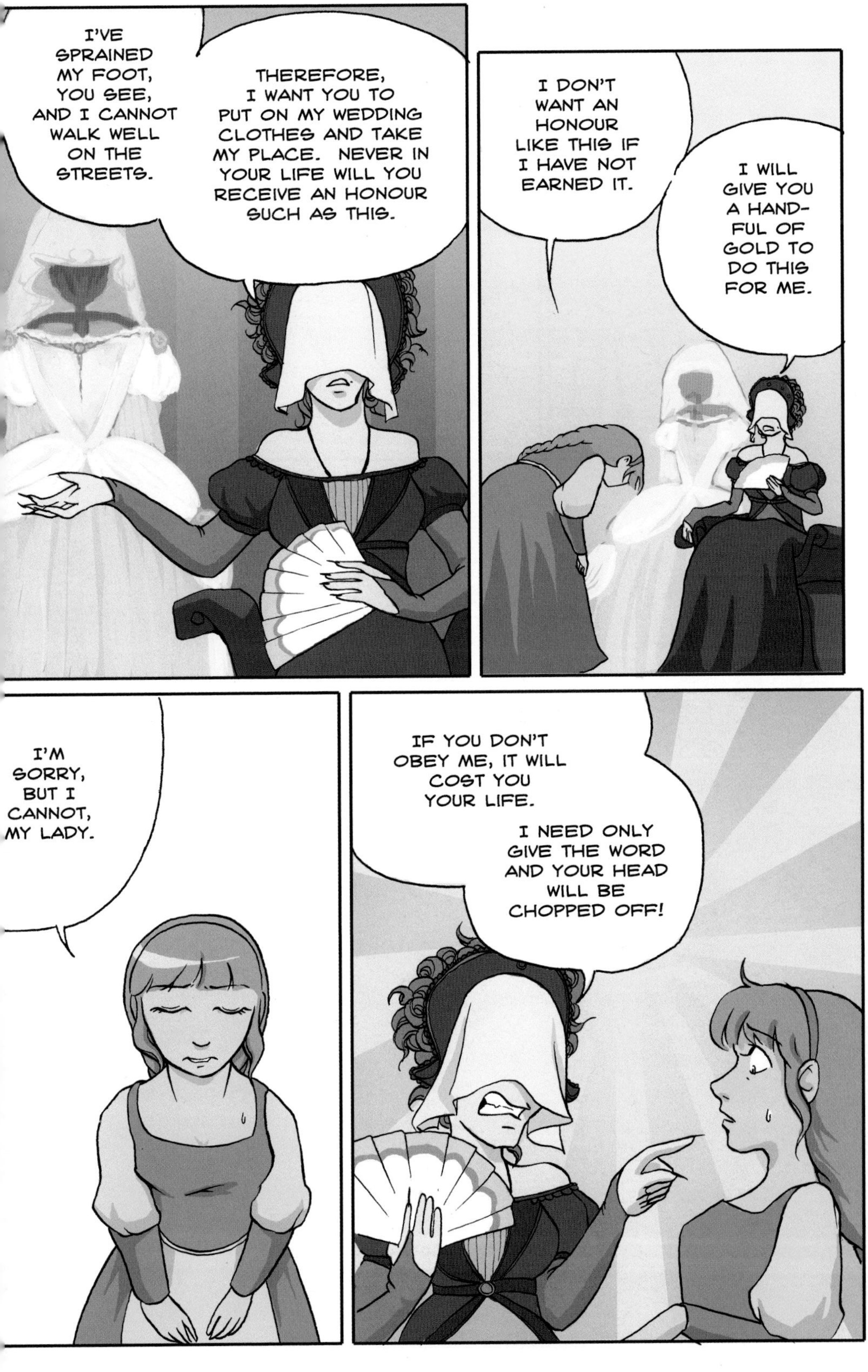
I'VE SPRAINED MY FOOT, YOU SEE, AND I CANNOT WALK WELL ON THE STREETS.
THEREFORE, I WANT YOU TO PUT ON MY WEDDING CLOTHES AND TAKE MY PLACE. NEVER IN YOUR LIFE WILL YOU RECEIVE AN HONOUR SUCH AS THIS.
I DON'T WANT AN HONOUR LIKE THIS IF I HAVE NOT EARNED IT.
I WILL GIVE YOU A HAND-FUL OF GOLD TO DO THIS FOR ME.
I'M SORRY, BUT I CANNOT, MY LADY.
IF YOU DON'T OBEY ME, IT WILL COST YOU YOUR LIFE.
I NEED ONLY GIVE THE WORD AND YOUR HEAD WILL BE CHOPPED OFF!

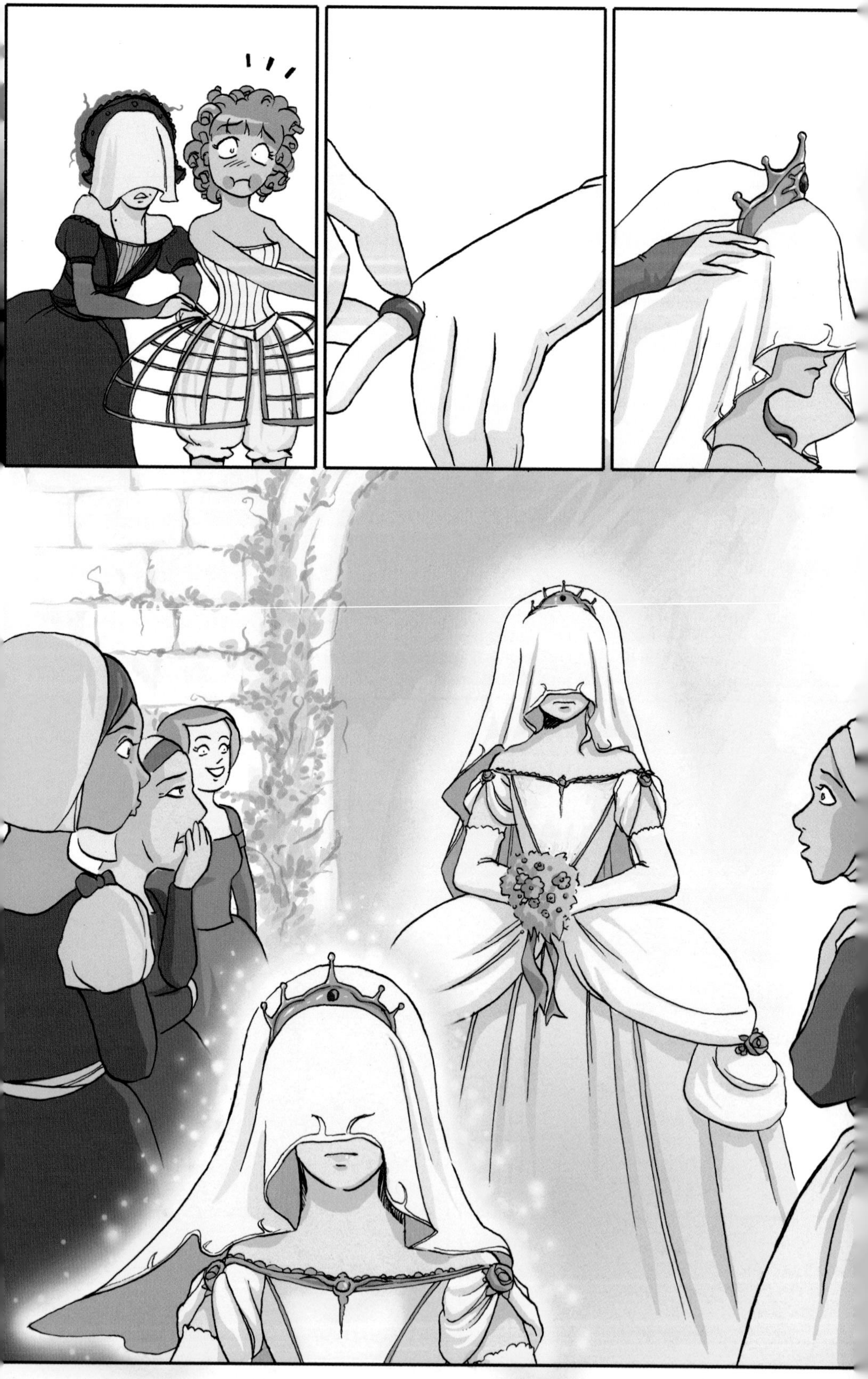

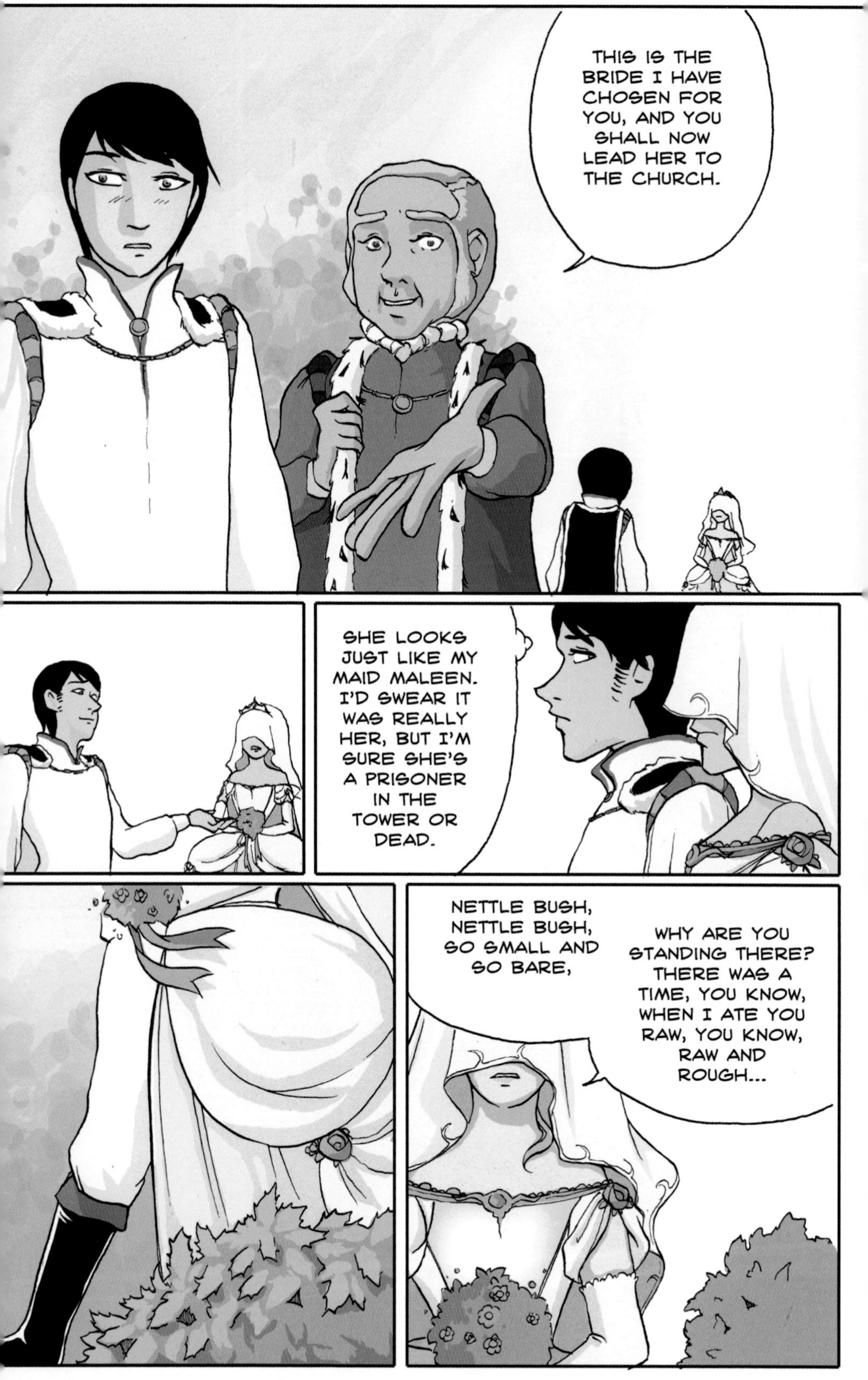
THIS IS THE BRIDE I HAVE CHOSEN FOR YOU, AND YOU SHALL NOW LEAD HER TO THE CHURCH.
SHE LOOKS JUST LIKE MY MAID MALEEN. I'D SWEAR IT WAS REALLY HER, BUT I'M SURE SHE'S A PRISONER IN THE TOWER OR DEAD.
NETTLE BUSH, NETTLE BUSH, SO SMALL AND SO BARE,
WHY ARE YOU STANDING THERE? THERE WAS A TIME, YOU KNOW, WHEN I ATE YOU RAW, YOU KNOW, RAW AND ROUGH...

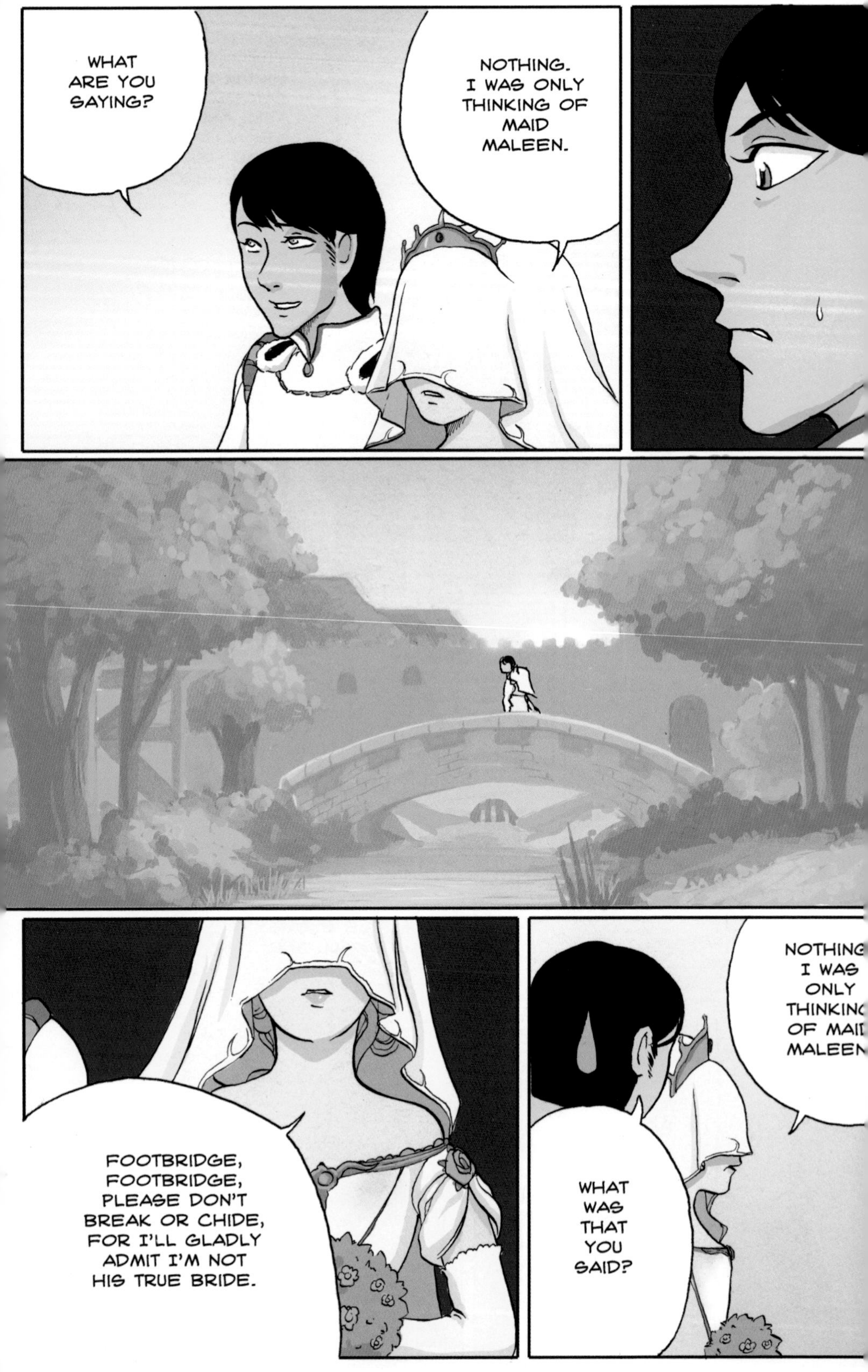
WHAT ARE YOU SAYING?
NOTHING. I WAS ONLY THINKING OF MAID MALEEN.
FOOTBRIDGE, FOOTBRIDGE, PLEASE DON'T BREAK OR CHIDE, FOR I'LL GLADLY ADMIT I'M NOT HIS TRUE BRIDE.
NOTHING I WAS ONLY THINKING OF MAI MALEEN
WHAT WAS THAT YOU SAID?

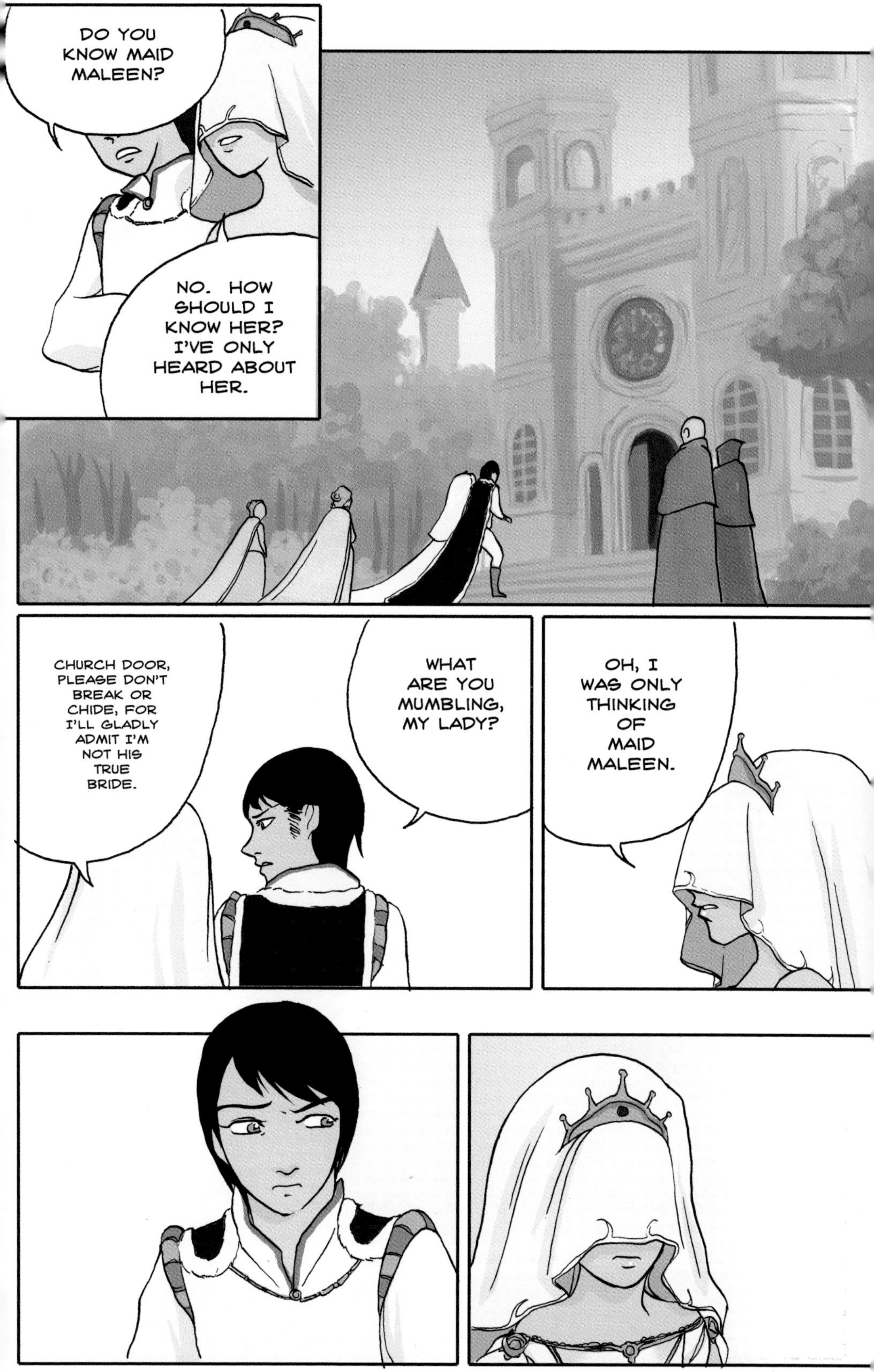
DO YOU KNOW MAID MALEEN?
NO. HOW SHOULD I KNOW HER? I'VE ONLY HEARD ABOUT HER.
CHURCH DOOR, PLEASE DON'T BREAK OR CHIDE, FOR I'LL GLADLY ADMIT I'M NOT HIS TRUE BRIDE.
WHAT ARE YOU MUMBLING, MY LADY?
OH, I WAS ONLY THINKING OF MAID MALEEN.

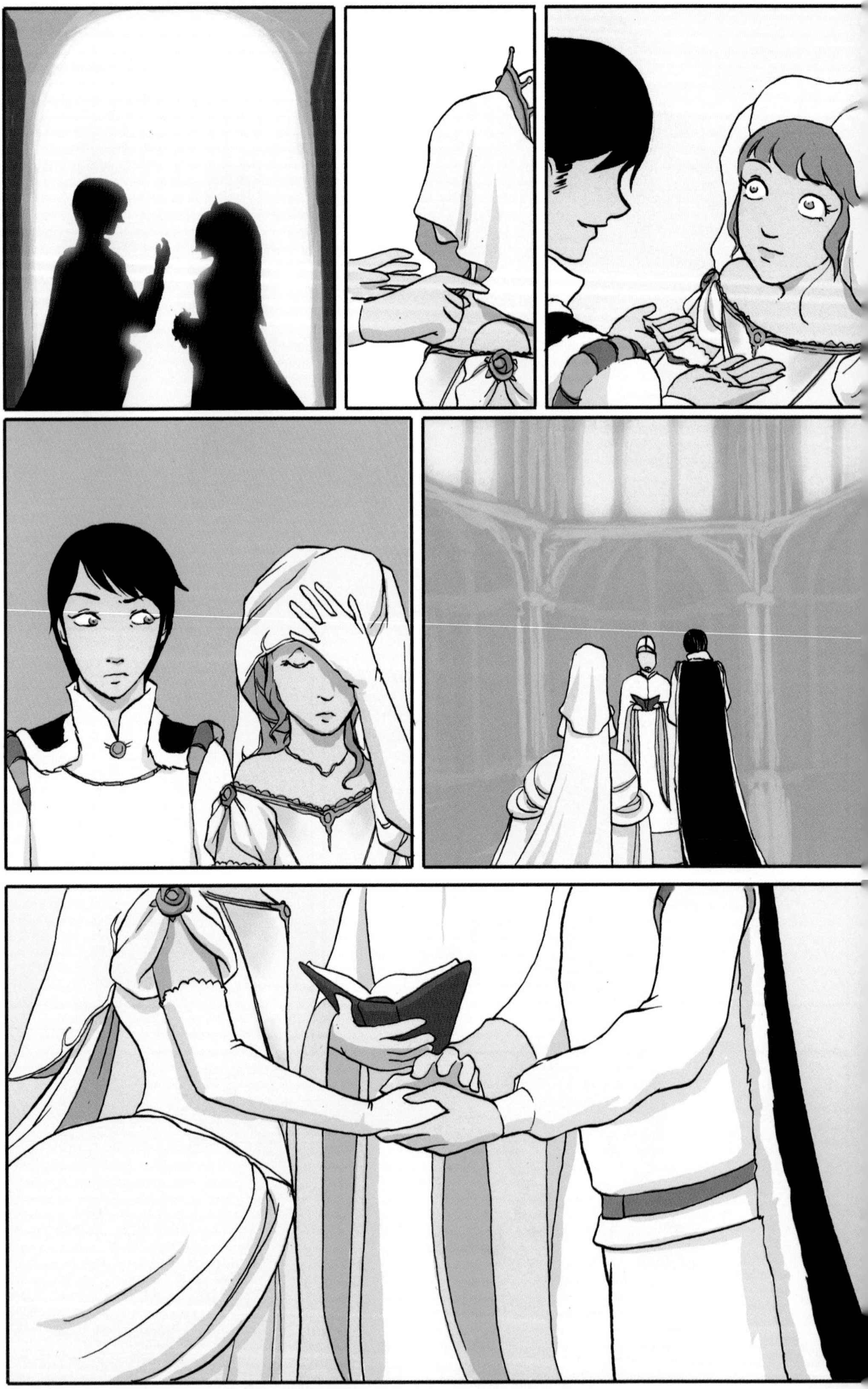

UNTIL TONIGHT THEN.

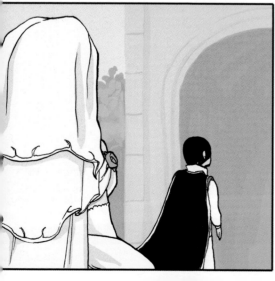

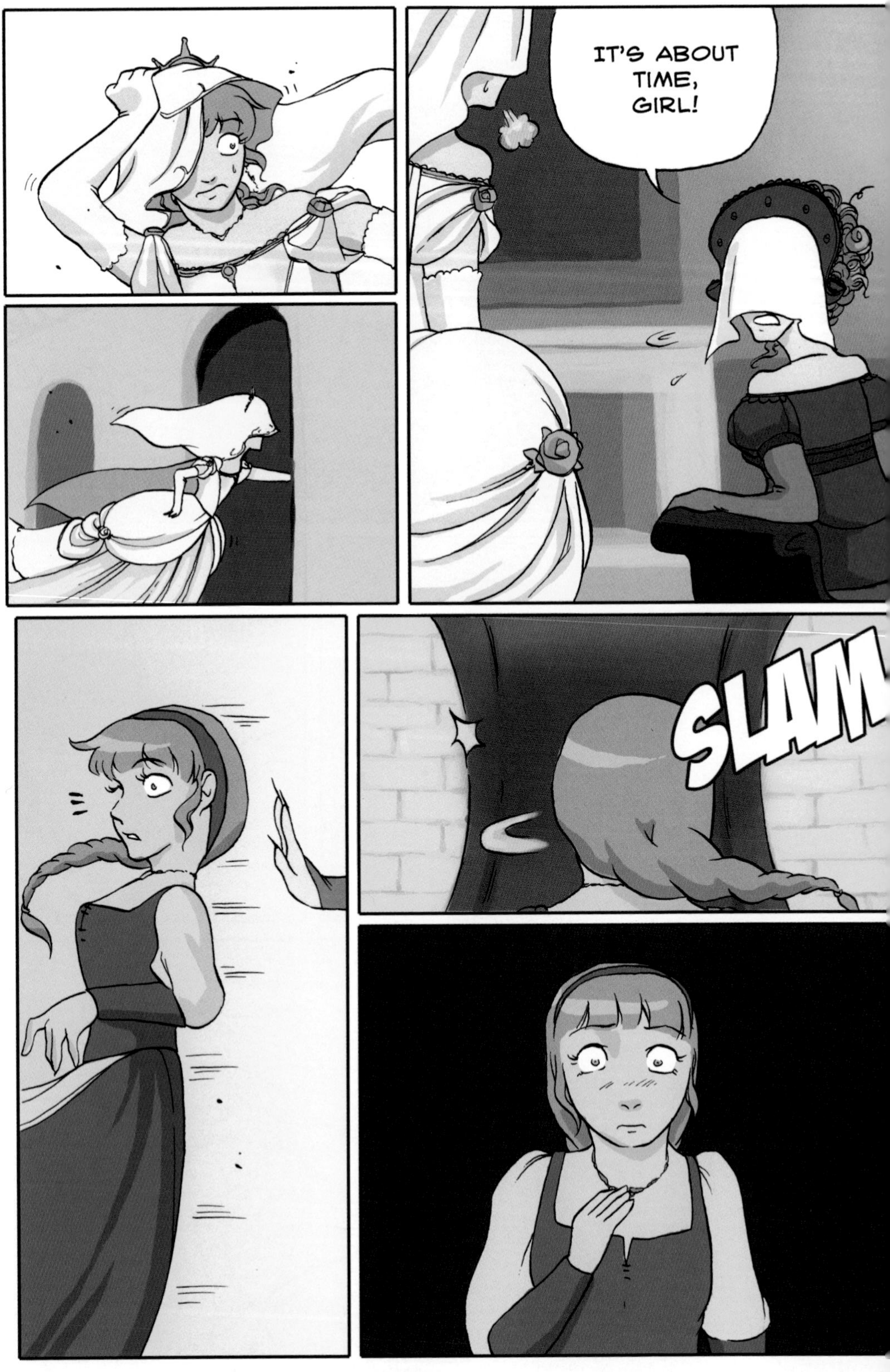
IT'S ABOUT TIME, GIRL!
SLAM

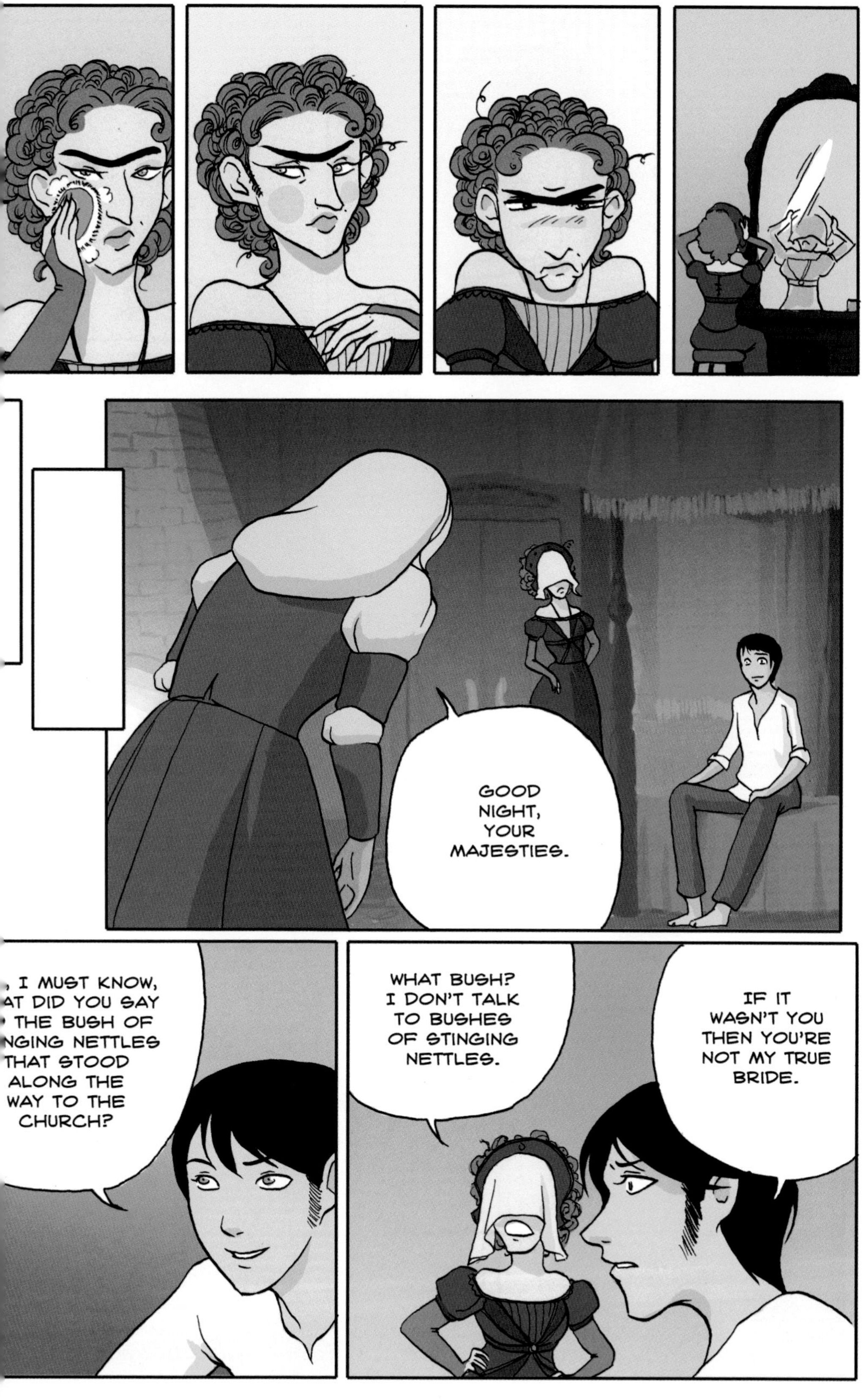
GOOD NIGHT, YOUR MAJESTIES.
, I MUST KNOW, AT DID YOU SAY THE BUSH OF NGING NETTLES THAT STOOD ALONG THE WAY TO THE CHURCH?
WHAT BUSH? I DON'T TALK TO BUSHES OF STINGING NETTLES.
IF IT WASN'T YOU THEN YOU'RE NOT MY TRUE BRIDE.

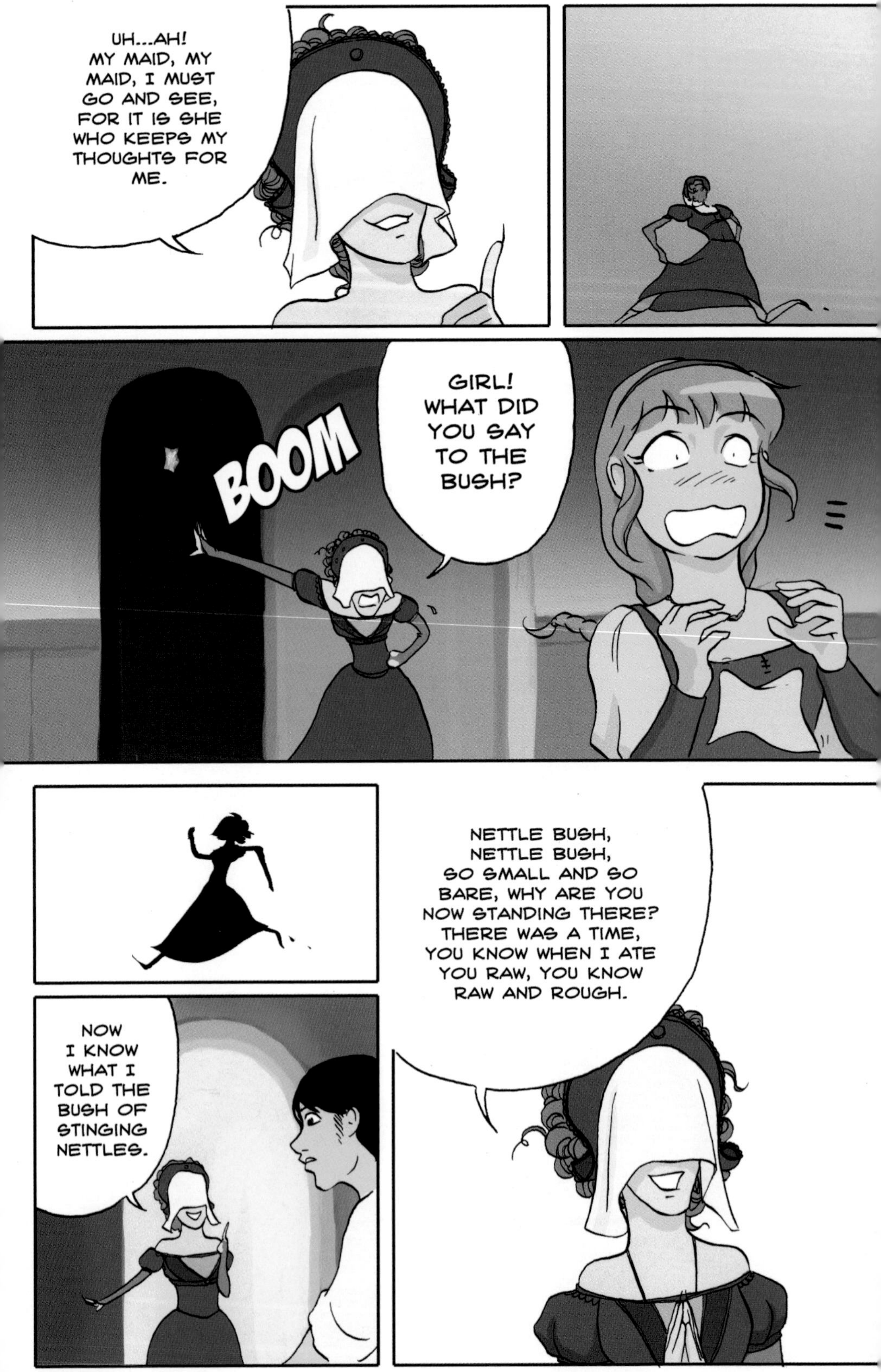
UH...AH! MY MAID, MY MAID, I MUST GO AND SEE, FOR IT IS SHE WHO KEEPS MY THOUGHTS FOR ME.
GIRL! WHAT DID YOU SAY TO THE BUSH?
BOOM
NETTLE BUSH, NETTLE BUSH, SO SMALL AND SO BARE, WHY ARE YOU NOW STANDING THERE? THERE WAS A TIME, YOU KNOW WHEN I ATE YOU RAW, YOU KNOW RAW AND ROUGH.
NOW I KNOW WHAT I TOLD THE BUSH OF STINGING NETTLES.

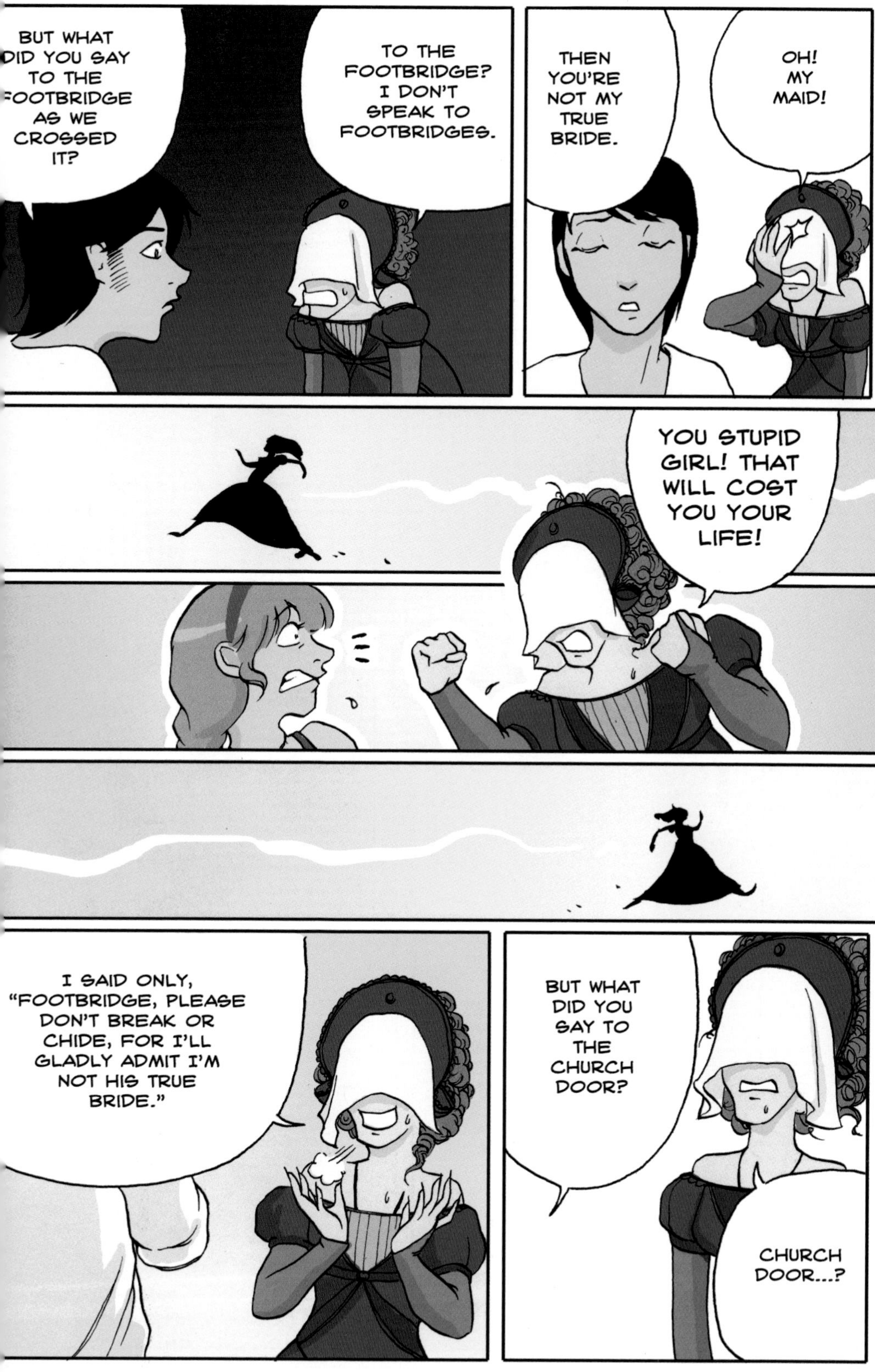
BUT WHAT DID YOU SAY TO THE FOOTBRIDGE AS WE CROSSED IT?
TO THE FOOTBRIDGE? I DON'T SPEAK TO FOOTBRIDGES.
THEN YOU'RE NOT MY TRUE BRIDE.
OH! MY MAID!
YOU STUPID GIRL! THAT WILL COST YOU YOUR LIFE!
I SAID ONLY, "FOOTBRIDGE, PLEASE DON'T BREAK OR CHIDE, FOR I'LL GLADLY ADMIT I'M NOT HIS TRUE BRIDE."
BUT WHAT DID YOU SAY TO THE CHURCH DOOR?
CHURCH DOOR...?

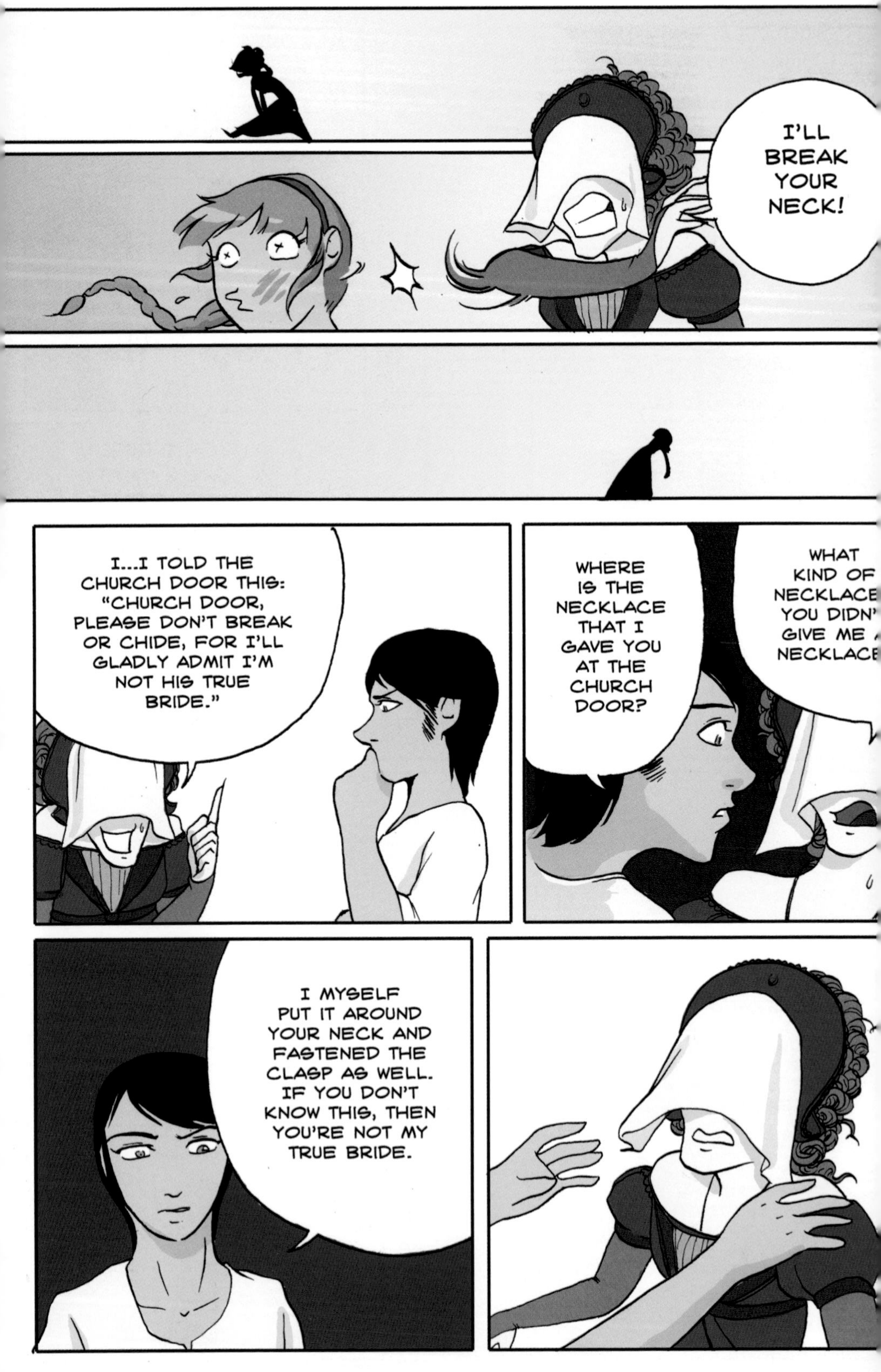
I'LL BREAK YOUR NECK!
I...I TOLD THE CHURCH DOOR THIS: "CHURCH DOOR, PLEASE DON'T BREAK OR CHIDE, FOR I'LL GLADLY ADMIT I'M NOT HIS TRUE BRIDE."
WHERE IS THE NECKLACE THAT I GAVE YOU AT THE CHURCH DOOR?
WHAT KIND OF NECKLACE YOU DIDN' GIVE ME NECKLAC
I MYSELF PUT IT AROUND YOUR NECK AND FASTENED THE CLASP AS WELL. IF YOU DON'T KNOW THIS, THEN YOU'RE NOT MY TRUE BRIDE.

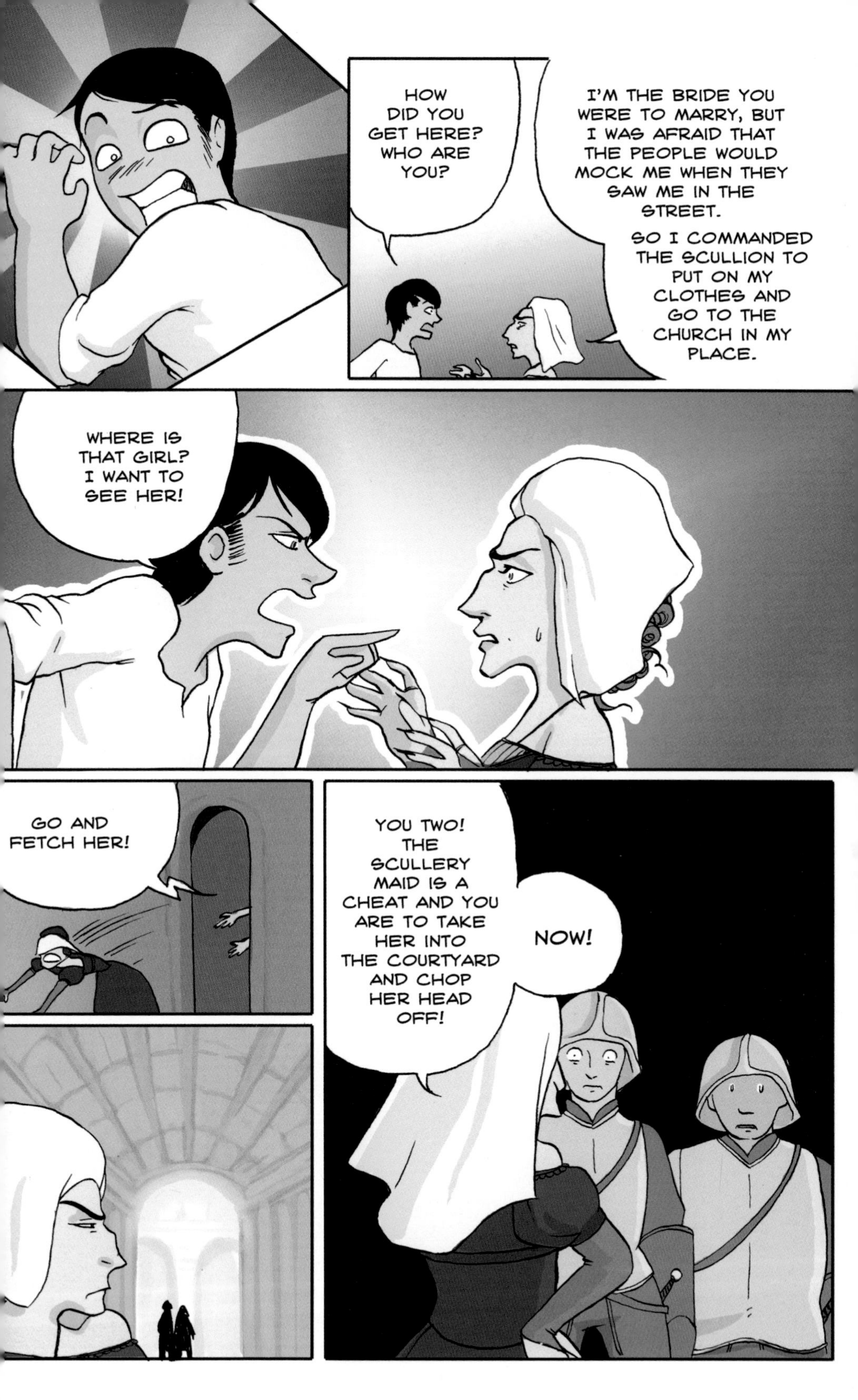
HOW DID YOU GET HERE? WHO ARE YOU?
I'M THE BRIDE YOU WERE TO MARRY, BUT I WAS AFRAID THAT THE PEOPLE WOULD MOCK ME WHEN THEY SAW ME IN THE STREET.
SO I COMMANDED THE SCULLION TO PUT ON MY CLOTHES AND GO TO THE CHURCH IN MY PLACE.
WHERE IS THAT GIRL? I WANT TO SEE HER!
GO AND FETCH HER!
YOU TWO! THE SCULLERY MAID IS A CHEAT AND YOU ARE TO TAKE HER INTO THE COURTYARD AND CHOP HER HEAD OFF!
NOW!

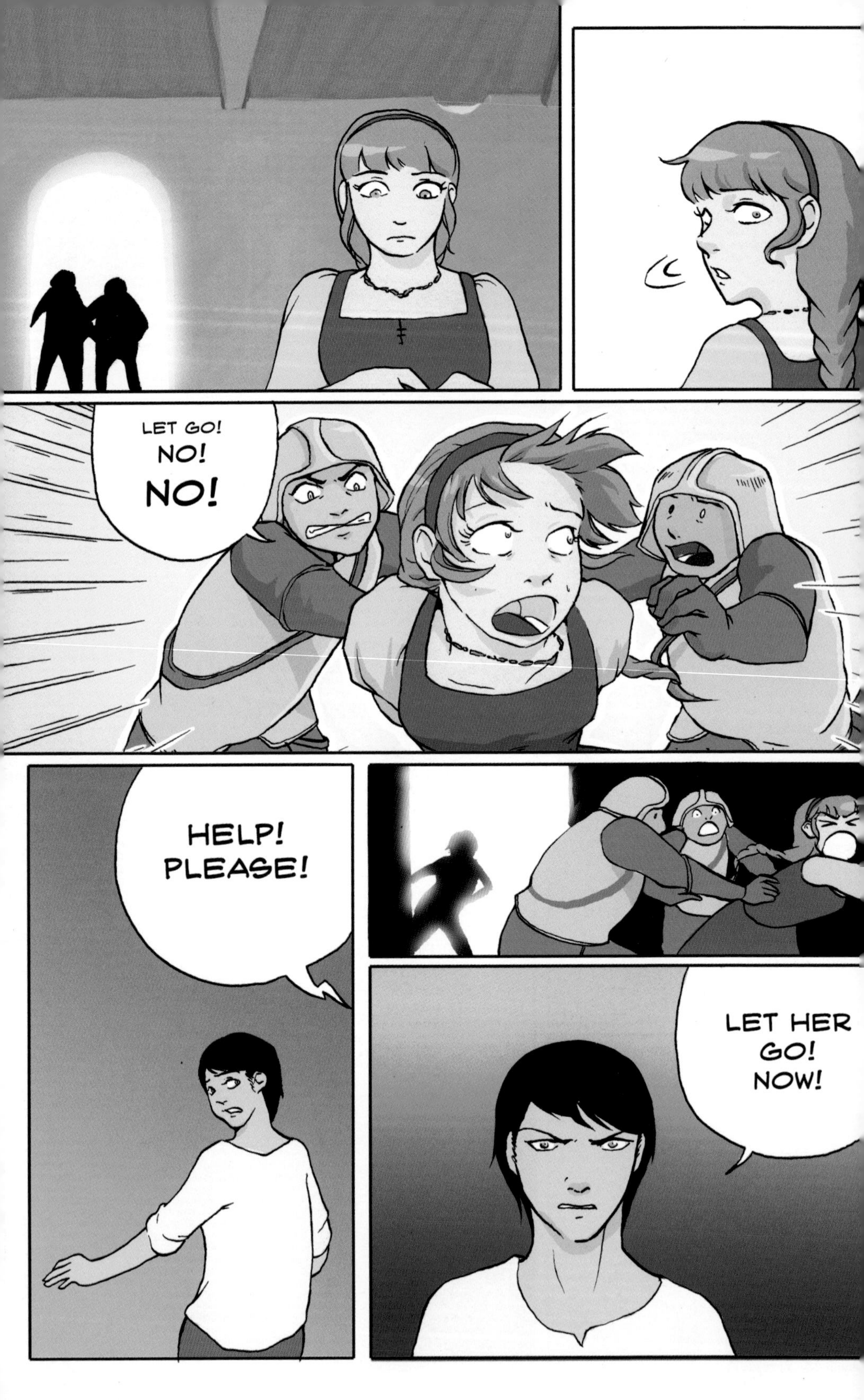
LET GO! NO! NO!
HELP! PLEASE!
LET HER GO! NOW!

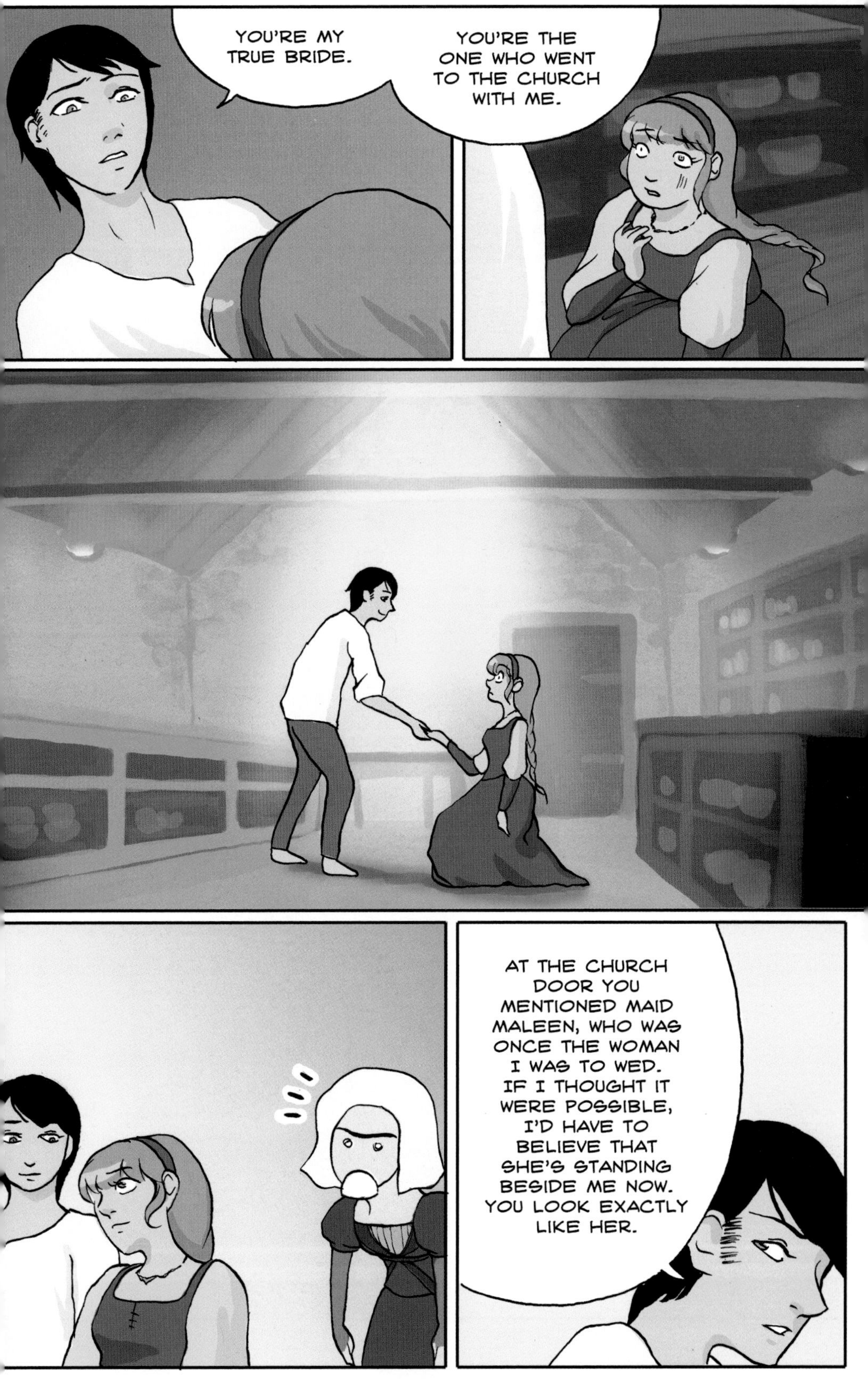
YOU'RE MY TRUE BRIDE.
YOU'RE THE ONE WHO WENT TO THE CHURCH WITH ME.
AT THE CHURCH DOOR YOU MENTIONED MAID MALEEN, WHO WAS ONCE THE WOMAN I WAS TO WED. IF I THOUGHT IT WERE POSSIBLE, I'D HAVE TO BELIEVE THAT SHE'S STANDING BESIDE ME NOW. YOU LOOK EXACTLY LIKE HER.

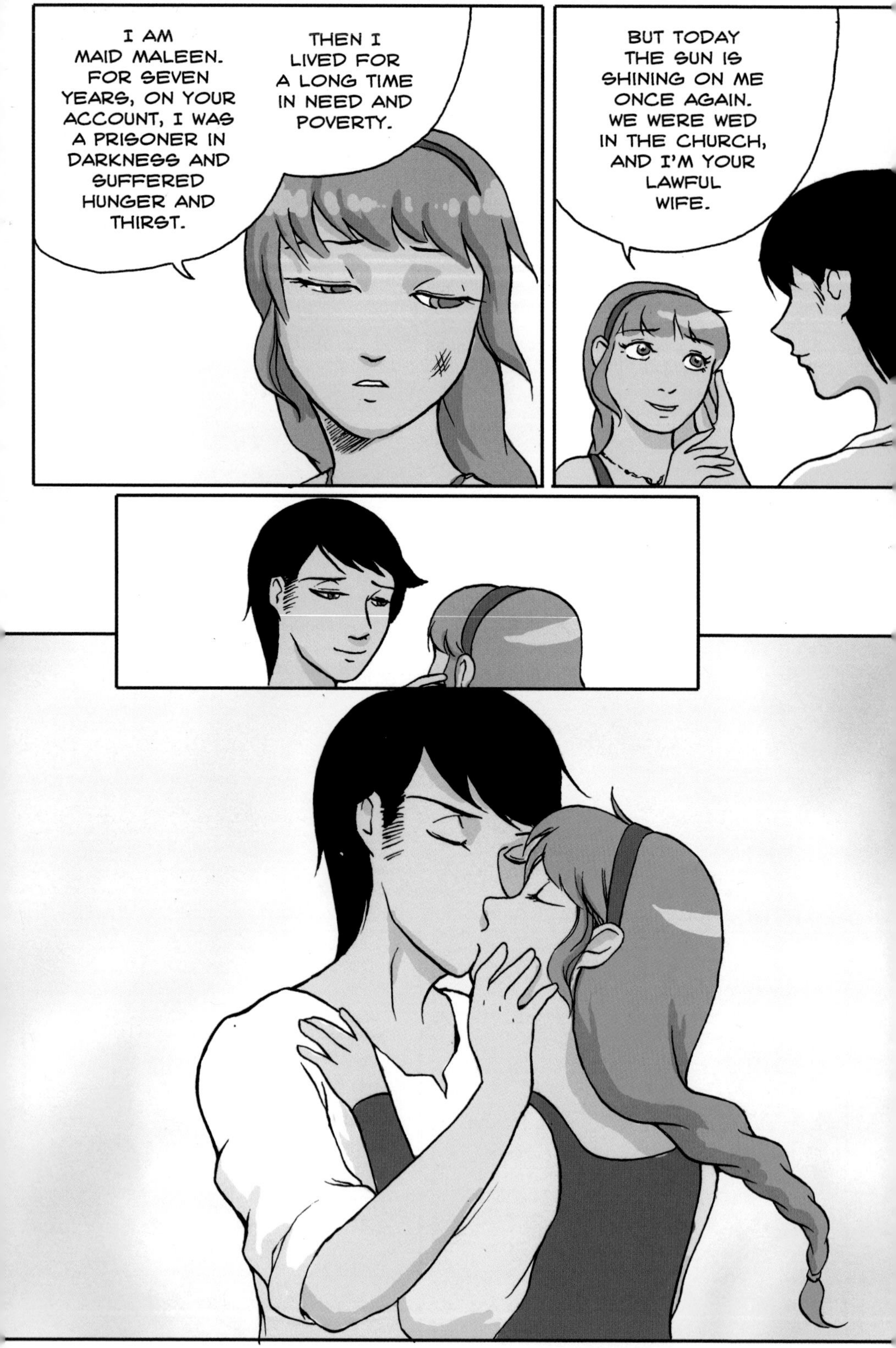
I AM MAID MALEEN. FOR SEVEN YEARS, ON YOUR ACCOUNT, I WAS A PRISONER IN DARKNESS AND SUFFERED HUNGER AND THIRST.
THEN I LIVED FOR A LONG TIME IN NEED AND POVERTY.
BUT TODAY THE SUN IS SHINING ON ME ONCE AGAIN. WE WERE WED IN THE CHURCH, AND I'M YOUR LAWFUL WIFE.

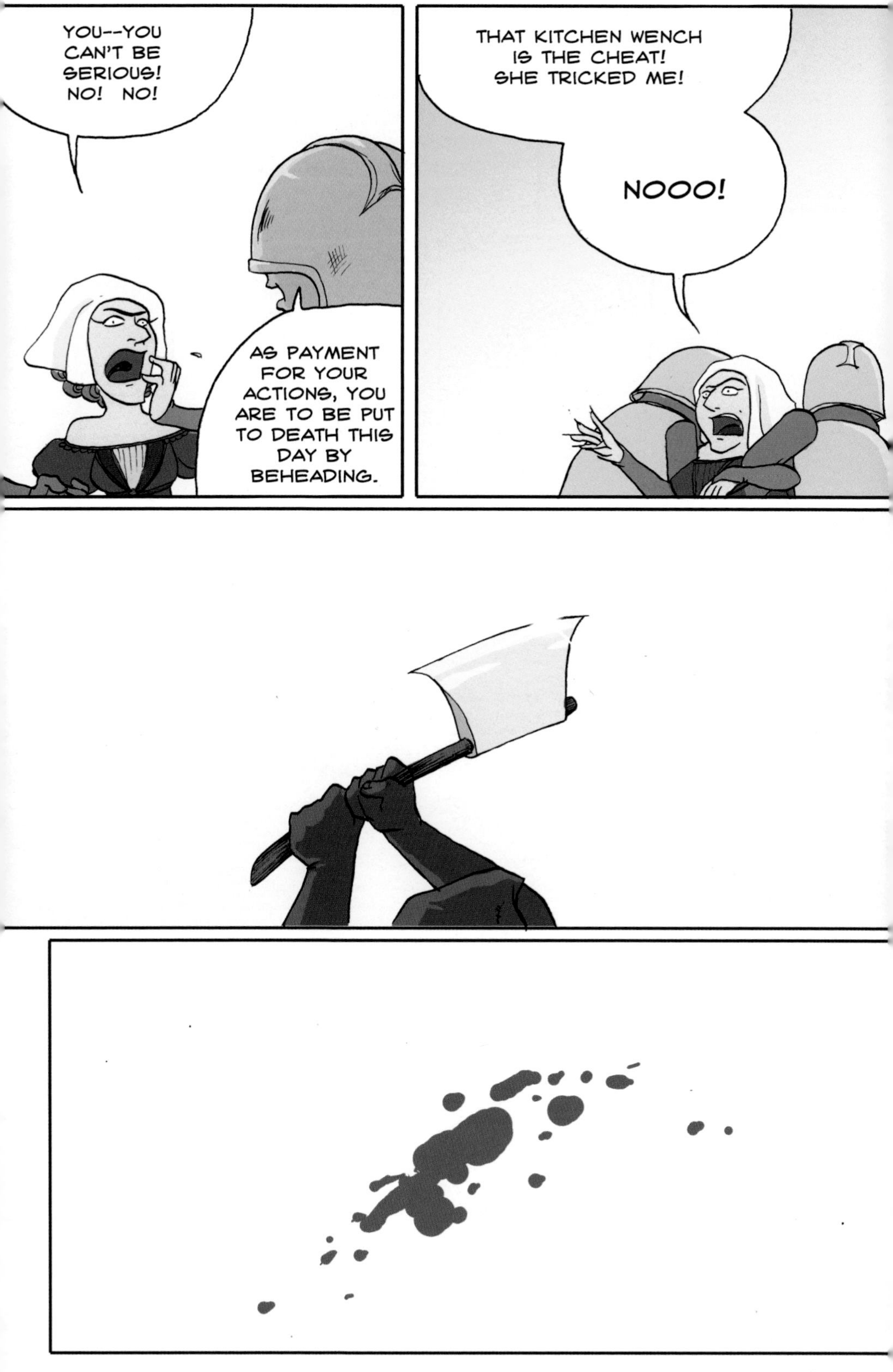
YOU--YOU CAN'T BE SERIOUS! NO! NO!
AS PAYMENT FOR YOUR ACTIONS, YOU ARE TO BE PUT TO DEATH THIS DAY BY BEHEADING.
THAT KITCHEN WENCH IS THE CHEAT! SHE TRICKED ME!
NOOO!

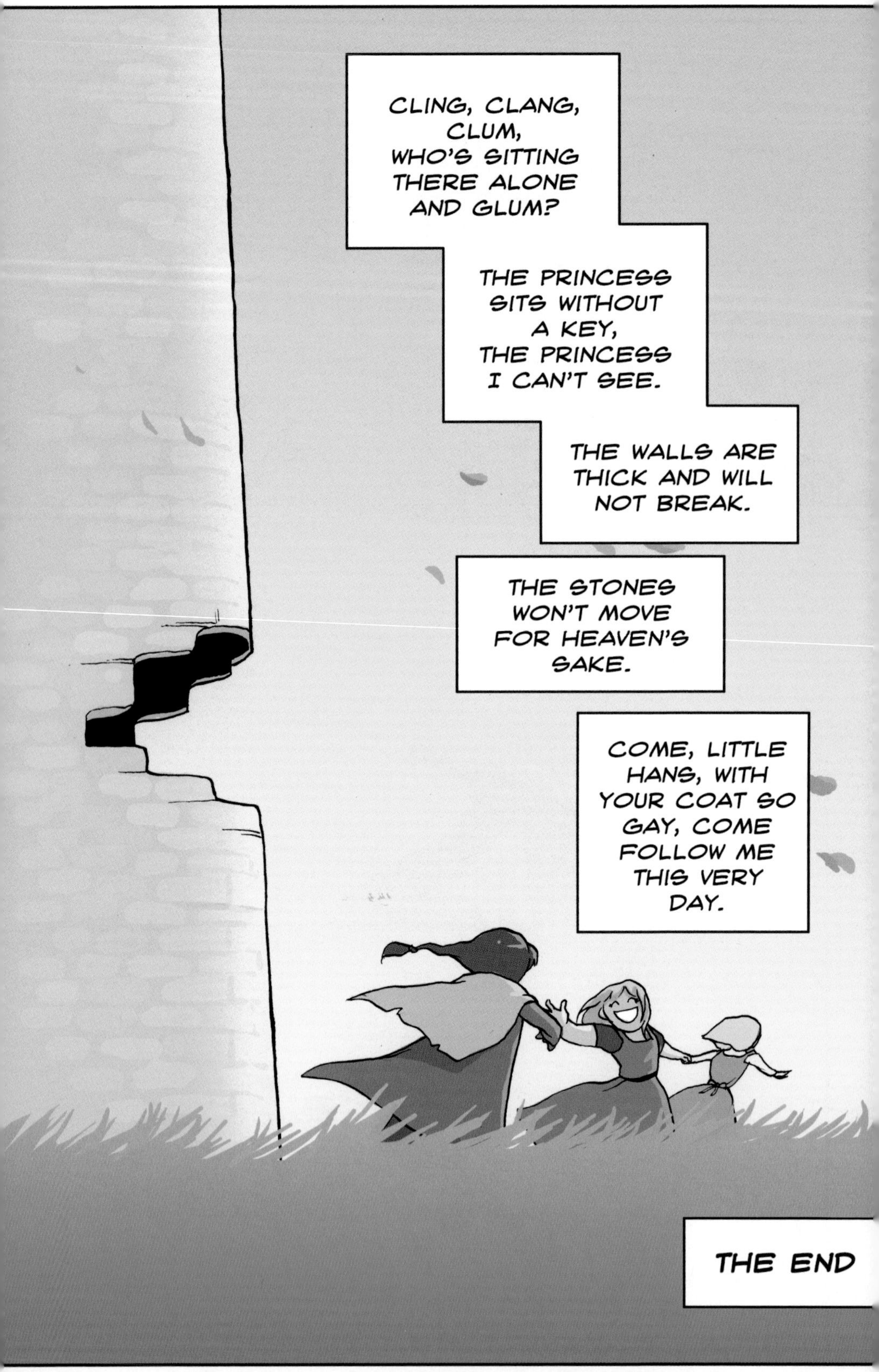
CLING, CLANG, CLUM, WHO'S SITTING THERE ALONE AND GLUM?
THE PRINCESS SITS WITHOUT A KEY, THE PRINCESS I CAN'T SEE.
THE WALLS ARE THICK AND WILL NOT BREAK.
THE STONES WON'T MOVE FOR HEAVEN'S SAKE.
COME, LITTLE HANS, WITH YOUR COAT SO GAY, COME FOLLOW ME THIS VERY DAY.
THE END

The BIRD, the MOUSE, and the SAUSAGE

STORY ADAPTED BY
GINA BIGGS

ILLUSTRATED BY
ELLE SKINNER

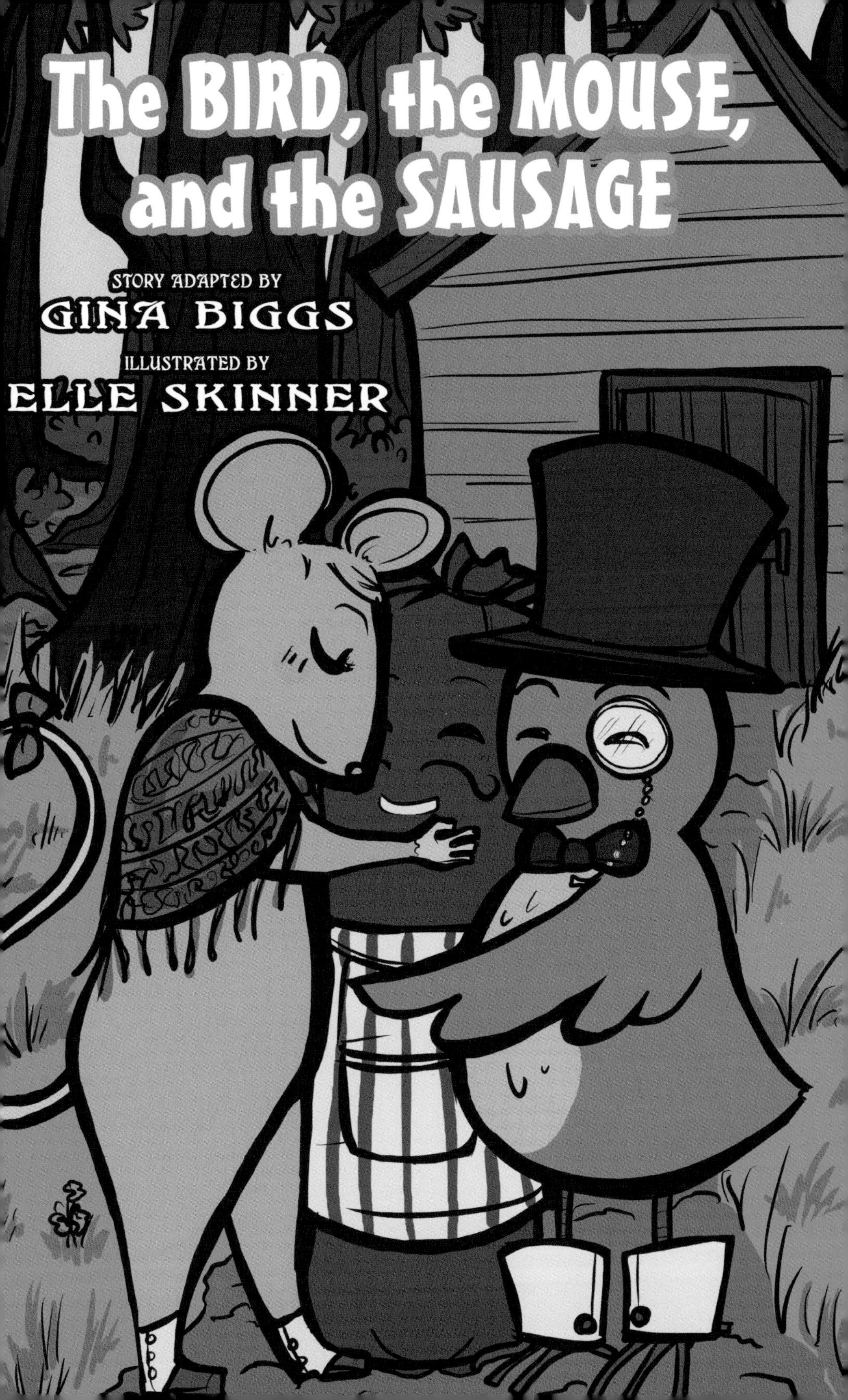

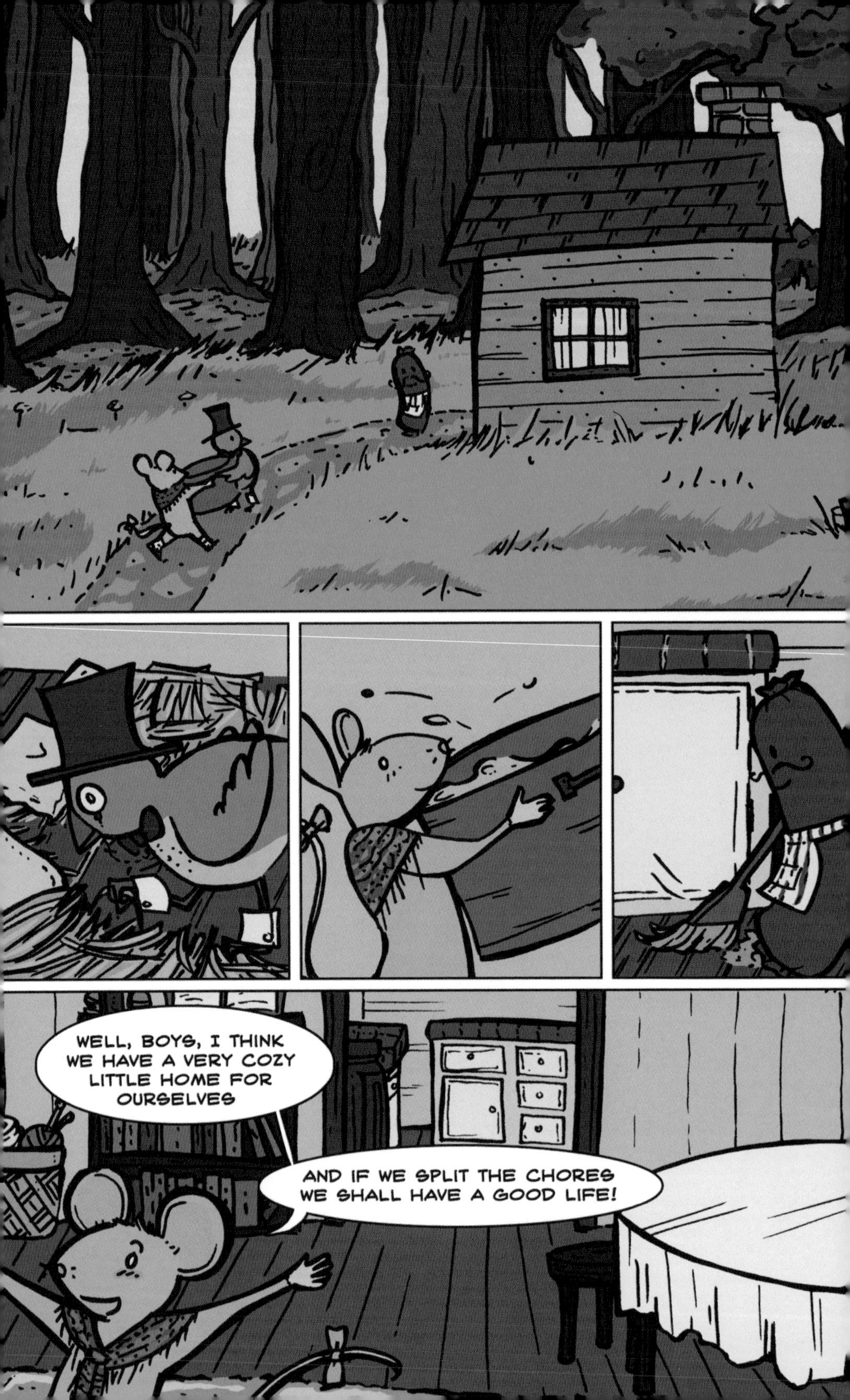
WELL, BOYS, I THINK WE HAVE A VERY COZY LITTLE HOME FOR OURSELVES
AND IF WE SPLIT THE CHORES WE SHALL HAVE A GOOD LIFE!

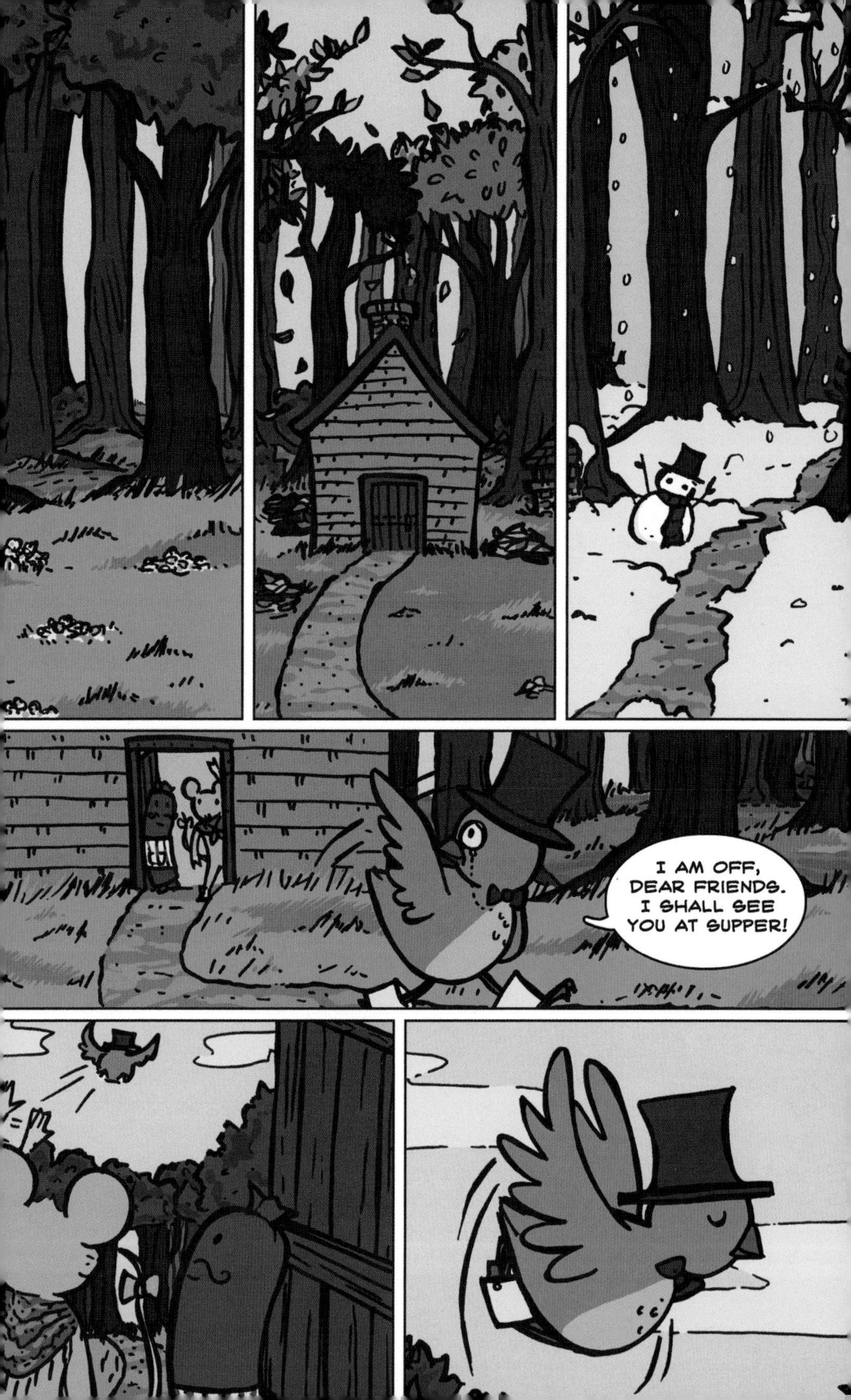
I AM OFF, DEAR FRIENDS. I SHALL SEE YOU AT SUPPER!

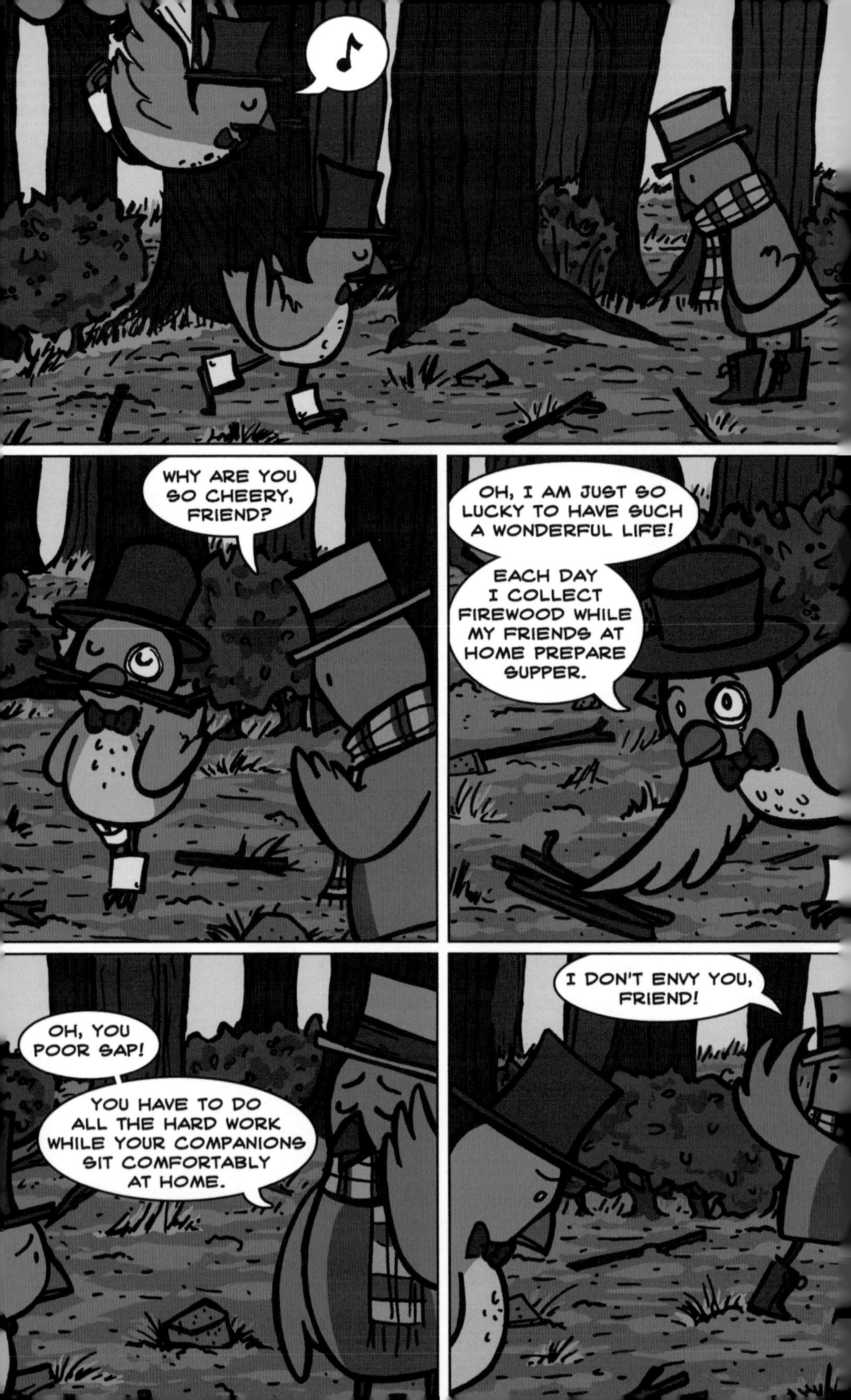
♪
WHY ARE YOU SO CHEERY, FRIEND?
OH, I AM JUST SO LUCKY TO HAVE SUCH A WONDERFUL LIFE!
EACH DAY I COLLECT FIREWOOD WHILE MY FRIENDS AT HOME PREPARE SUPPER.
OH, YOU POOR SAP!
YOU HAVE TO DO ALL THE HARD WORK WHILE YOUR COMPANIONS SIT COMFORTABLY AT HOME.
I DON'T ENVY YOU, FRIEND!

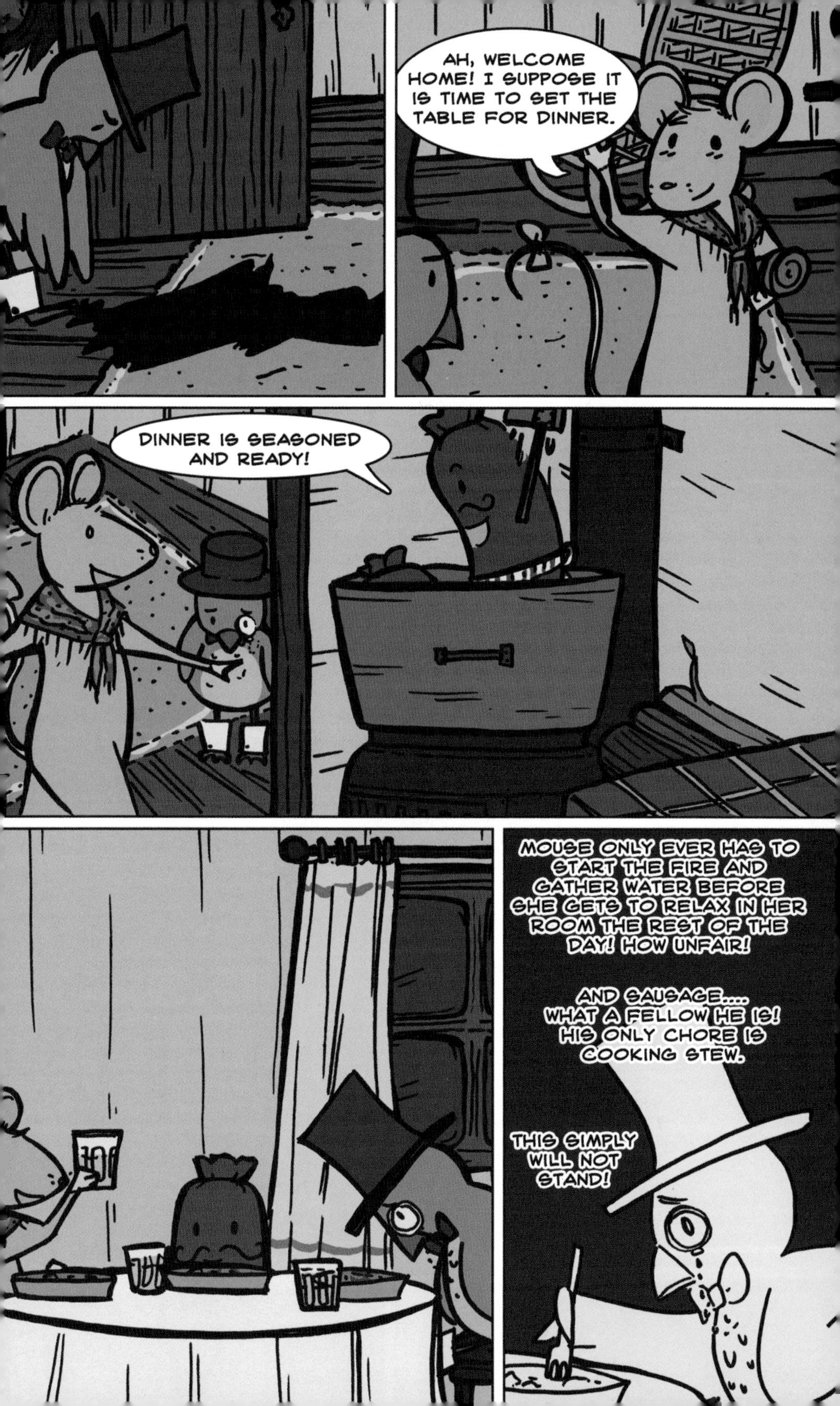

AH, WELCOME HOME! I SUPPOSE IT IS TIME TO SET THE TABLE FOR DINNER.
DINNER IS SEASONED AND READY!
MOUSE ONLY EVER HAS TO START THE FIRE AND GATHER WATER BEFORE SHE GETS TO RELAX IN HER ROOM THE REST OF THE DAY! HOW UNFAIR!
AND SAUSAGE.... WHAT A FELLOW HE IS! HIS ONLY CHORE IS COOKING STEW.
THIS SIMPLY WILL NOT STAND!

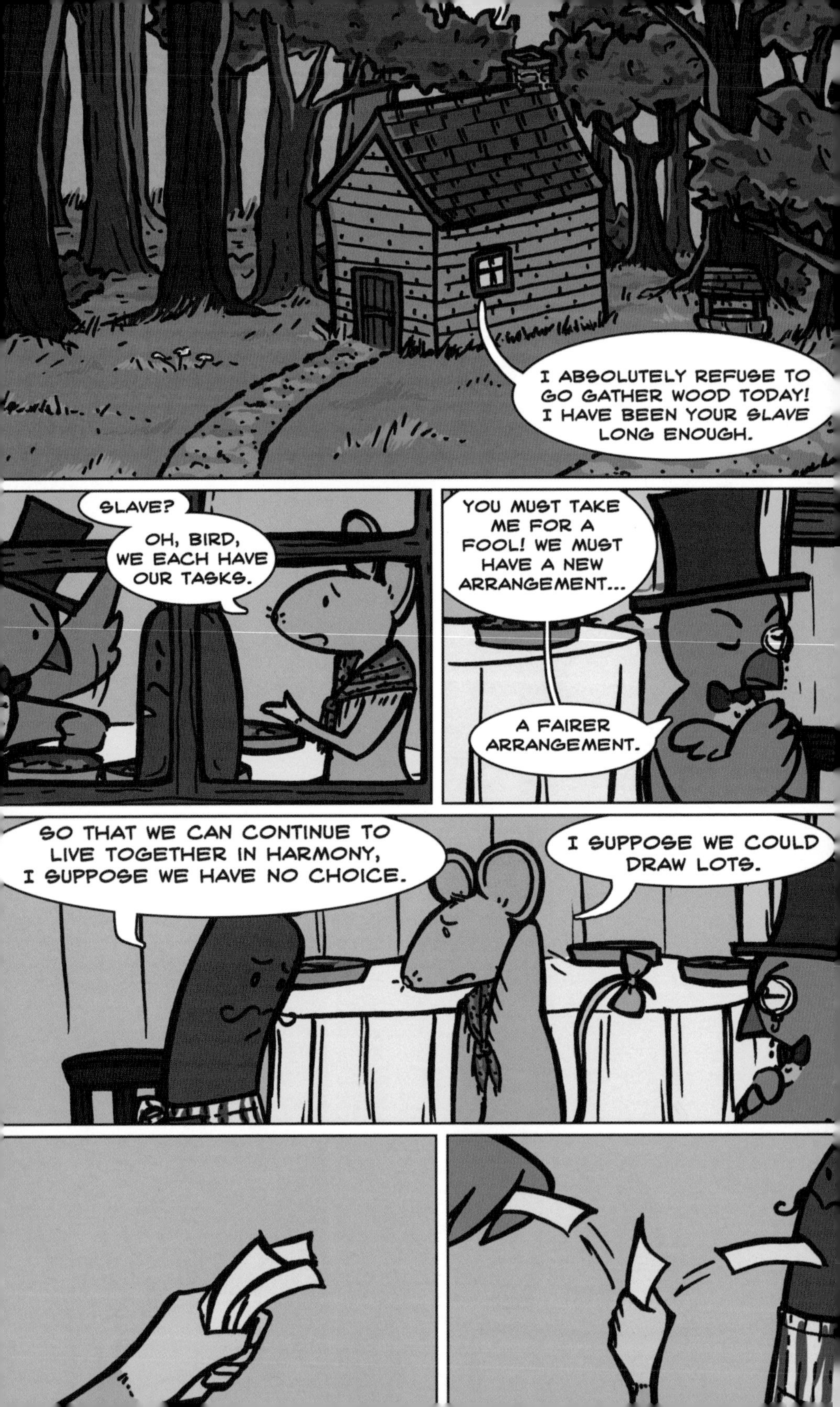
I ABSOLUTELY REFUSE TO GO GATHER WOOD TODAY! I HAVE BEEN YOUR SLAVE LONG ENOUGH.
SLAVE?
OH, BIRD, WE EACH HAVE OUR TASKS.
YOU MUST TAKE ME FOR A FOOL! WE MUST HAVE A NEW ARRANGEMENT...
A FAIRER ARRANGEMENT.
SO THAT WE CAN CONTINUE TO LIVE TOGETHER IN HARMONY, I SUPPOSE WE HAVE NO CHOICE.
I SUPPOSE WE COULD DRAW LOTS.

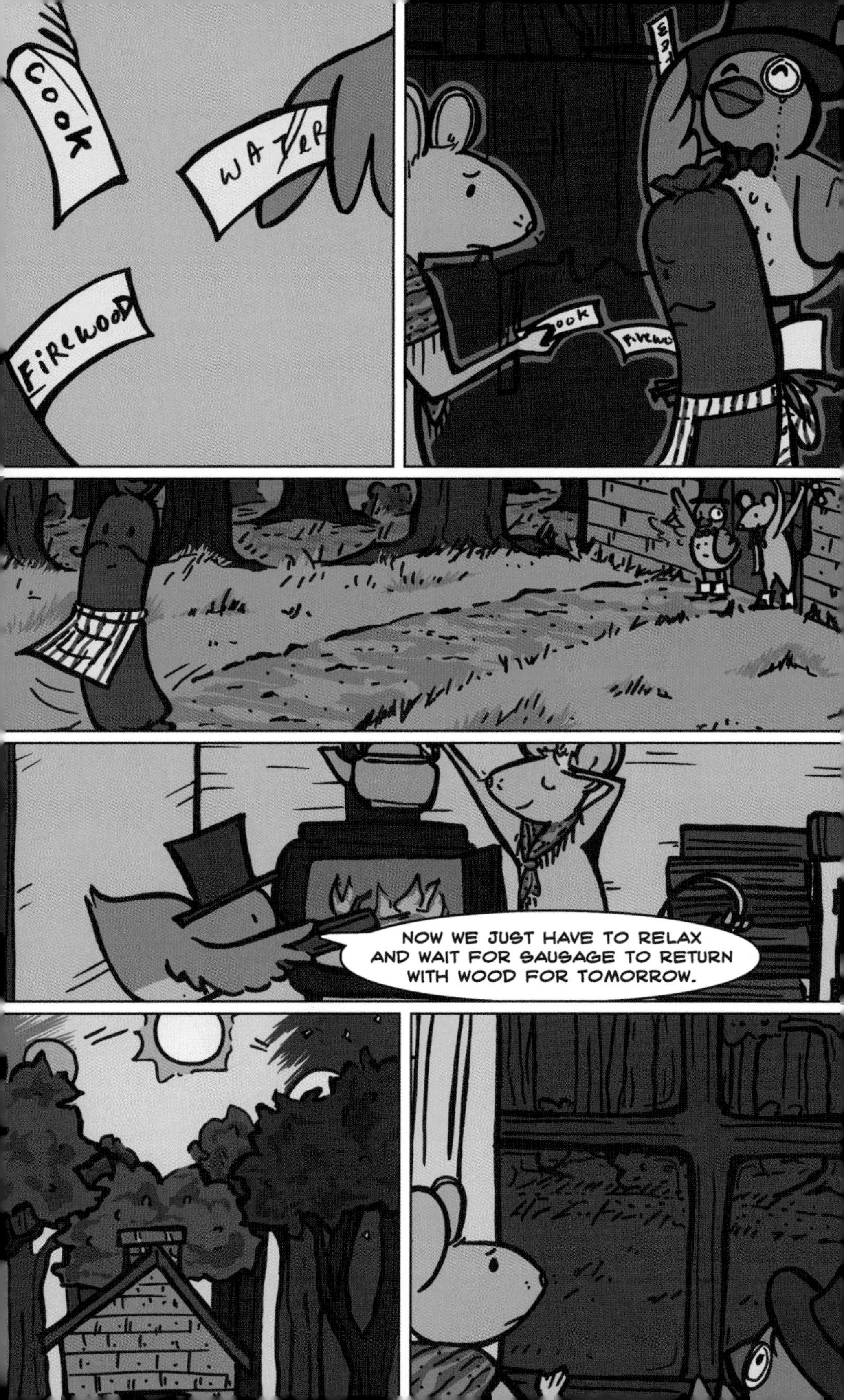
COOK
WATER
FIREWOOD
NOW WE JUST HAVE TO RELAX AND WAIT FOR SAUSAGE TO RETURN WITH WOOD FOR TOMORROW.

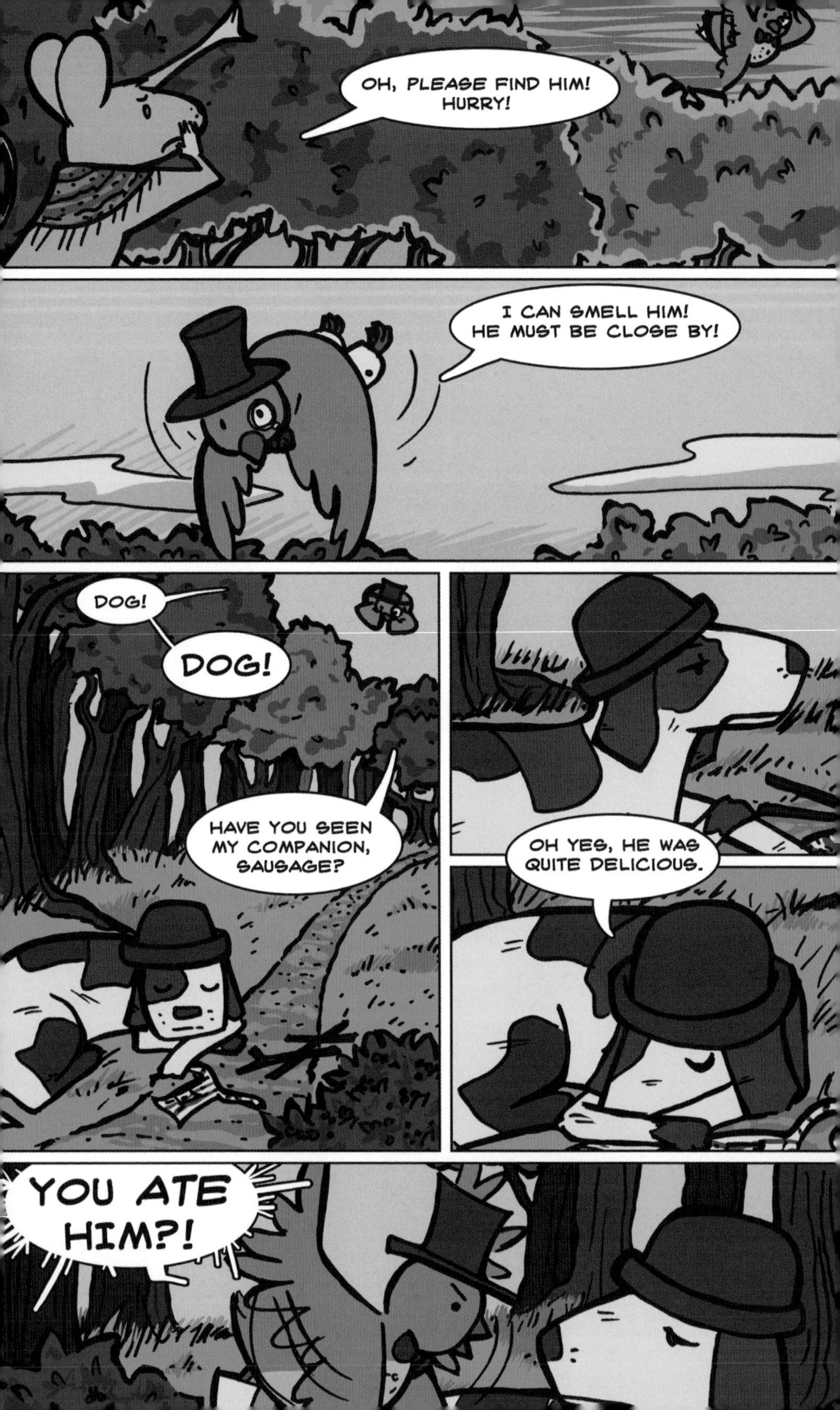

OH, PLEASE FIND HIM! HURRY!
I CAN SMELL HIM! HE MUST BE CLOSE BY!
DOG!
DOG!
HAVE YOU SEEN MY COMPANION, SAUSAGE?
OH YES, HE WAS QUITE DELICIOUS.
YOU ATE HIM?!

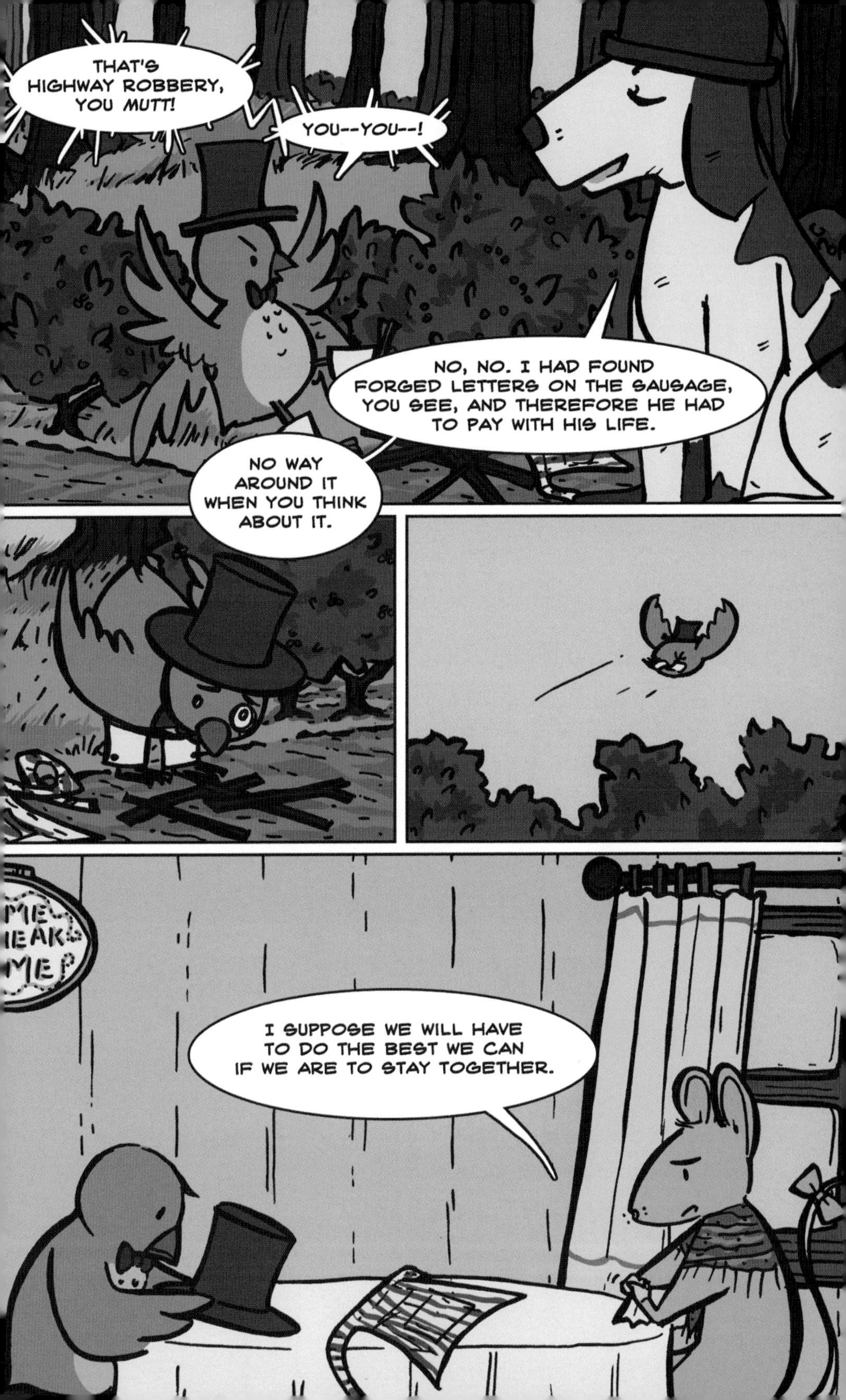
THAT'S HIGHWAY ROBBERY, YOU MUTT!
YOU--YOU--!
NO, NO. I HAD FOUND FORGED LETTERS ON THE SAUSAGE, YOU SEE, AND THEREFORE HE HAD TO PAY WITH HIS LIFE.
NO WAY AROUND IT WHEN YOU THINK ABOUT IT.
I SUPPOSE WE WILL HAVE TO DO THE BEST WE CAN IF WE ARE TO STAY TOGETHER.

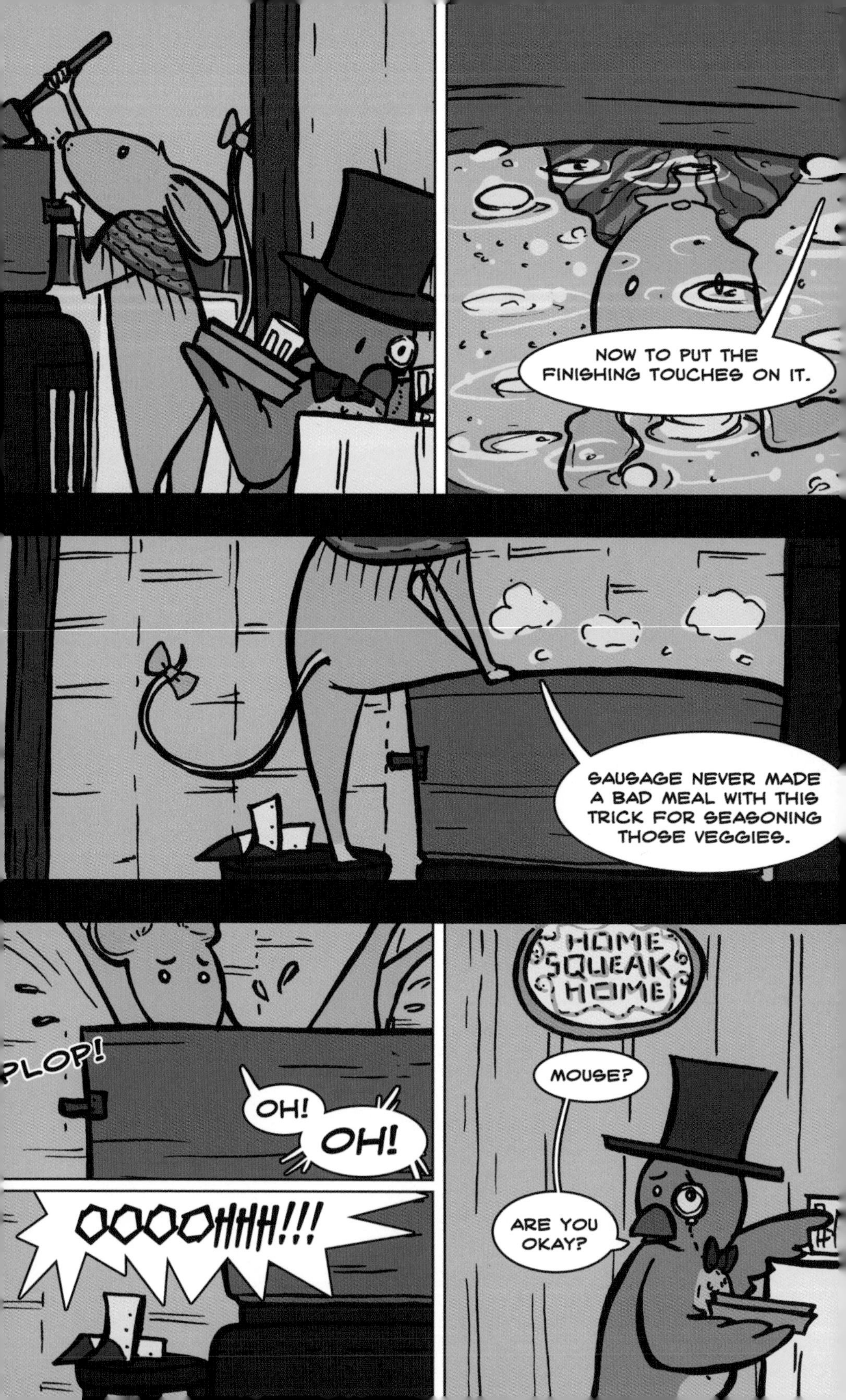
NOW TO PUT THE FINISHING TOUCHES ON IT.
SAUSAGE NEVER MADE A BAD MEAL WITH THIS TRICK FOR SEASONING THOSE VEGGIES.
PLOP!
OH!
OH!
OOOOHHH!!!
HOME SQUEAK HOME
MOUSE?
ARE YOU OKAY?

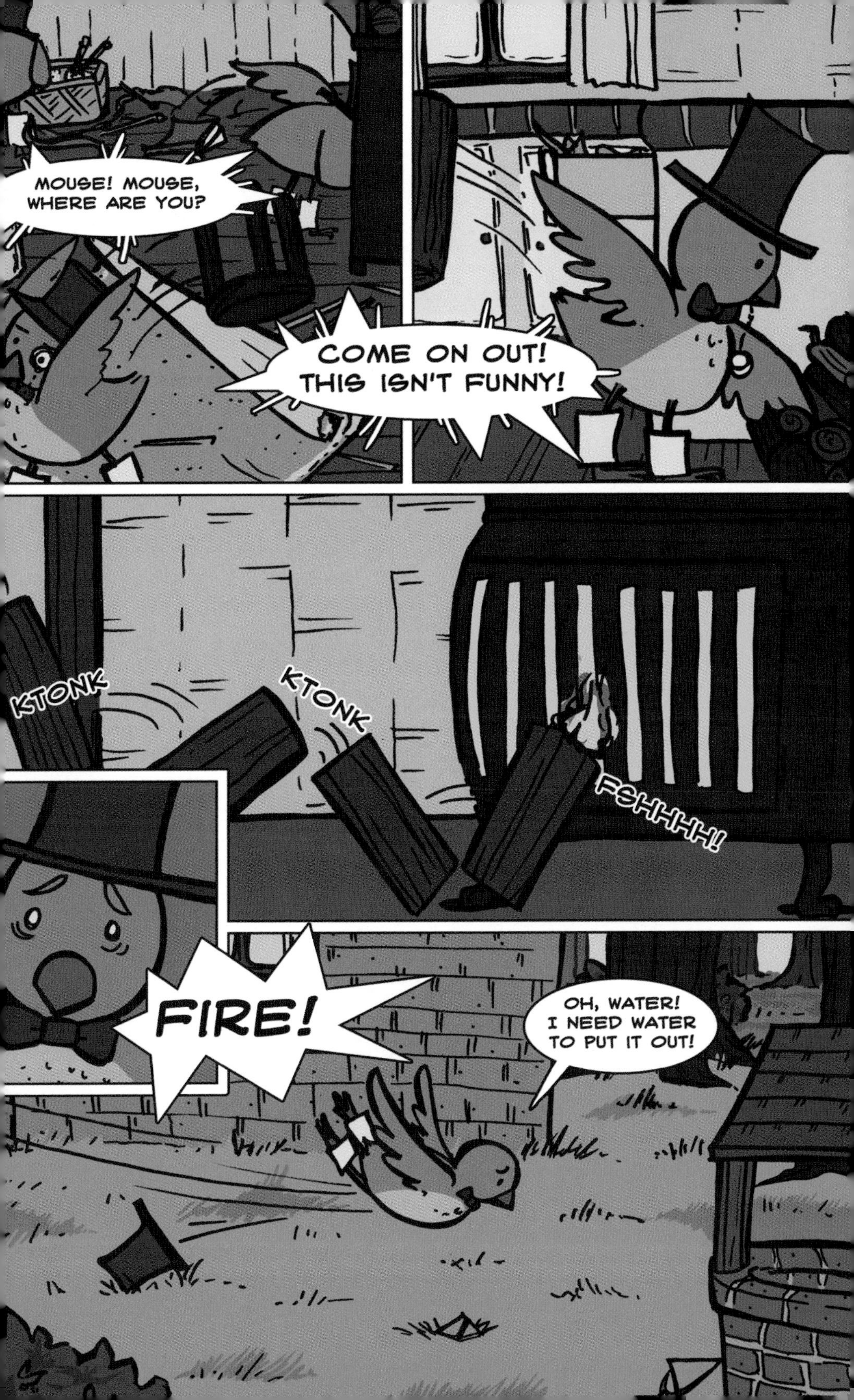
MOUSE! MOUSE, WHERE ARE YOU?
COME ON OUT! THIS ISN'T FUNNY!
KTONK
KTONK
FSHHHH!
FIRE!
OH, WATER! I NEED WATER TO PUT IT OUT!

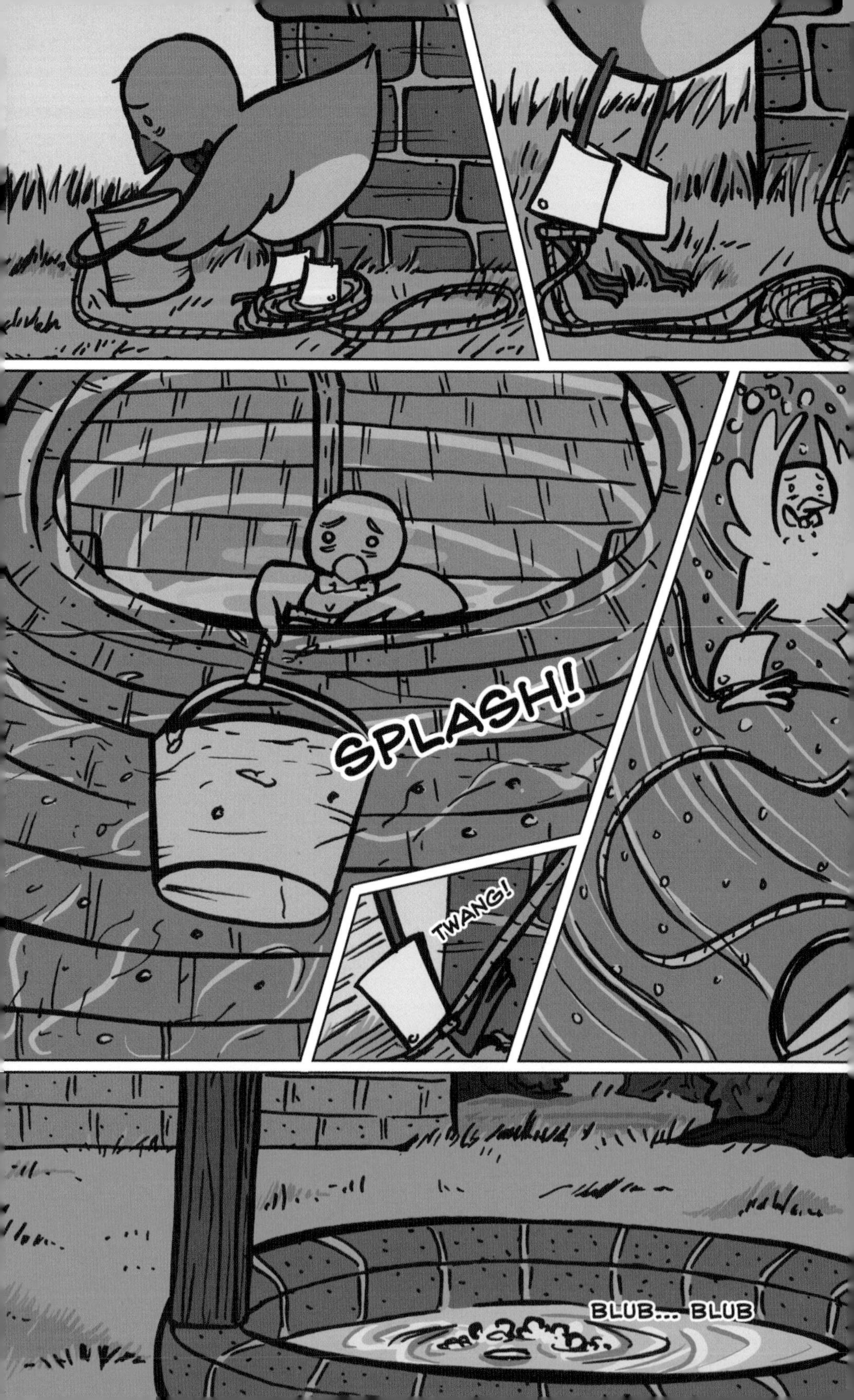
SPLASH!
TWANG!
BLUB... BLUB

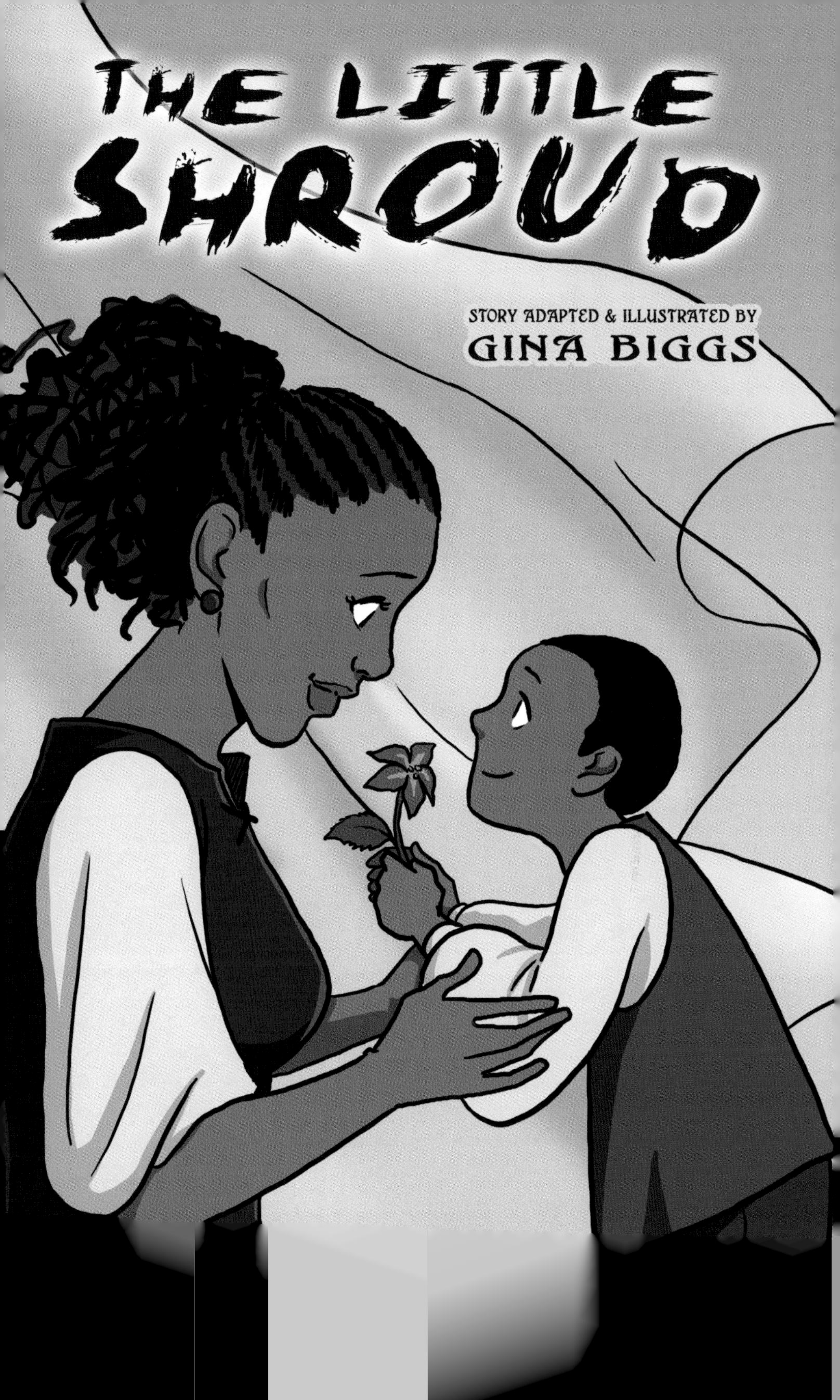
THE LITTLE SHROUD
STORY ADAPTED & ILLUSTRATED BY
GINA BIGGS

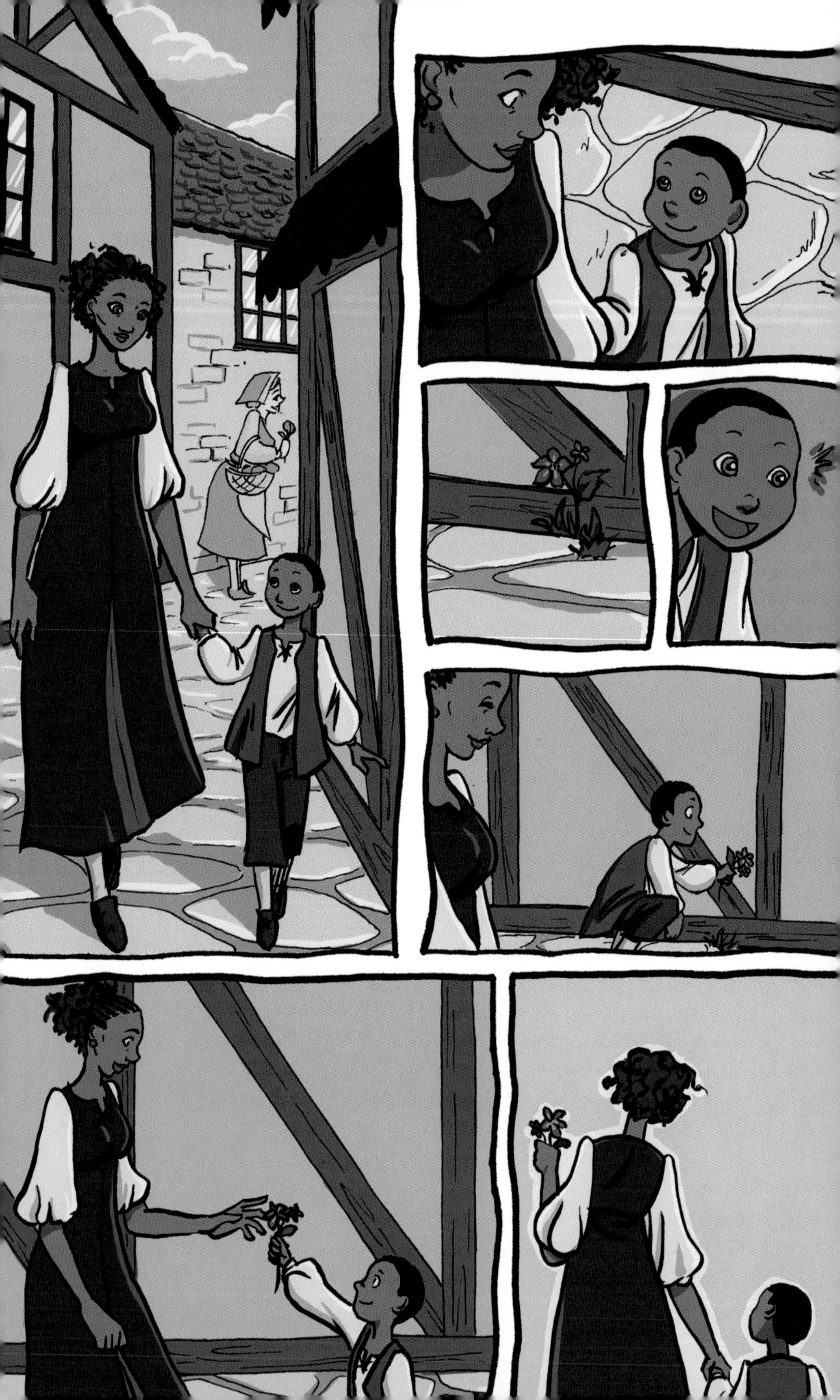

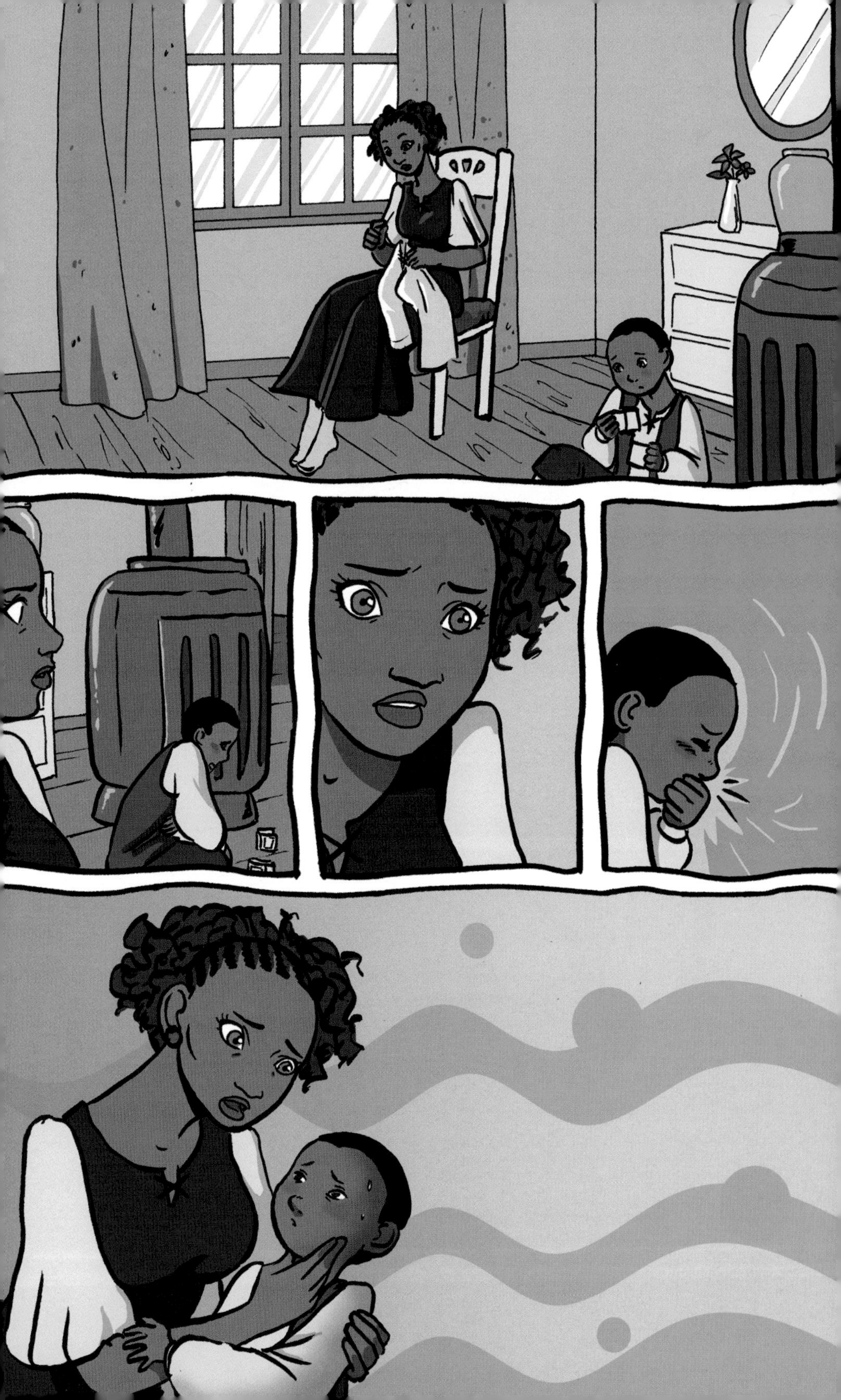

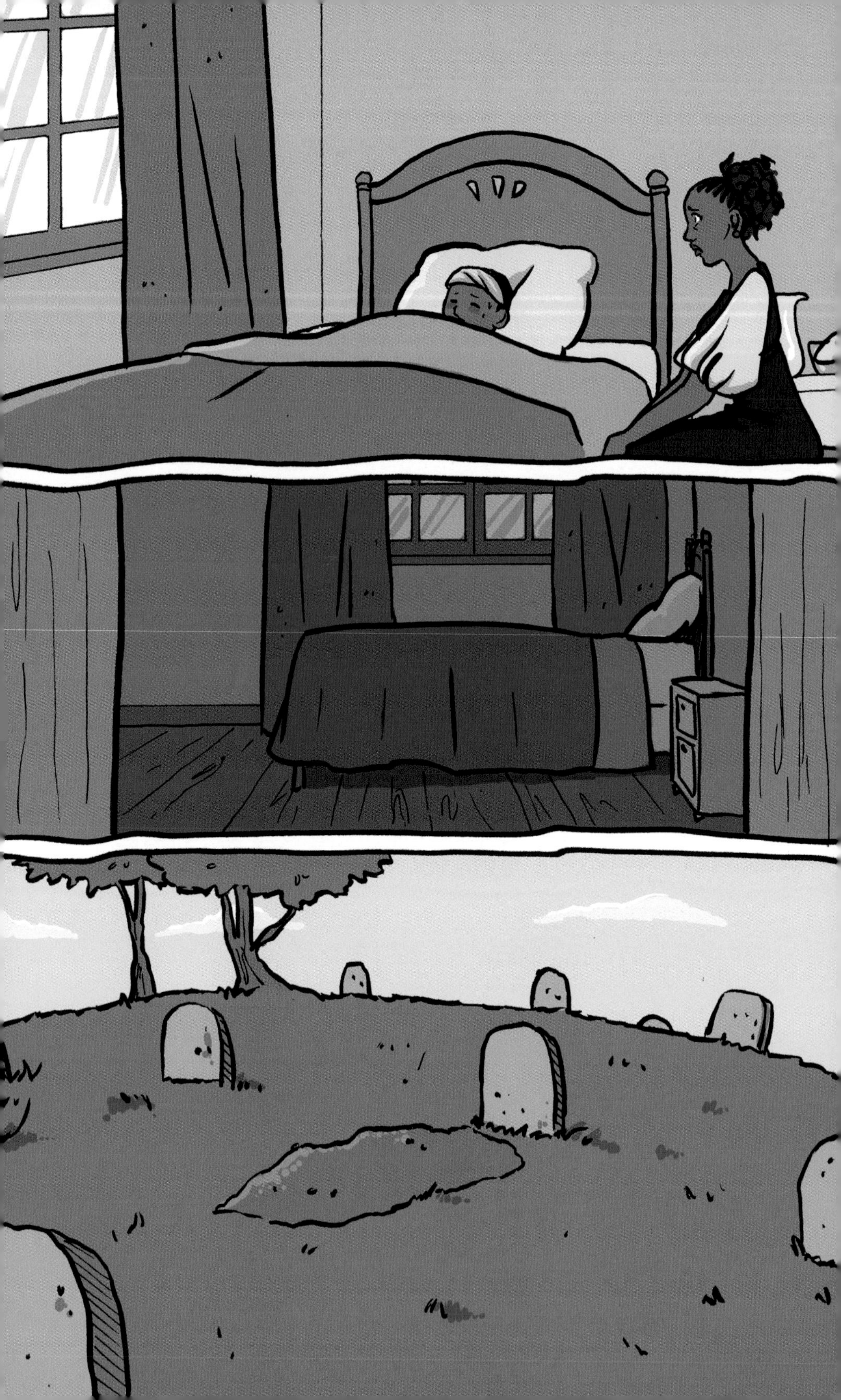

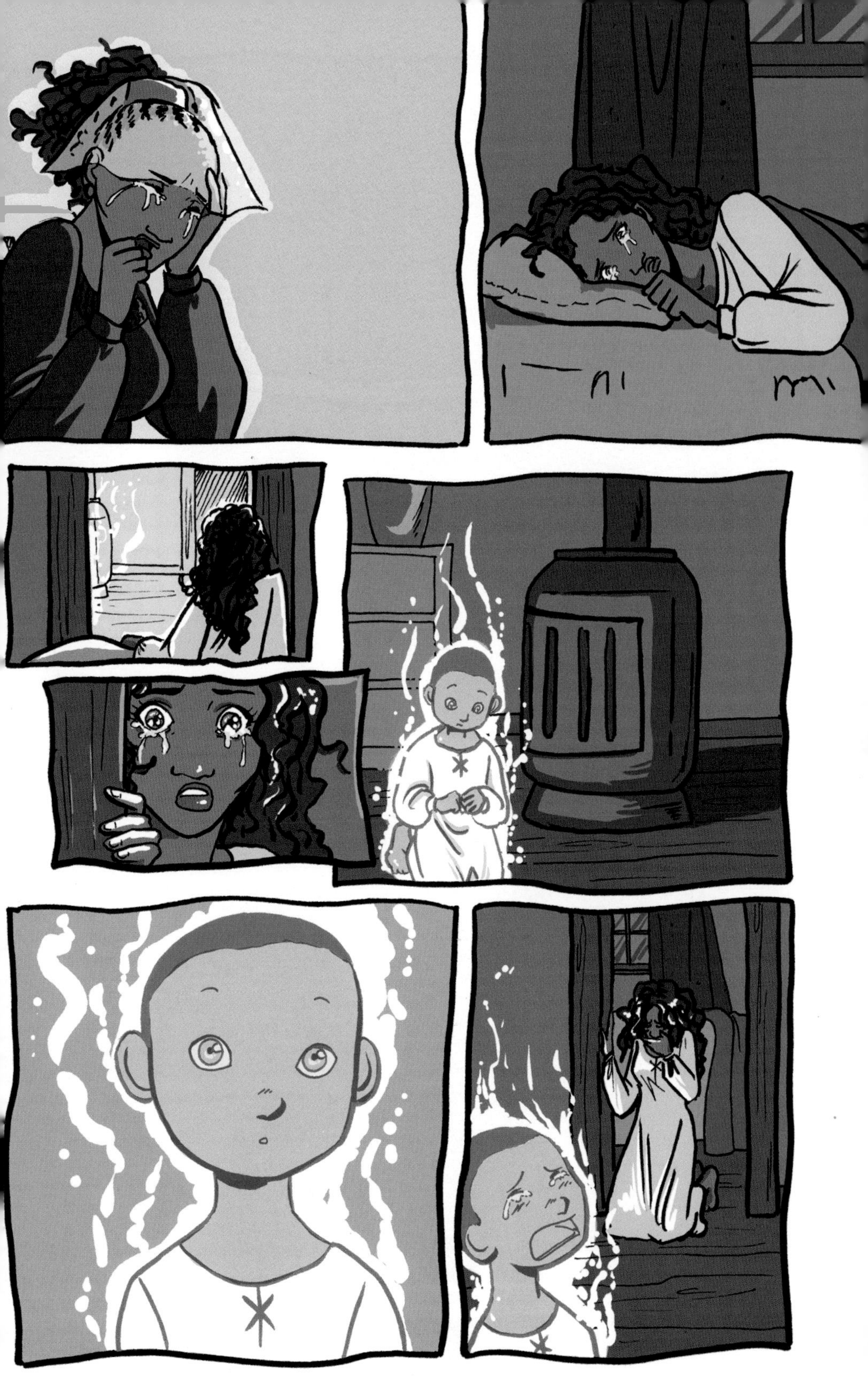

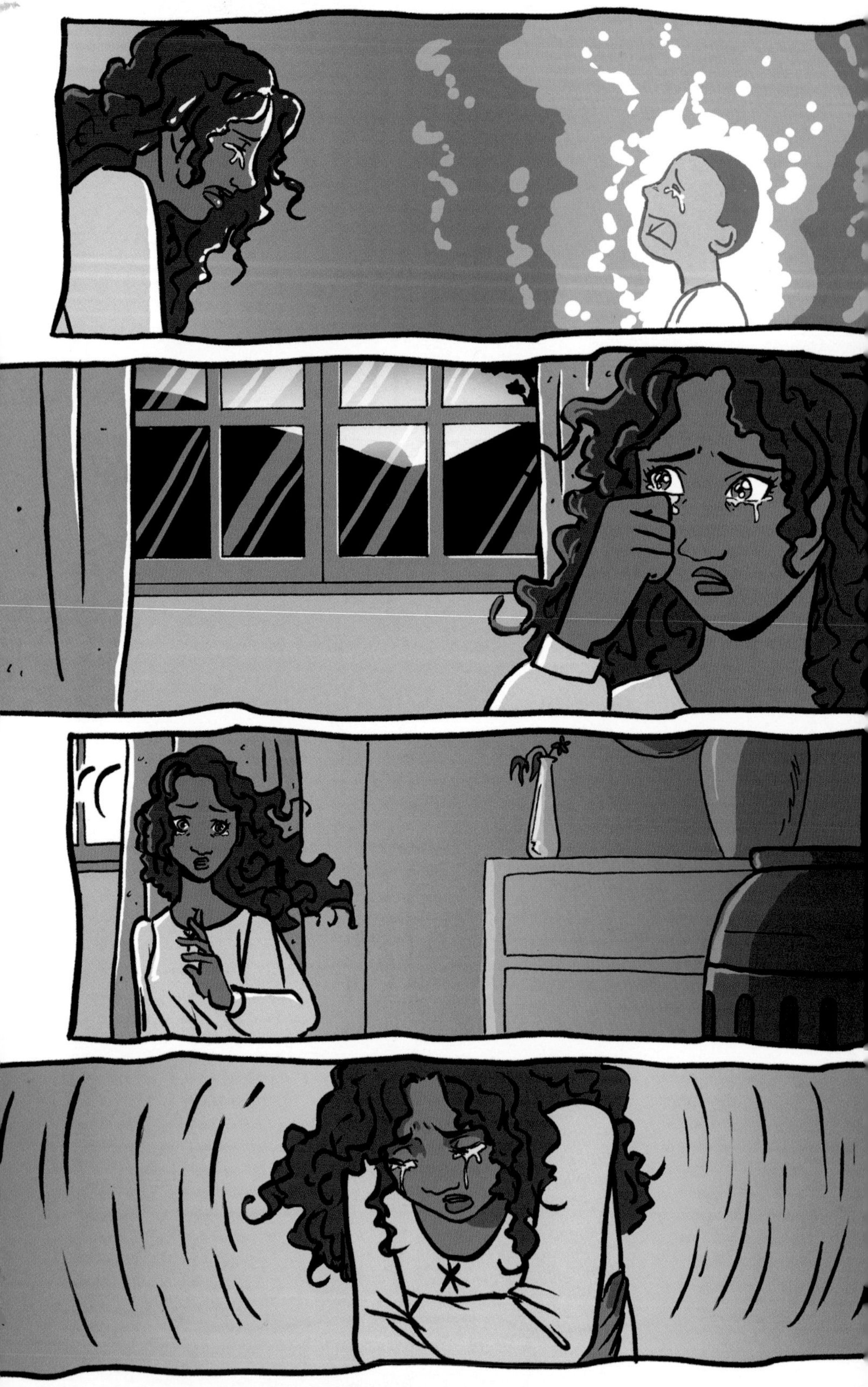

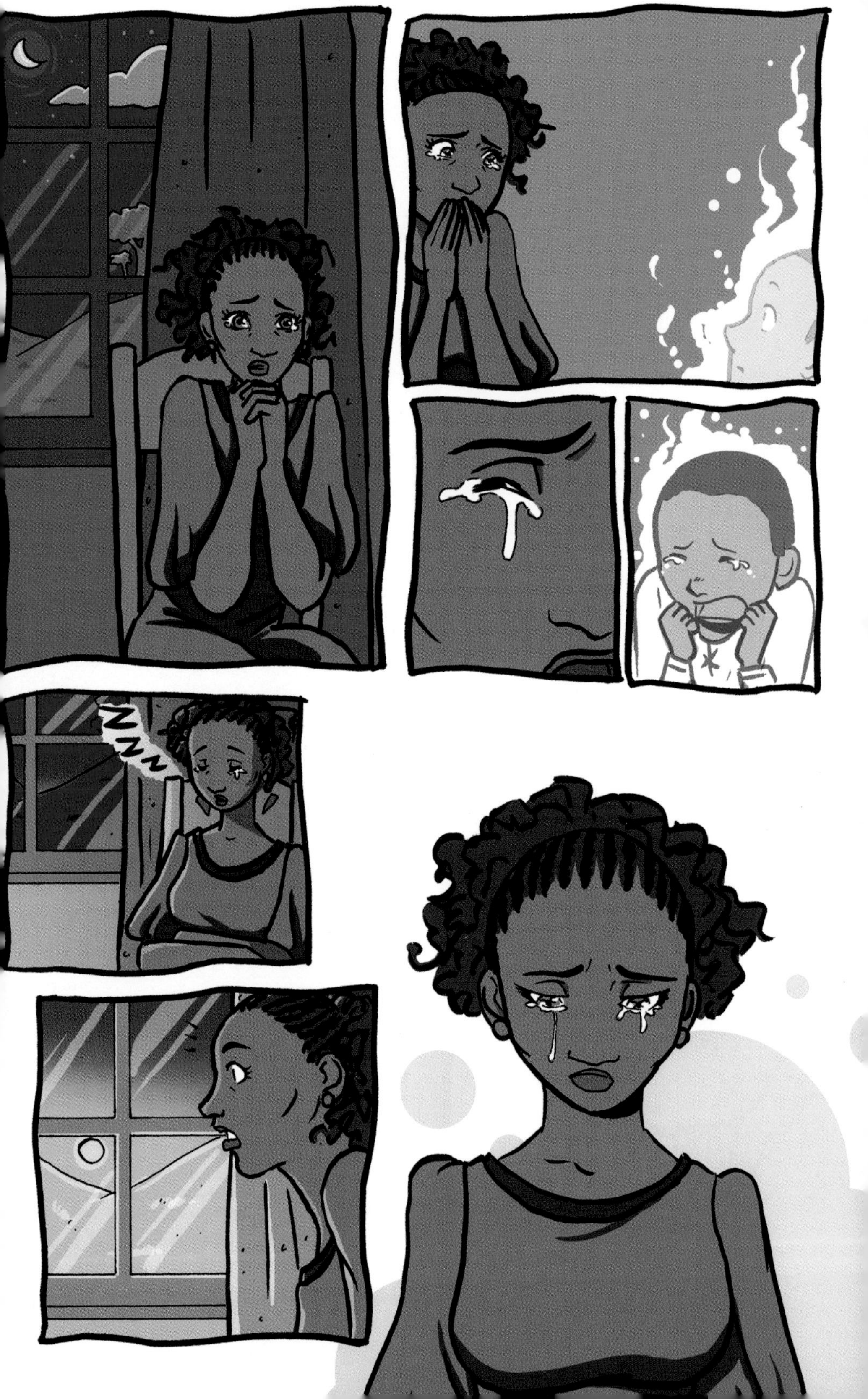
ZZZ

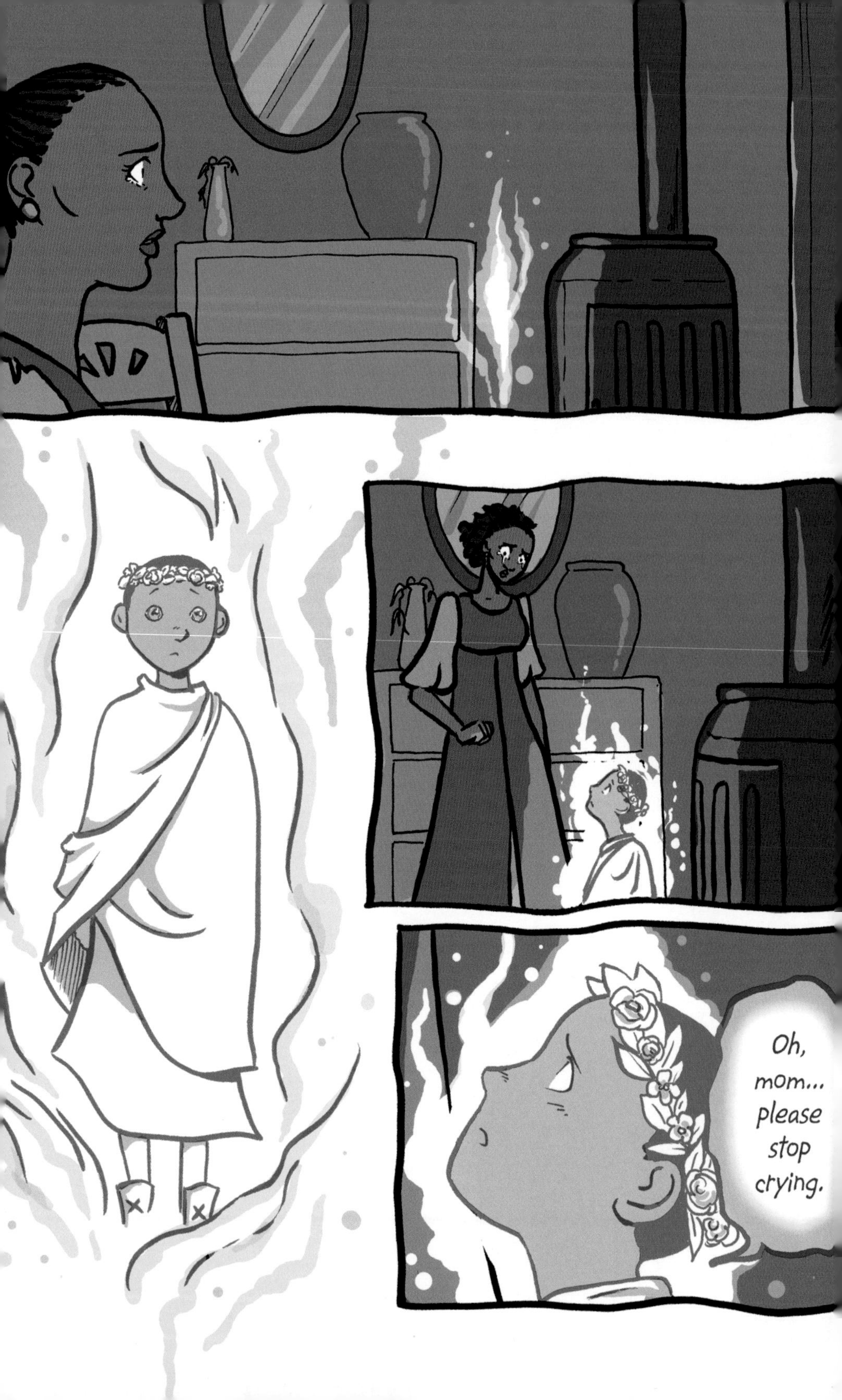
Oh, mom... please stop crying.

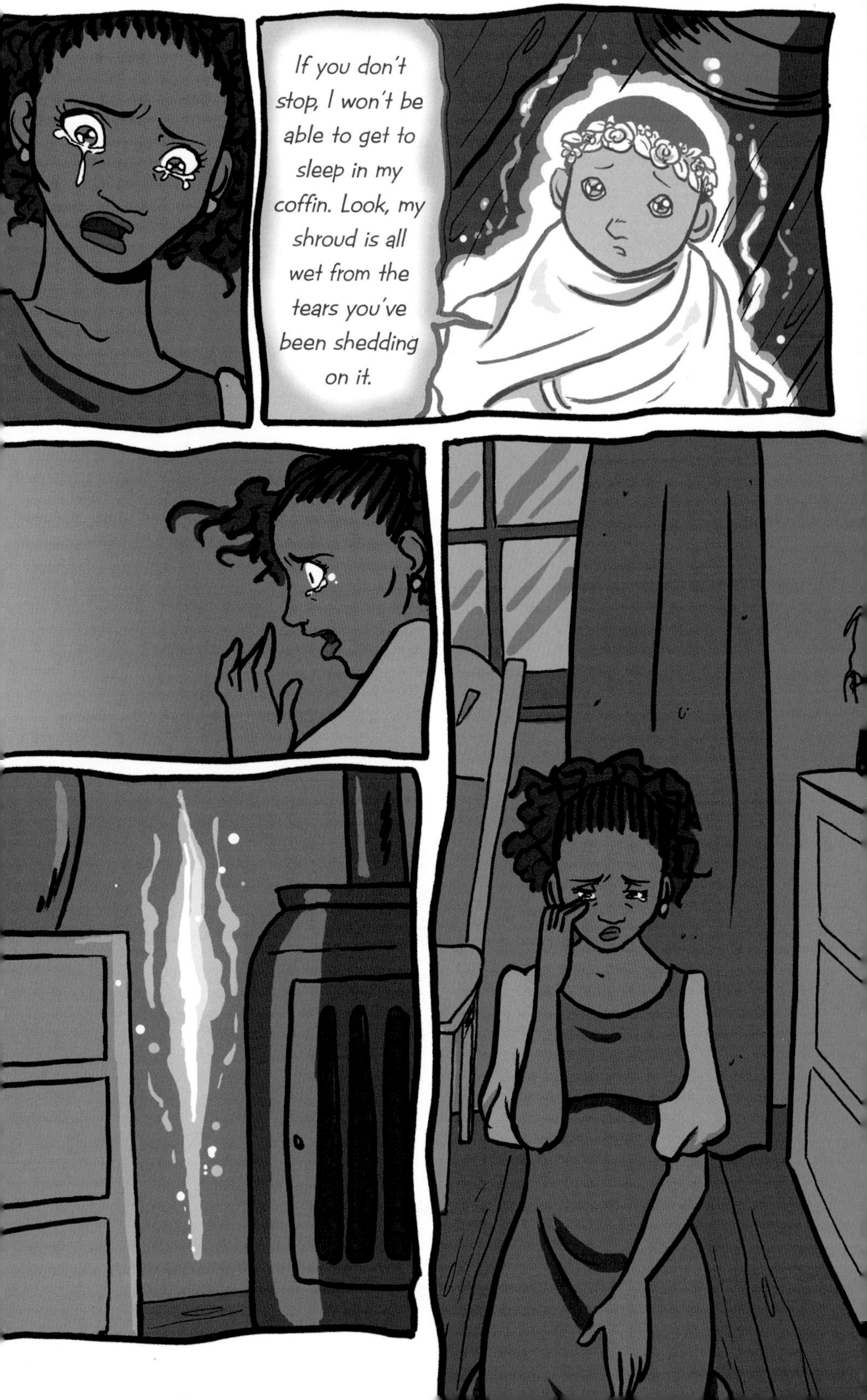
If you don't stop, I won't be able to get to sleep in my coffin. Look, my shroud is all wet from the tears you've been shedding on it.

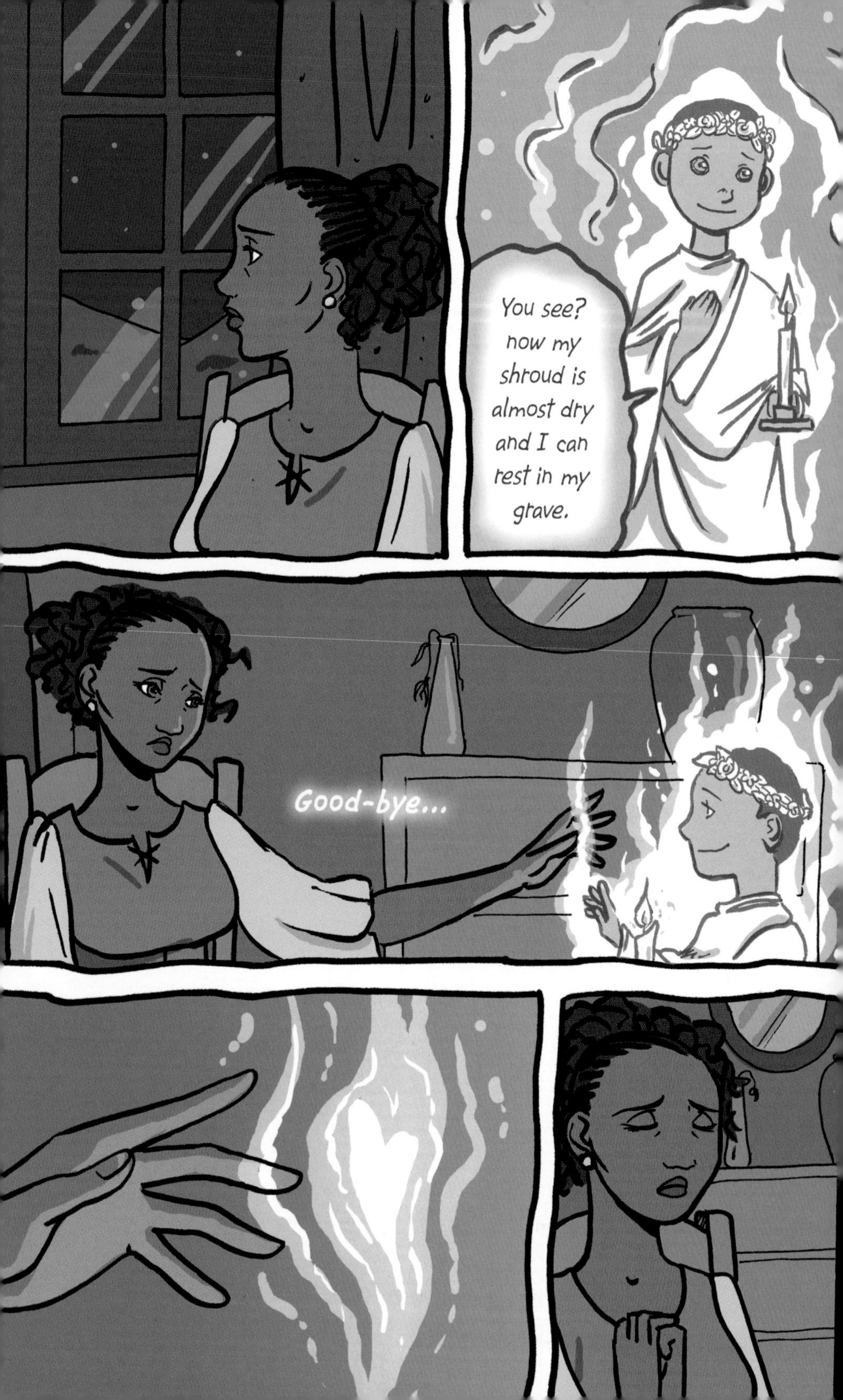
You see? now my shroud is almost dry and I can rest in my grave.
Good-bye...

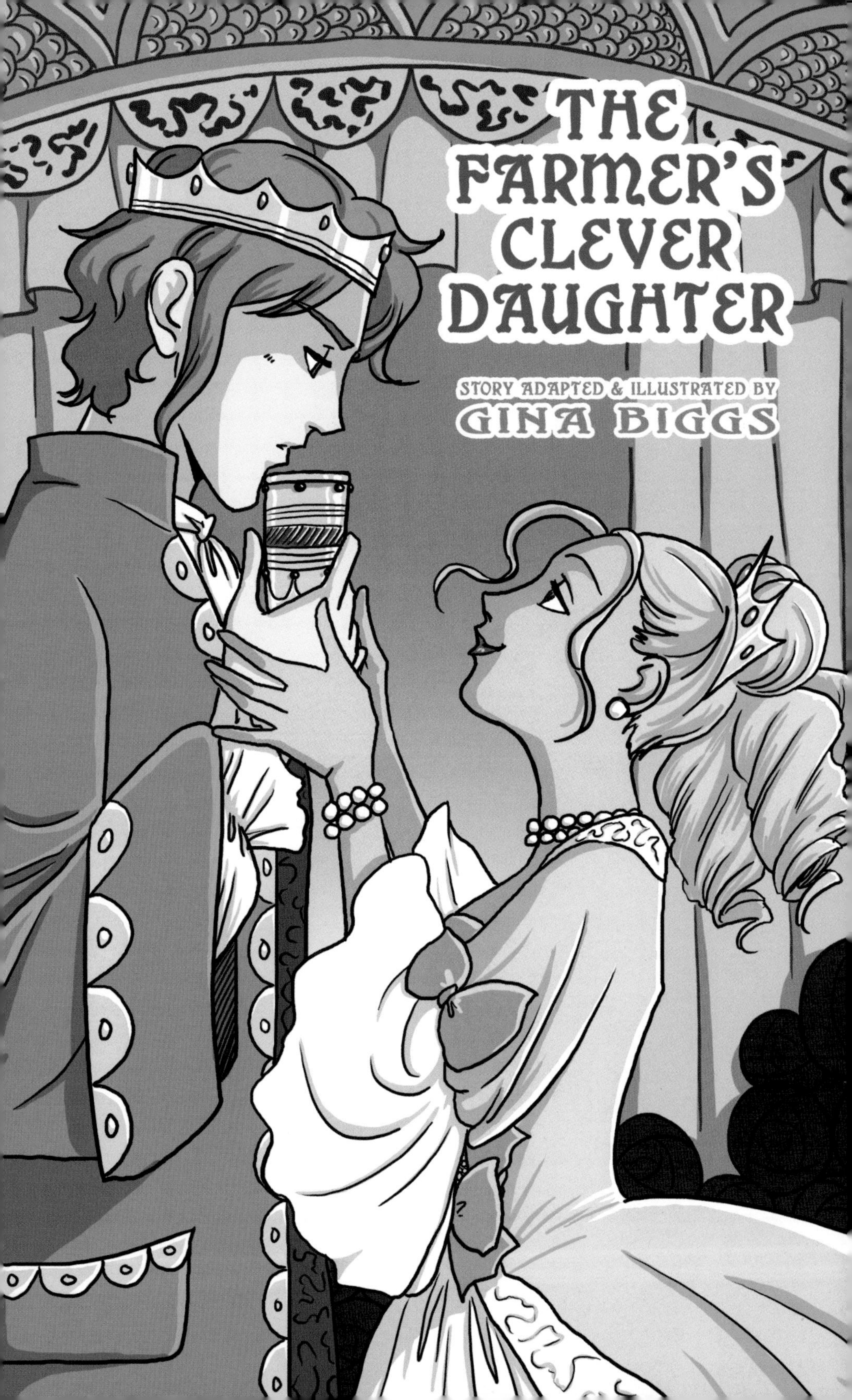
THE FARMER'S CLEVER DAUGHTER
STORY ADAPTED & ILLUSTRATED BY
GINA BIGGS

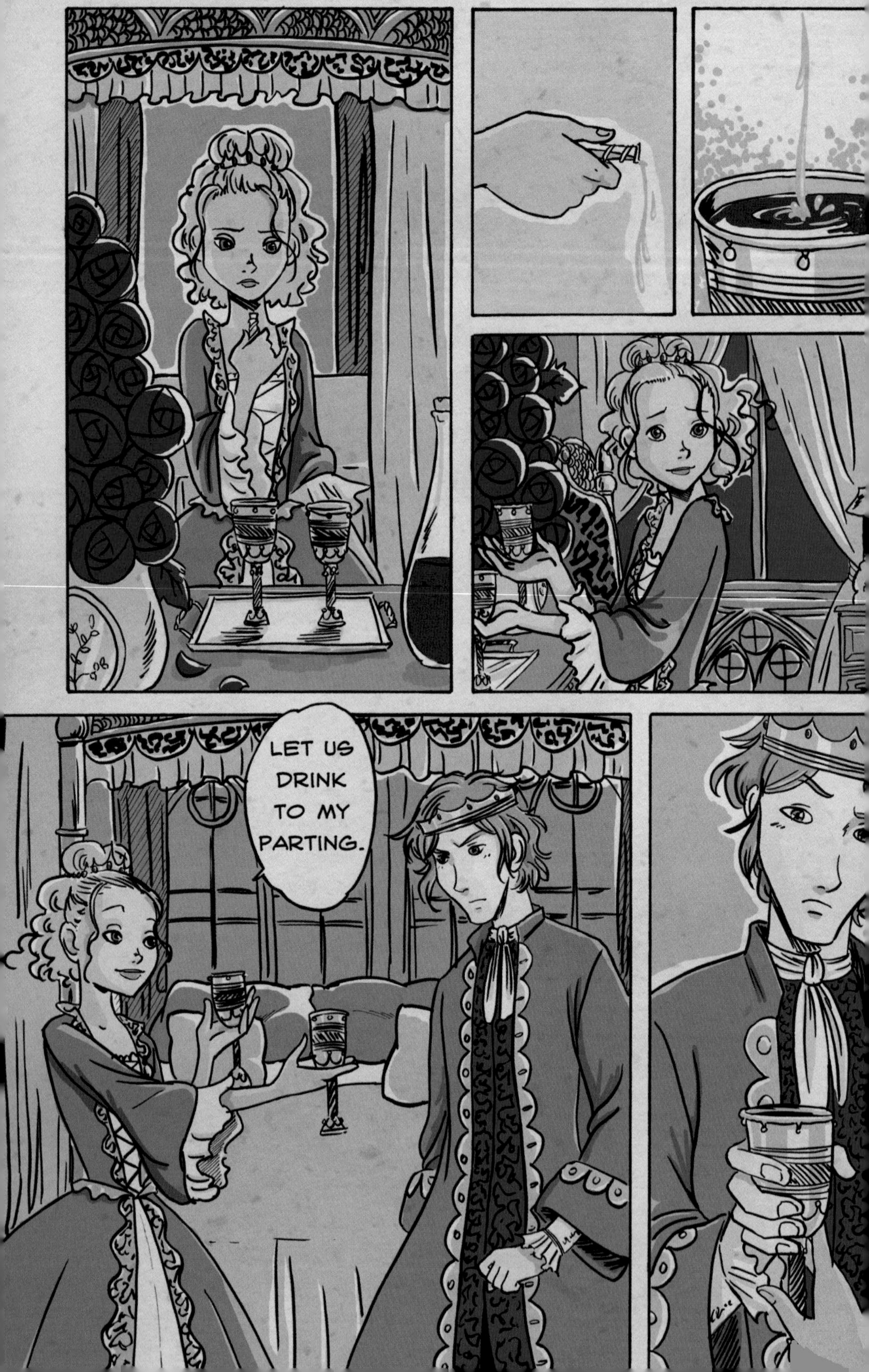
LET US DRINK TO MY PARTING.

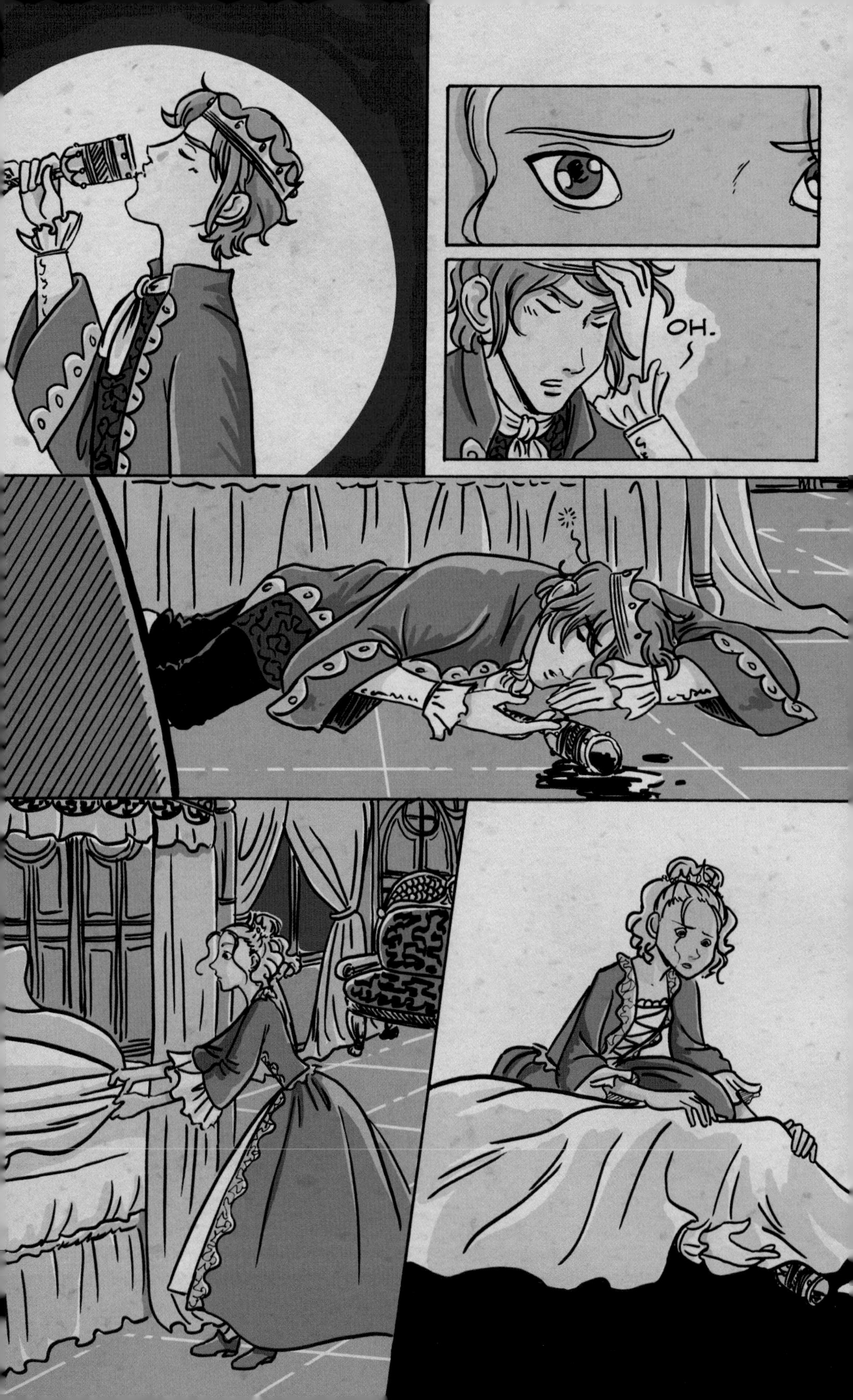
OH.

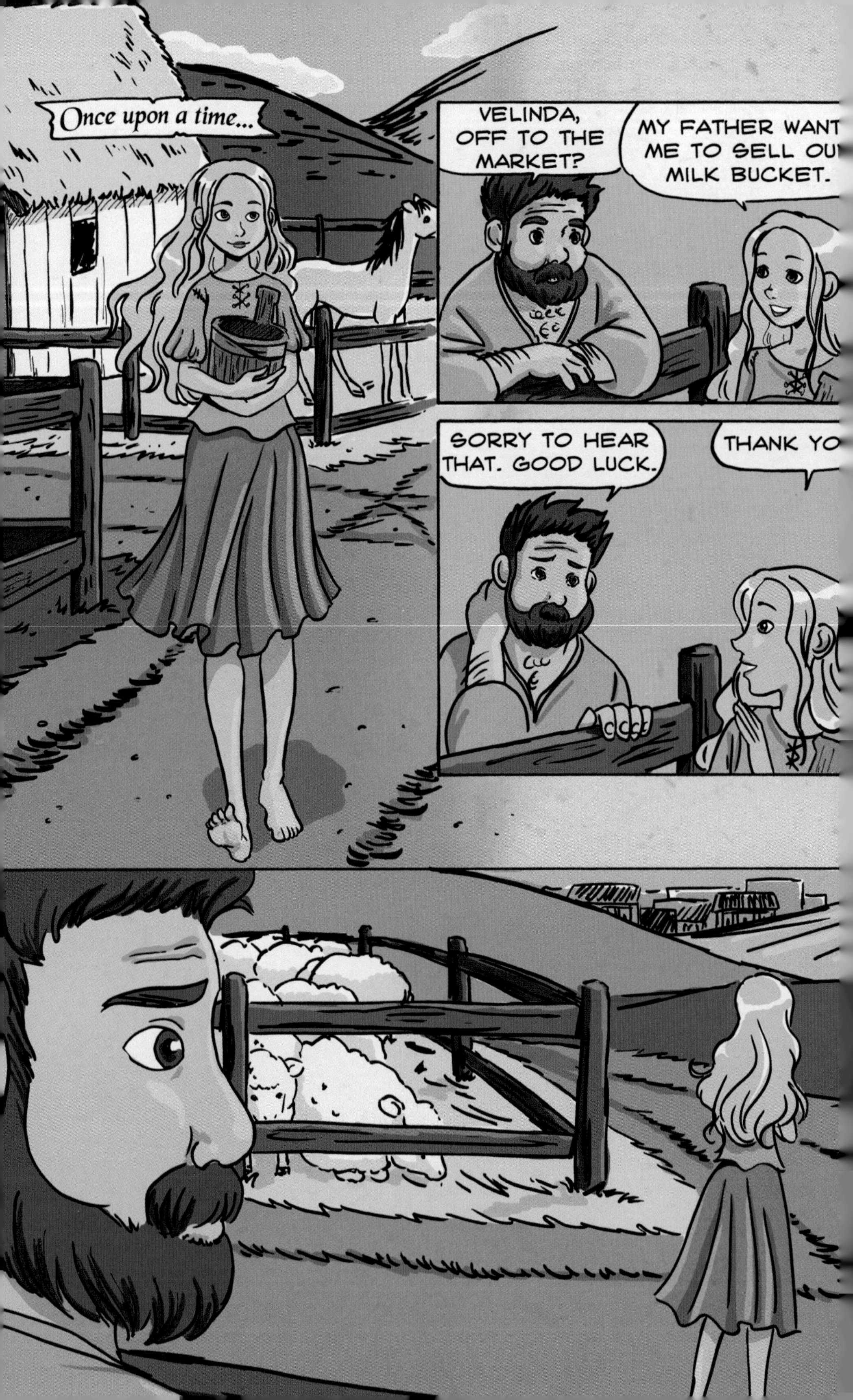
Once upon a time...
VELINDA, OFF TO THE MARKET?
MY FATHER WANT ME TO SELL OU MILK BUCKET.
SORRY TO HEAR THAT. GOOD LUCK.
THANK YO

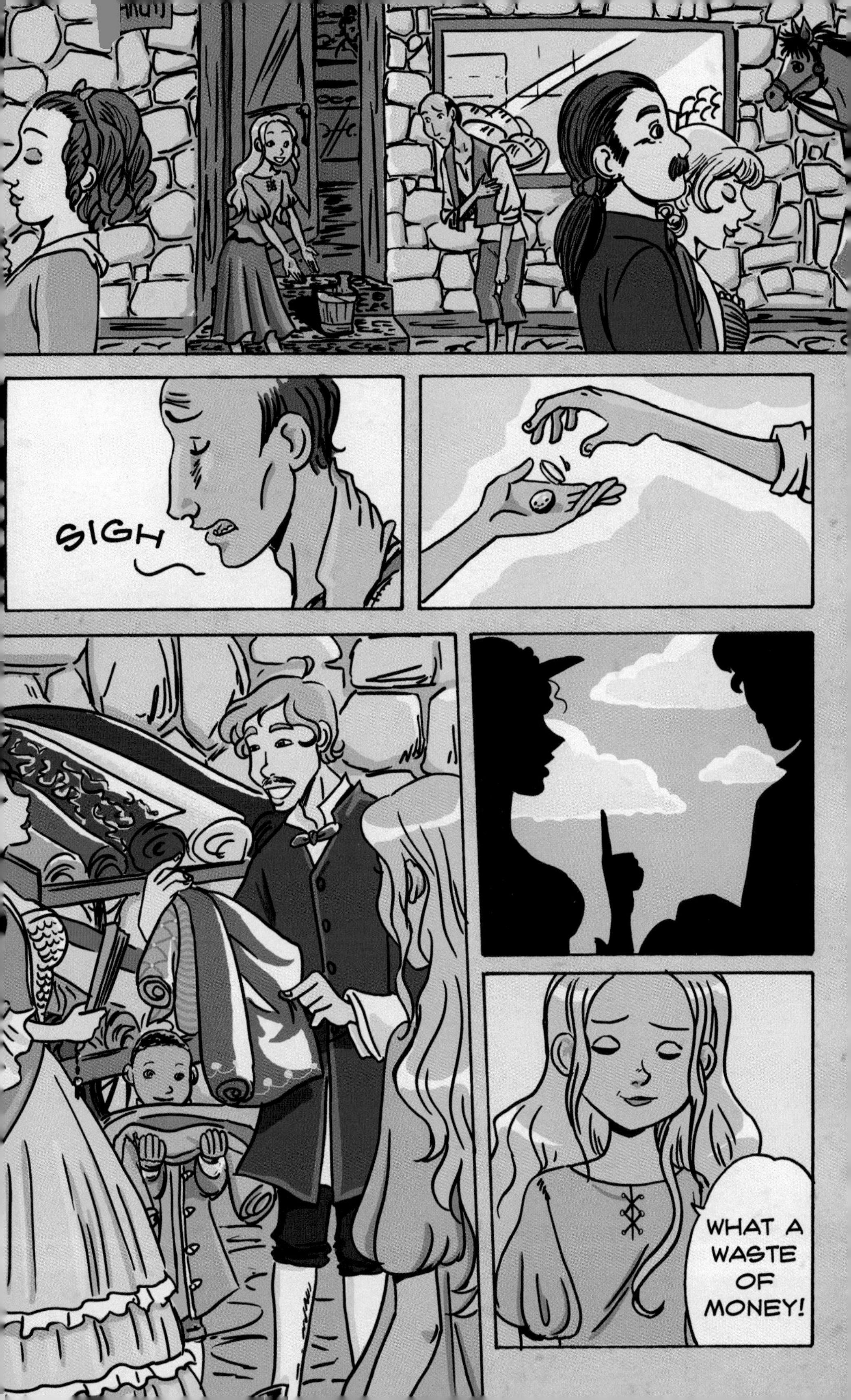
SIGH
WHAT A WASTE OF MONEY!

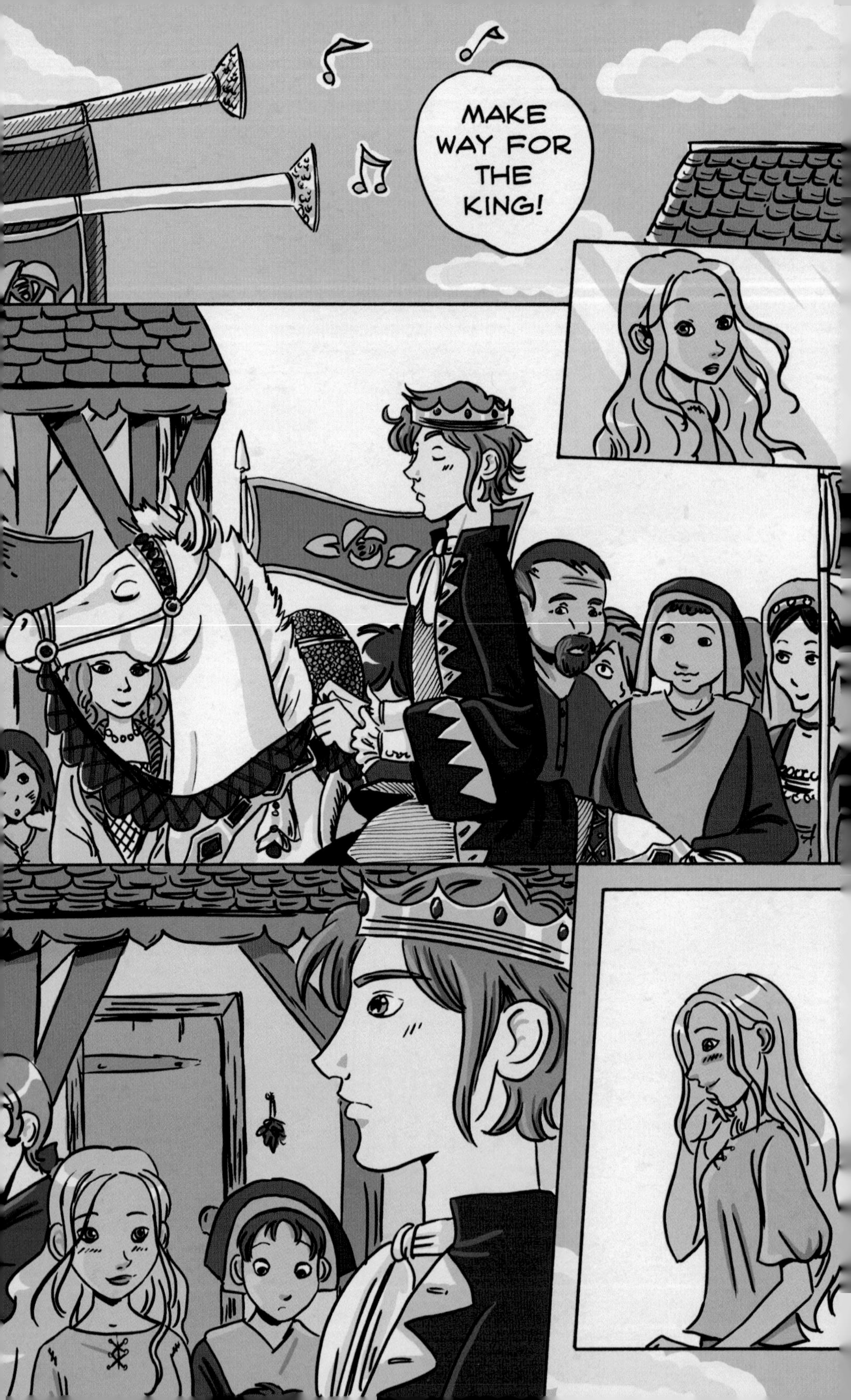
MAKE WAY FOR THE KING!

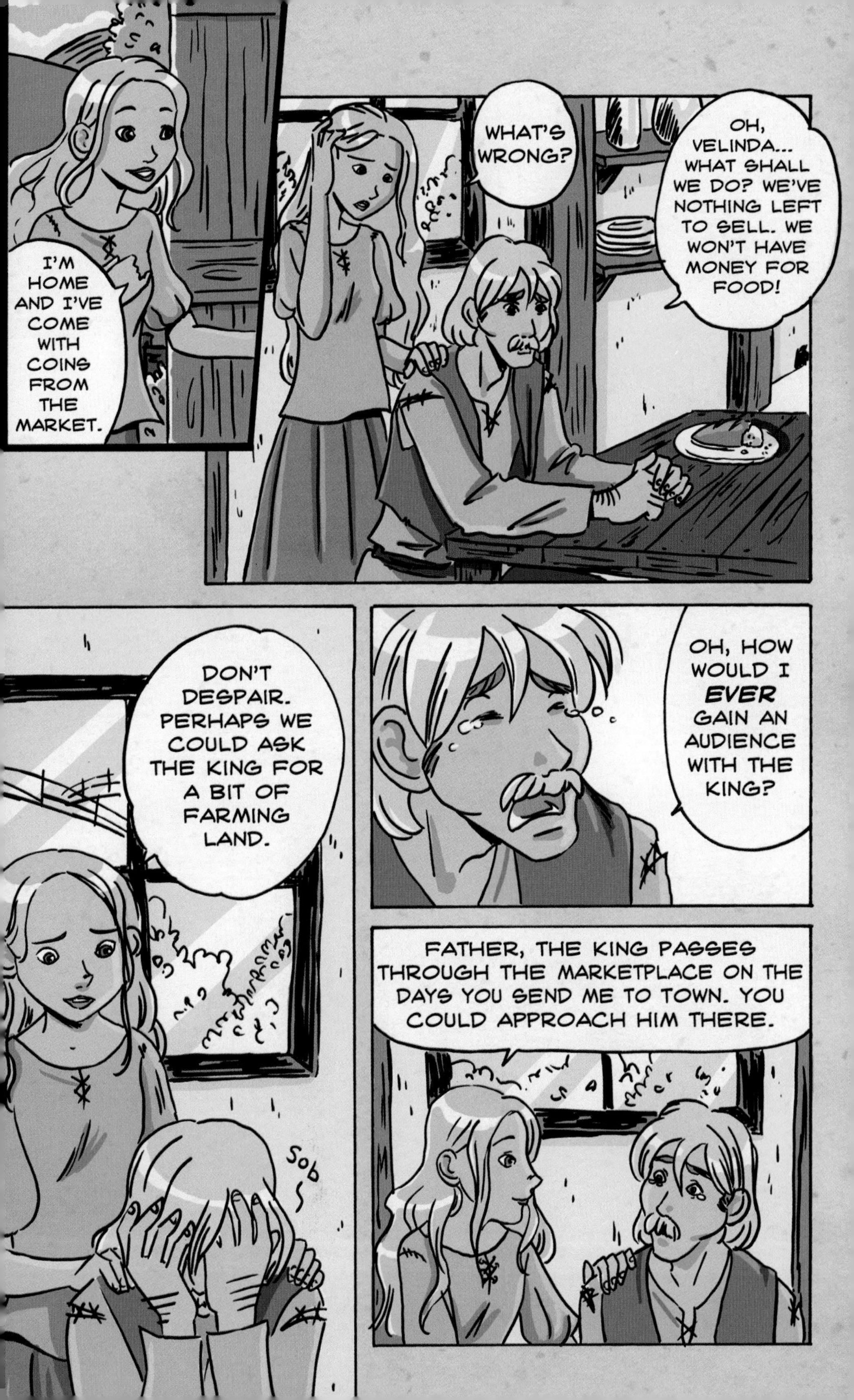
I'M HOME AND I'VE COME WITH COINS FROM THE MARKET.
WHAT'S WRONG?
OH, VELINDA... WHAT SHALL WE DO? WE'VE NOTHING LEFT TO SELL. WE WON'T HAVE MONEY FOR FOOD!
DON'T DESPAIR. PERHAPS WE COULD ASK THE KING FOR A BIT OF FARMING LAND.
Sob
OH, HOW WOULD I ***EVER*** GAIN AN AUDIENCE WITH THE KING?
FATHER, THE KING PASSES THROUGH THE MARKETPLACE ON THE DAYS YOU SEND ME TO TOWN. YOU COULD APPROACH HIM THERE.

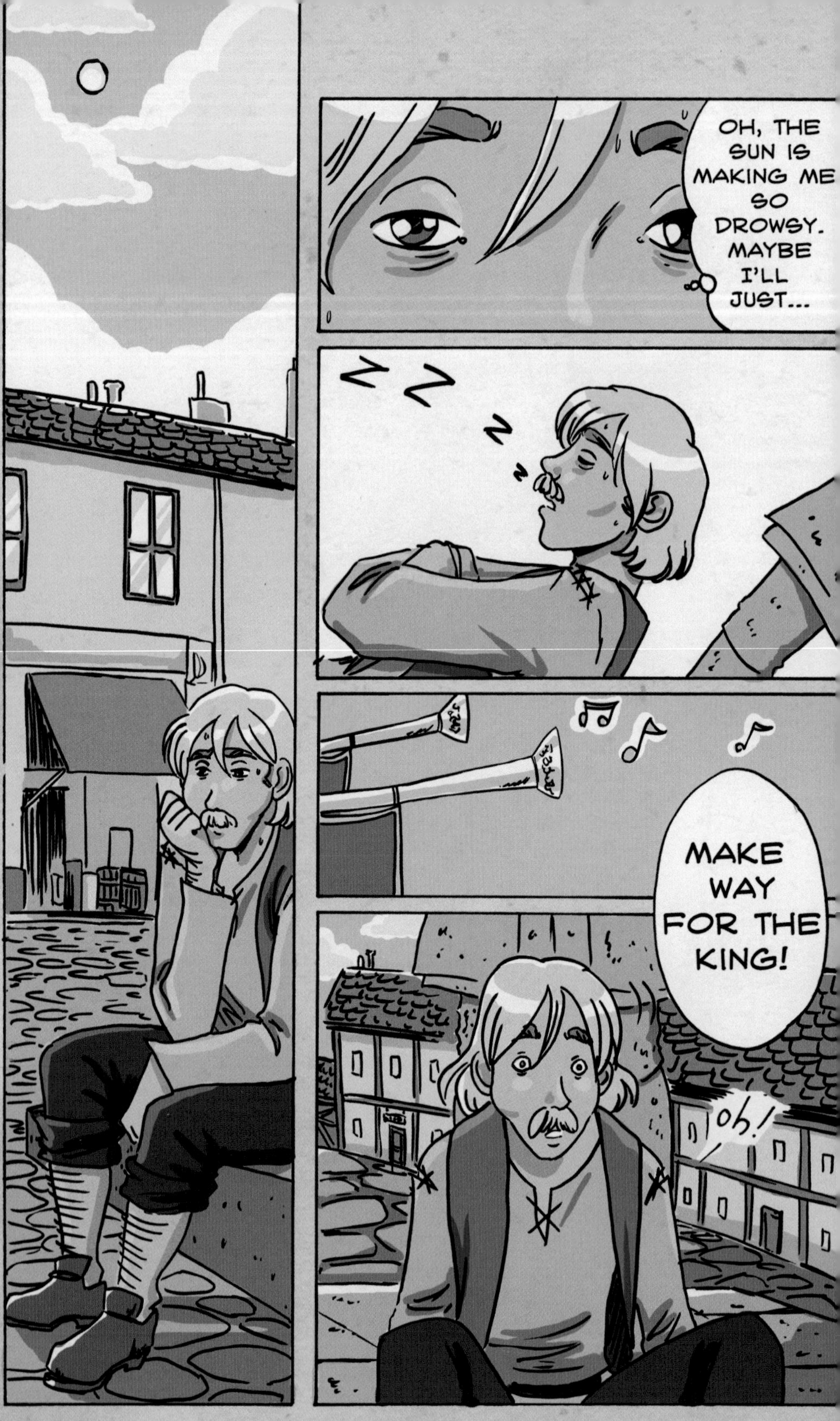
OH, THE SUN IS MAKING ME SO DROWSY. MAYBE I'LL JUST...
Z Z Z Z
MAKE WAY FOR THE KING!
oh!

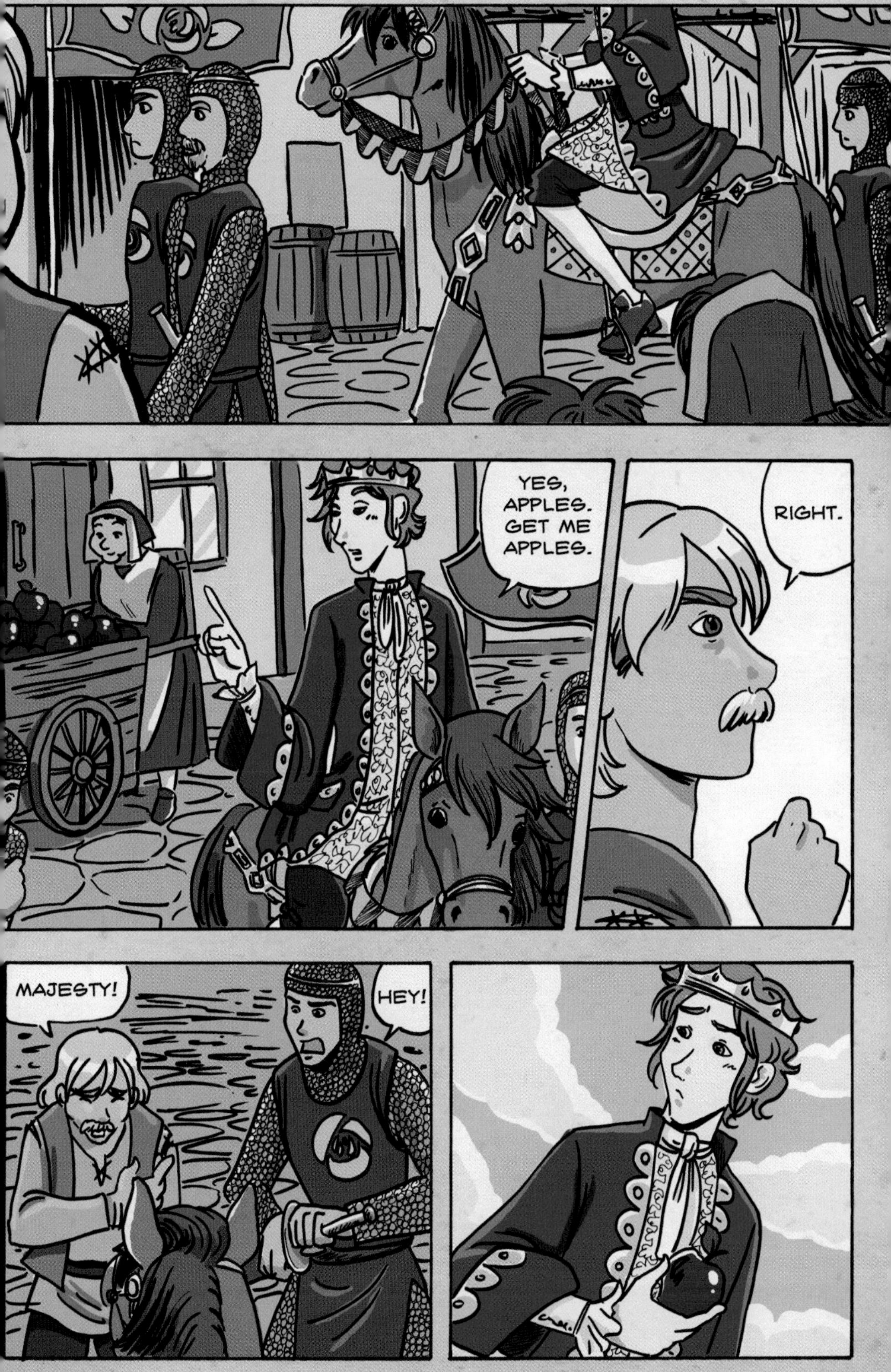
YES, APPLES. GET ME APPLES.
RIGHT.
MAJESTY!
HEY!

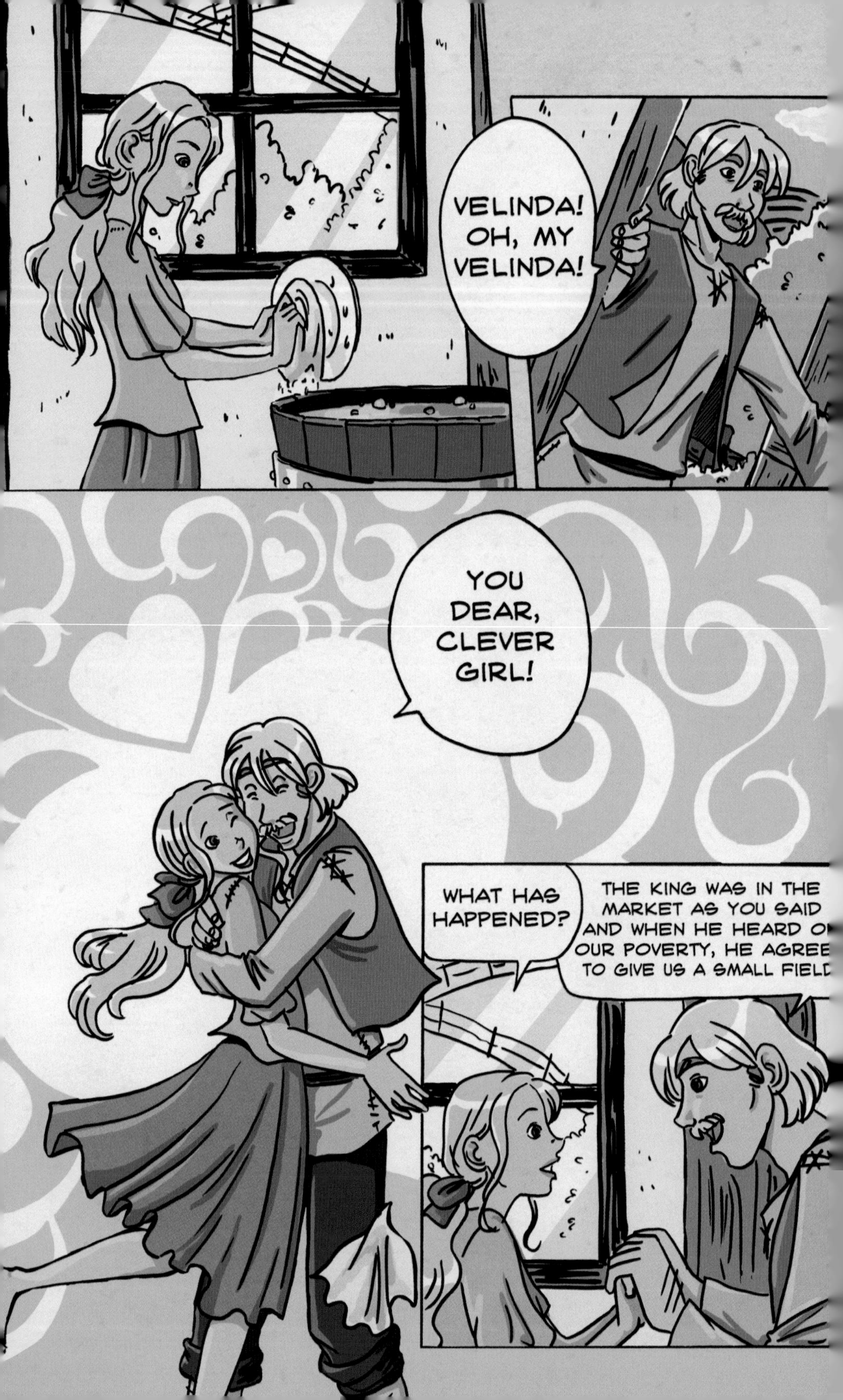
VELINDA! OH, MY VELINDA!
YOU DEAR, CLEVER GIRL!
WHAT HAS HAPPENED?
THE KING WAS IN THE MARKET AS YOU SAID AND WHEN HE HEARD O OUR POVERTY, HE AGREE TO GIVE US A SMALL FIELD

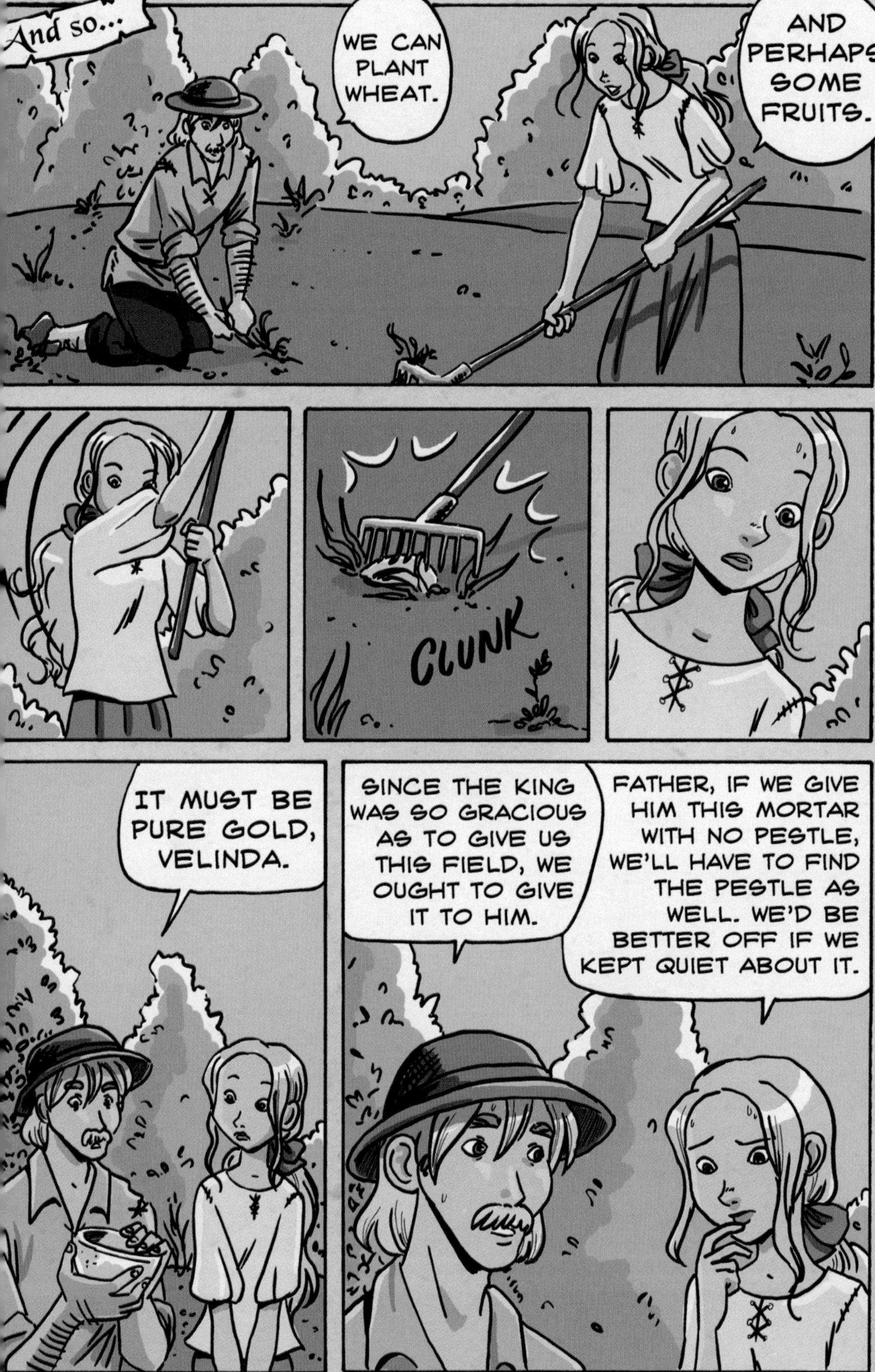
And so...
WE CAN PLANT WHEAT.
AND PERHAPS SOME FRUITS.
CLUNK
IT MUST BE PURE GOLD, VELINDA.
SINCE THE KING WAS SO GRACIOUS AS TO GIVE US THIS FIELD, WE OUGHT TO GIVE IT TO HIM.
FATHER, IF WE GIVE HIM THIS MORTAR WITH NO PESTLE, WE'LL HAVE TO FIND THE PESTLE AS WELL. WE'D BE BETTER OFF IF WE KEPT QUIET ABOUT IT.

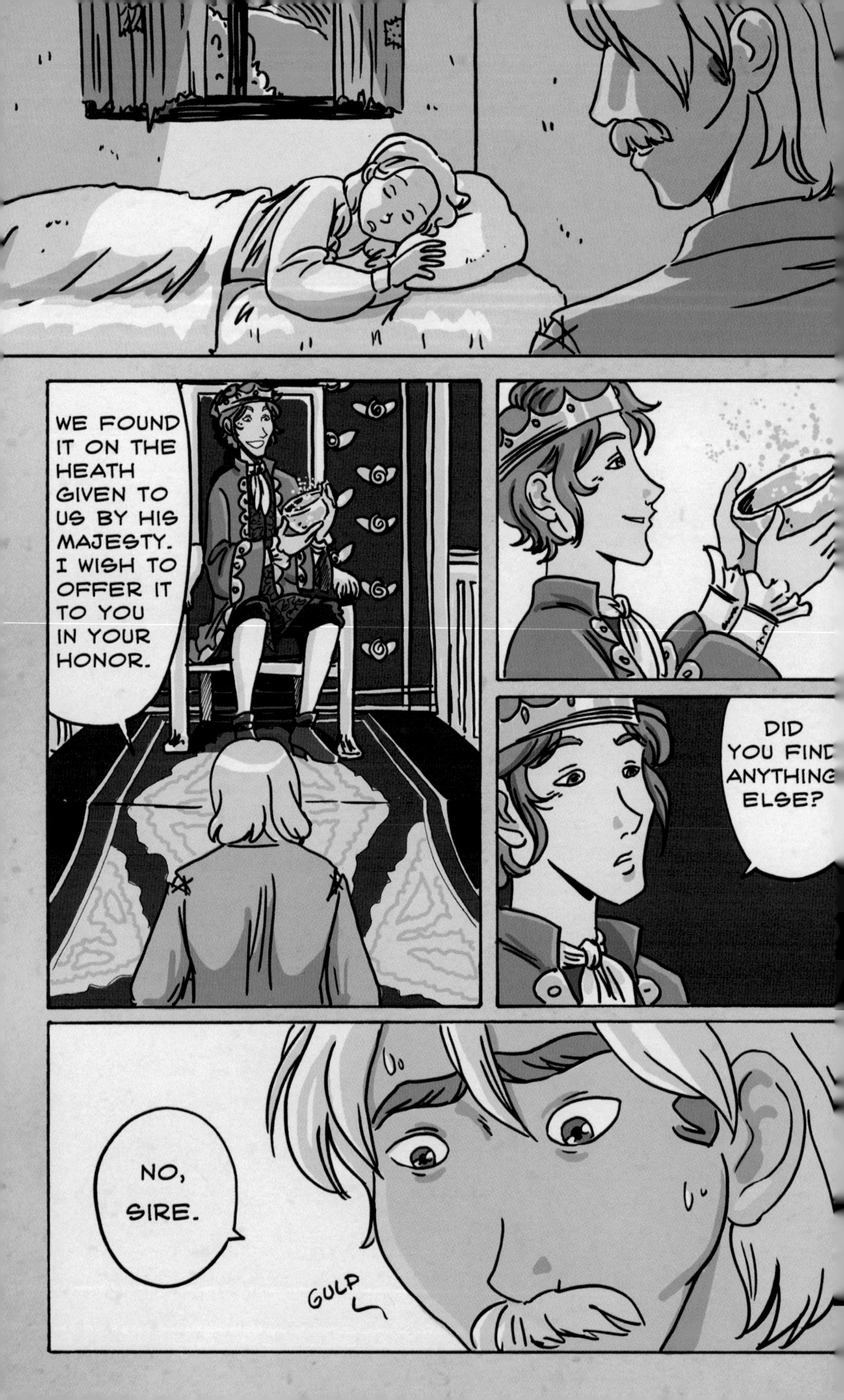
WE FOUND IT ON THE HEATH GIVEN TO US BY HIS MAJESTY. I WISH TO OFFER IT TO YOU IN YOUR HONOR.
DID YOU FIND ANYTHING ELSE?
NO, SIRE.
GULP

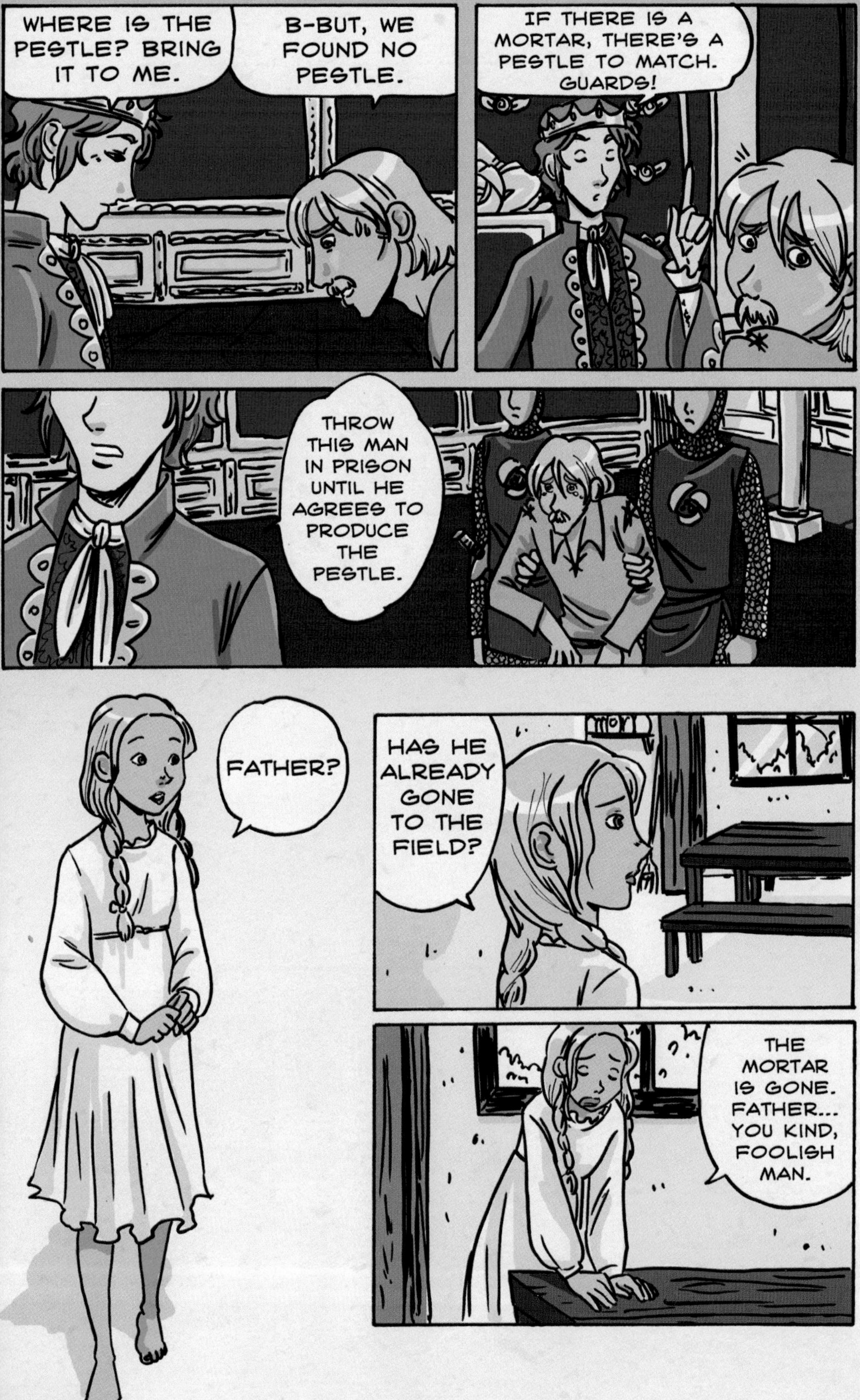
WHERE IS THE PESTLE? BRING IT TO ME.
B-BUT, WE FOUND NO PESTLE.
IF THERE IS A MORTAR, THERE'S A PESTLE TO MATCH. GUARDS!
THROW THIS MAN IN PRISON UNTIL HE AGREES TO PRODUCE THE PESTLE.
FATHER?
HAS HE ALREADY GONE TO THE FIELD?
THE MORTAR IS GONE. FATHER... YOU KIND, FOOLISH MAN.

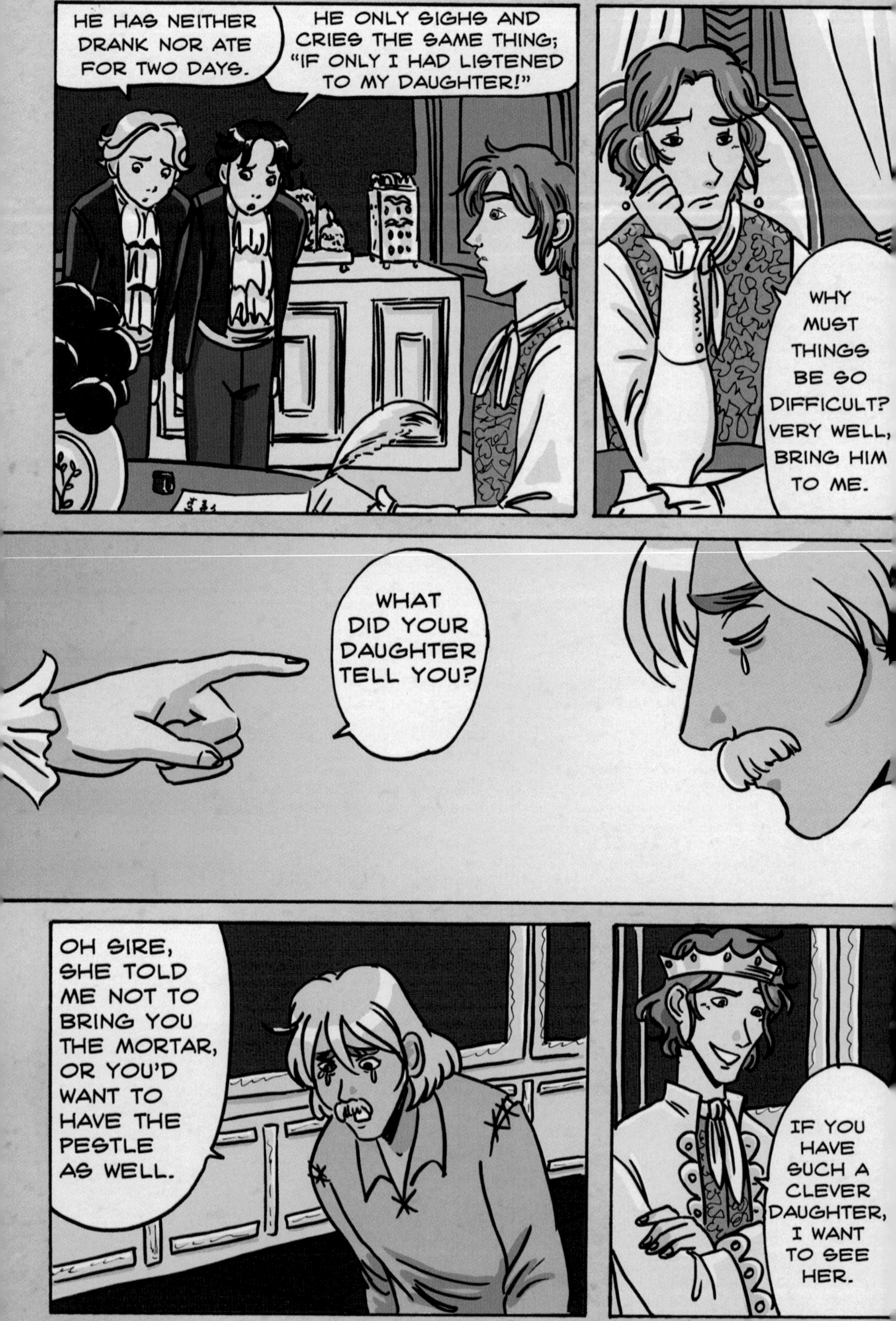
HE HAS NEITHER DRANK NOR ATE FOR TWO DAYS.
HE ONLY SIGHS AND CRIES THE SAME THING; "IF ONLY I HAD LISTENED TO MY DAUGHTER!"
WHY MUST THINGS BE SO DIFFICULT? VERY WELL, BRING HIM TO ME.
WHAT DID YOUR DAUGHTER TELL YOU?
OH SIRE, SHE TOLD ME NOT TO BRING YOU THE MORTAR, OR YOU'D WANT TO HAVE THE PESTLE AS WELL.
IF YOU HAVE SUCH A CLEVER DAUGHTER, I WANT TO SEE HER.

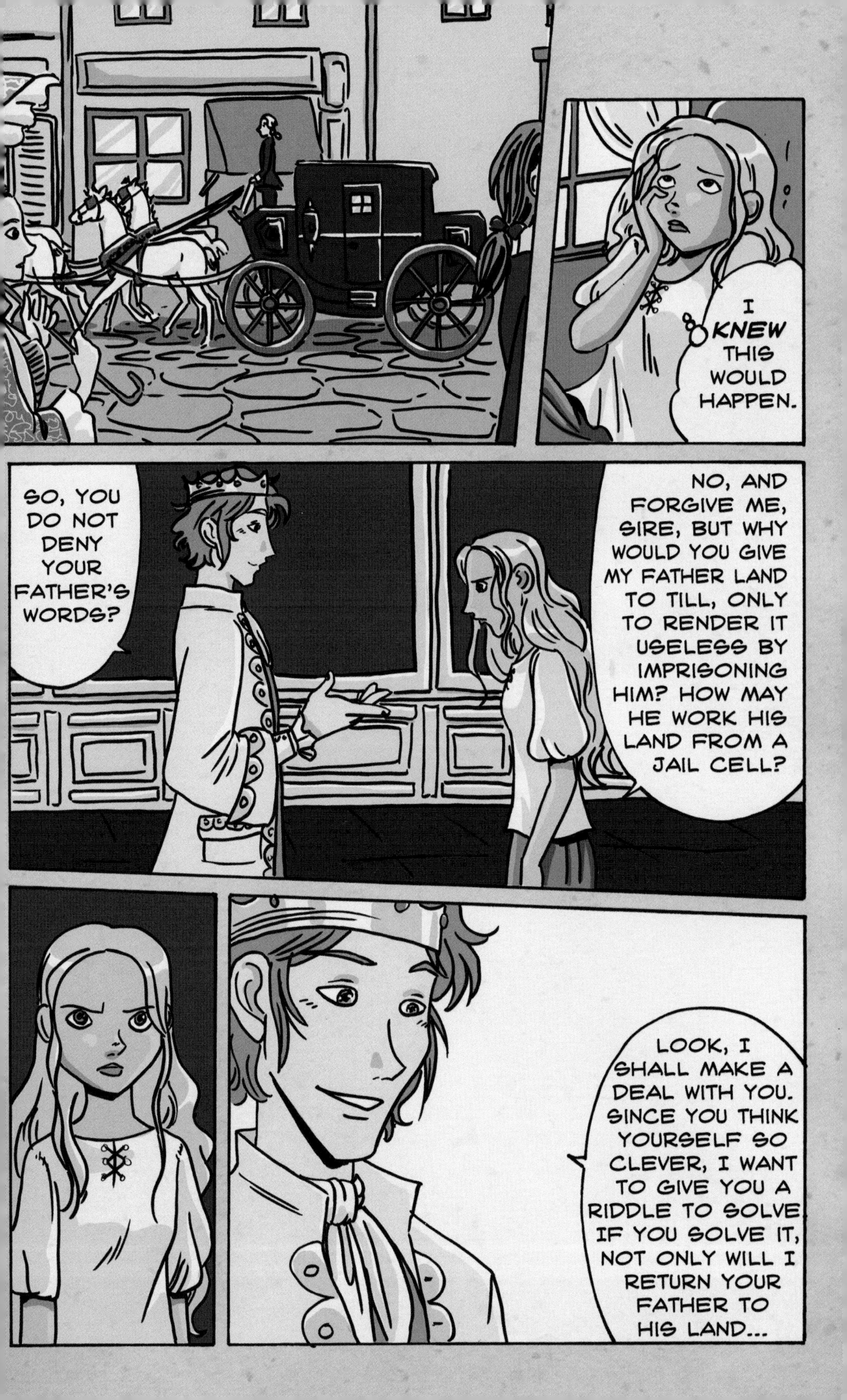
I KNEW THIS WOULD HAPPEN.
SO, YOU DO NOT DENY YOUR FATHER'S WORDS?
NO, AND FORGIVE ME, SIRE, BUT WHY WOULD YOU GIVE MY FATHER LAND TO TILL, ONLY TO RENDER IT USELESS BY IMPRISONING HIM? HOW MAY HE WORK HIS LAND FROM A JAIL CELL?
LOOK, I SHALL MAKE A DEAL WITH YOU. SINCE YOU THINK YOURSELF SO CLEVER, I WANT TO GIVE YOU A RIDDLE TO SOLVE. IF YOU SOLVE IT, NOT ONLY WILL I RETURN YOUR FATHER TO HIS LAND...

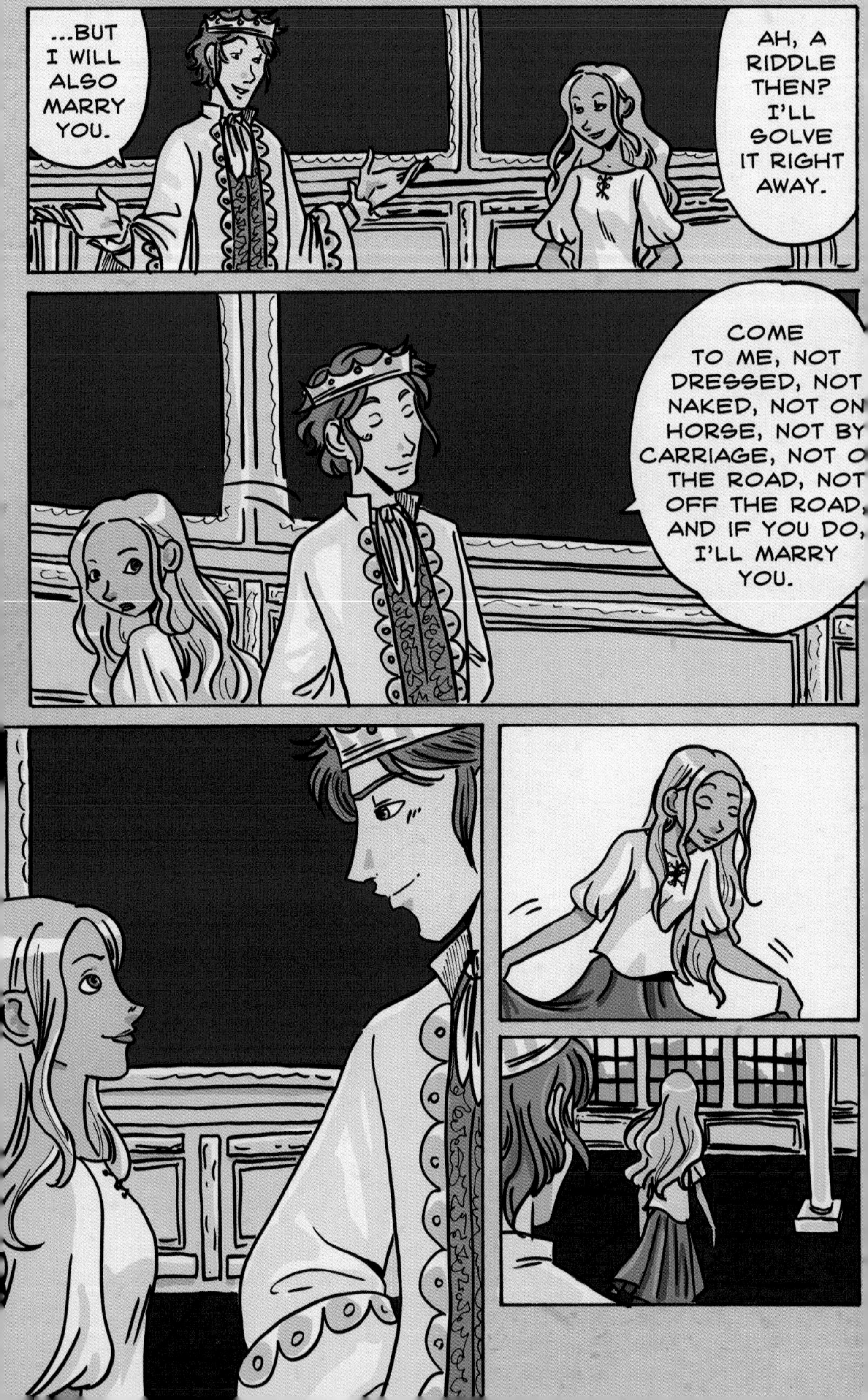
...BUT I WILL ALSO MARRY YOU.
AH, A RIDDLE THEN? I'LL SOLVE IT RIGHT AWAY.
COME TO ME, NOT DRESSED, NOT NAKED, NOT ON HORSE, NOT BY CARRIAGE, NOT O THE ROAD, NOT OFF THE ROAD, AND IF YOU DO, I'LL MARRY YOU.

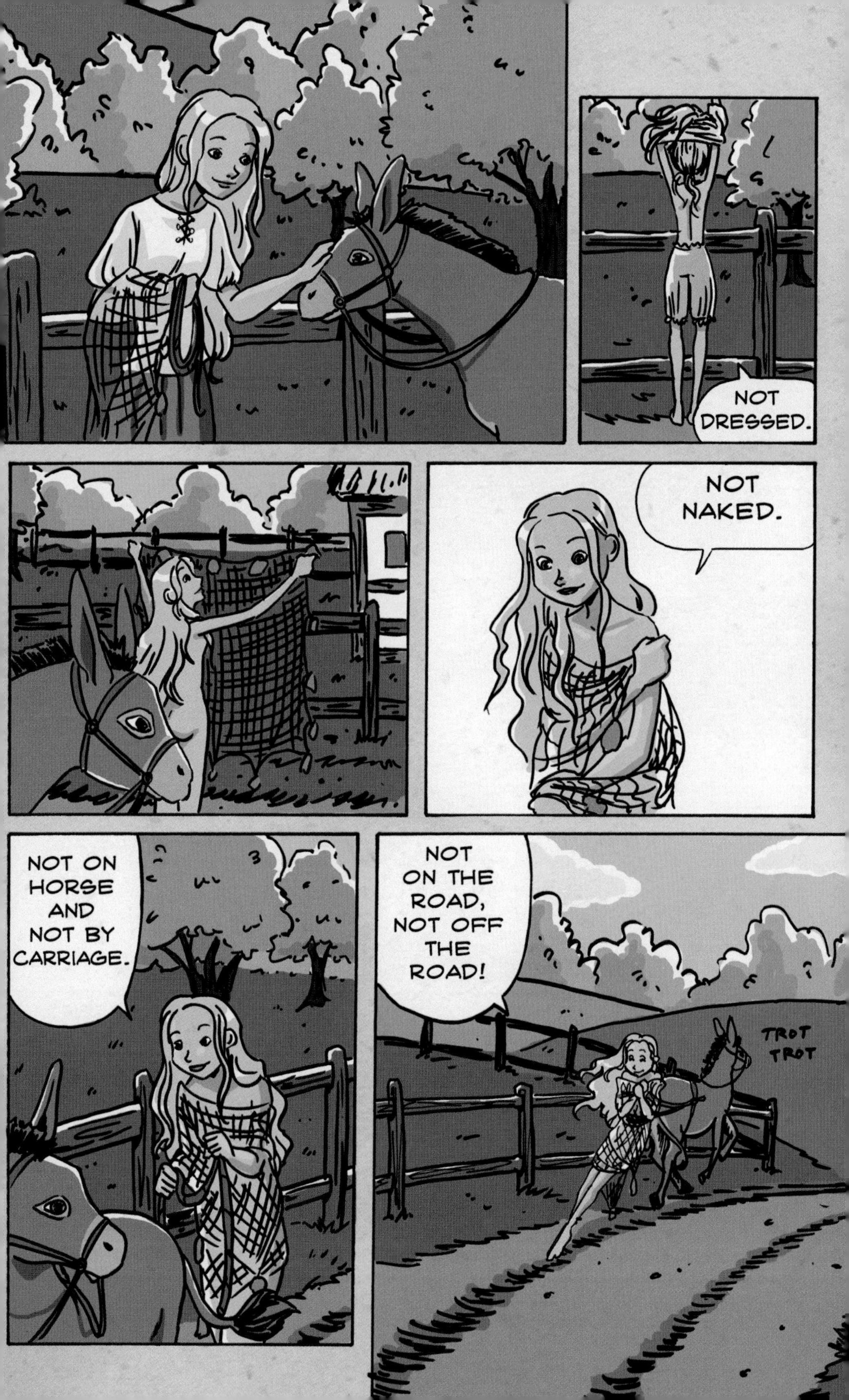
NOT DRESSED.
NOT NAKED.
NOT ON HORSE AND NOT BY CARRIAGE.
NOT ON THE ROAD, NOT OFF THE ROAD!
TROT TROT

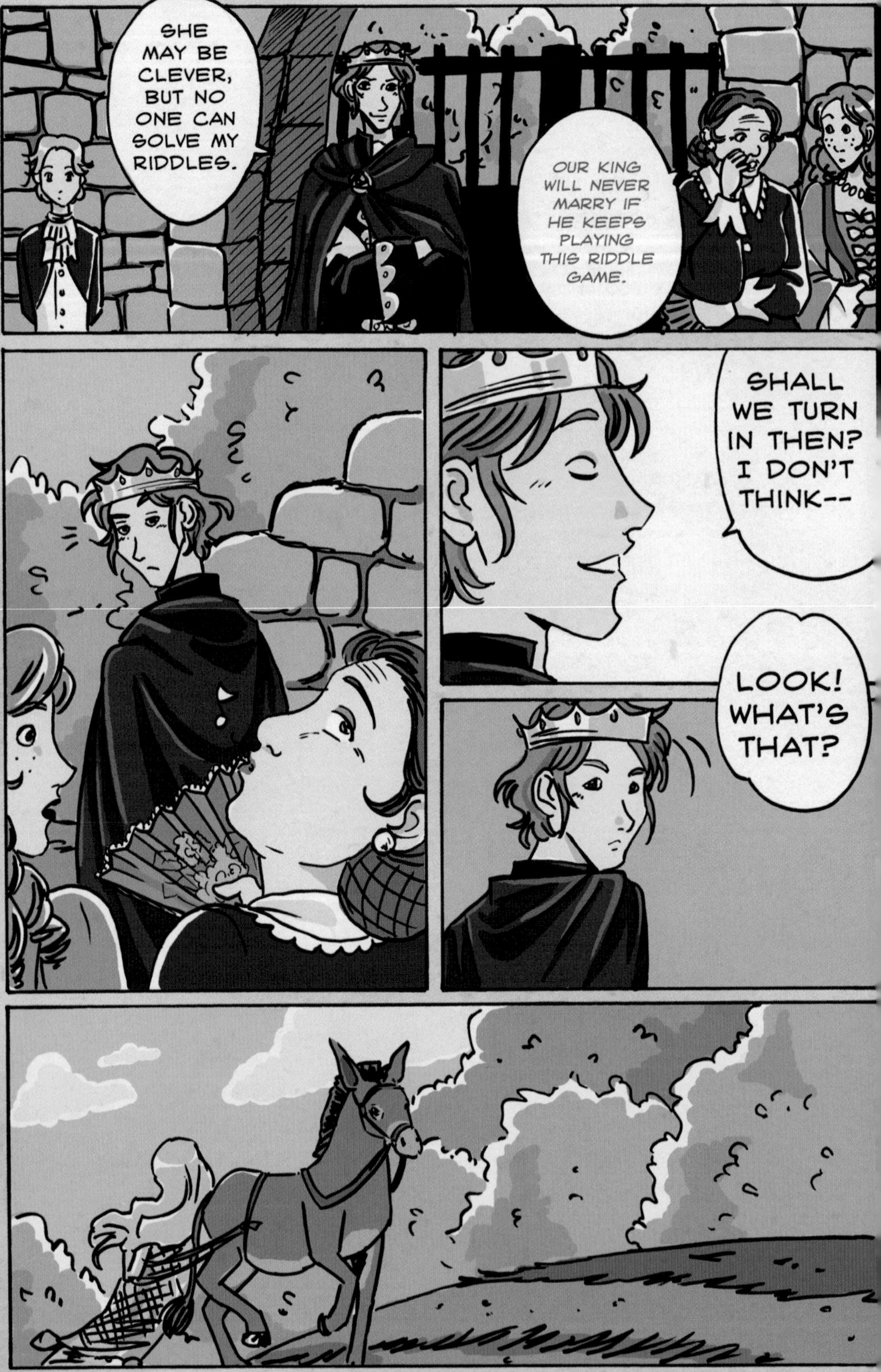
SHE MAY BE CLEVER, BUT NO ONE CAN SOLVE MY RIDDLES.
OUR KING WILL NEVER MARRY IF HE KEEPS PLAYING THIS RIDDLE GAME.
SHALL WE TURN IN THEN? I DON'T THINK--
LOOK! WHAT'S THAT?

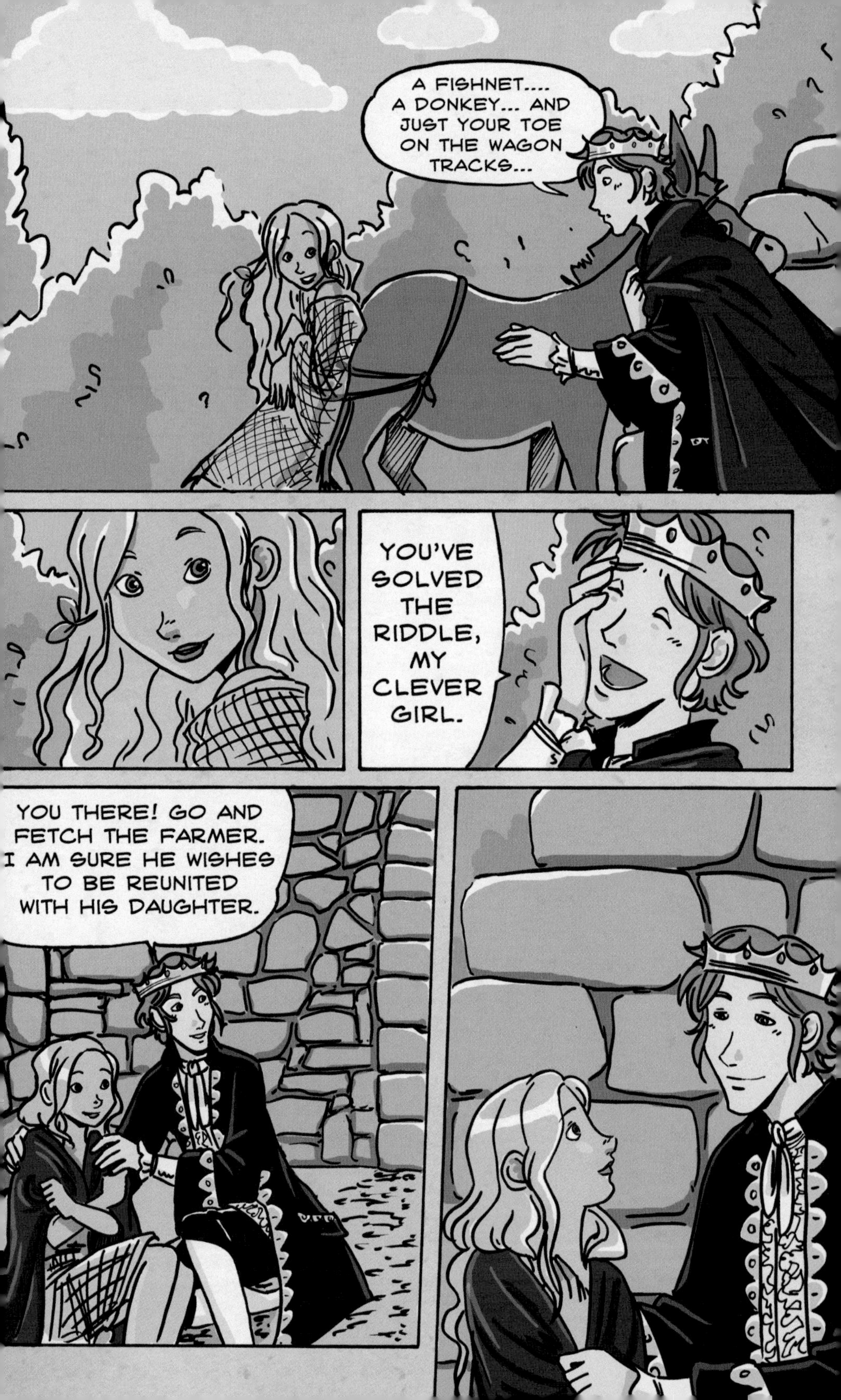
A FISHNET....
A DONKEY... AND
JUST YOUR TOE
ON THE WAGON
TRACKS...
YOU'VE SOLVED THE RIDDLE, MY CLEVER GIRL.
YOU THERE! GO AND FETCH THE FARMER. I AM SURE HE WISHES TO BE REUNITED WITH HIS DAUGHTER.

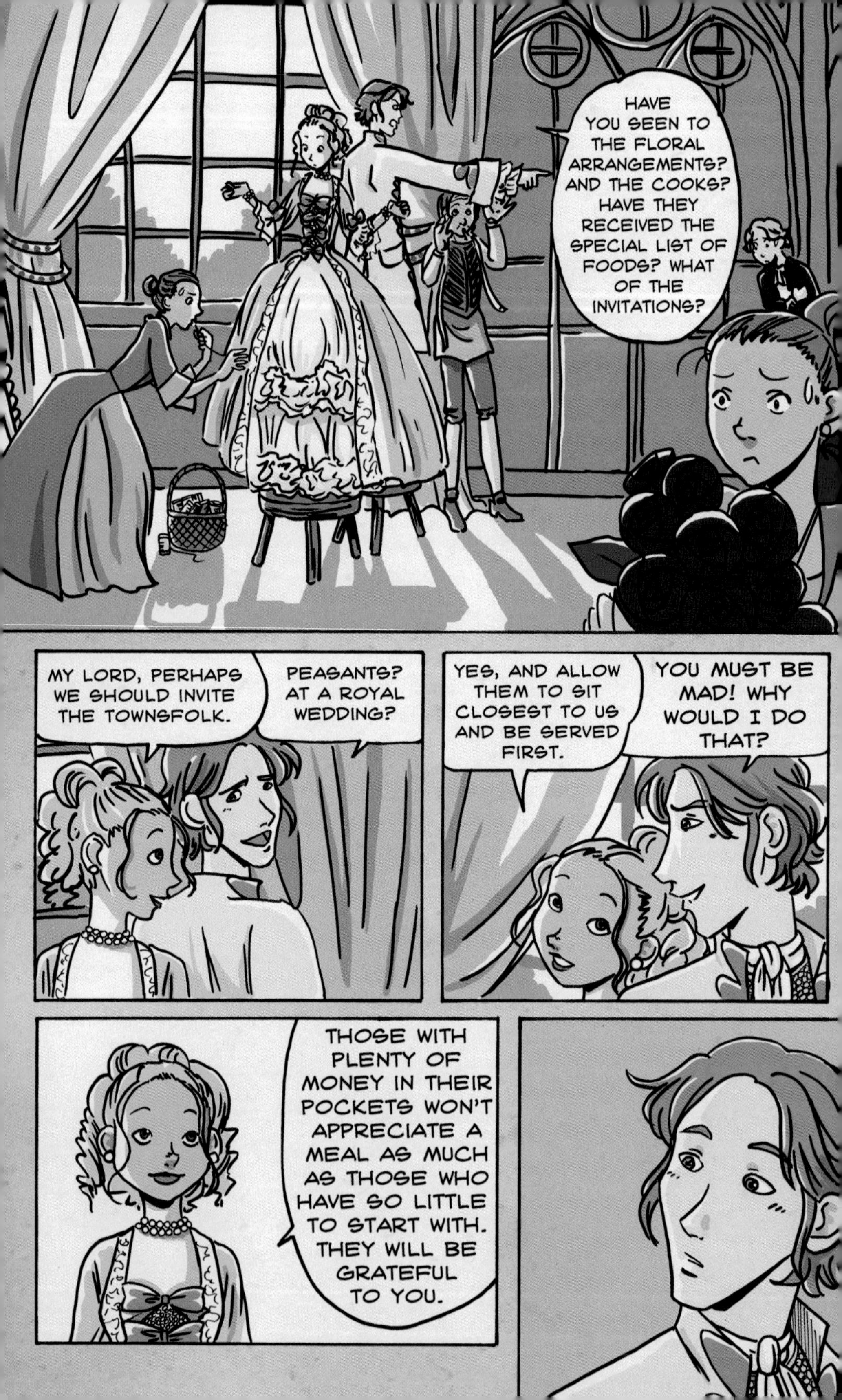
HAVE YOU SEEN TO THE FLORAL ARRANGEMENTS? AND THE COOKS? HAVE THEY RECEIVED THE SPECIAL LIST OF FOODS? WHAT OF THE INVITATIONS?
MY LORD, PERHAPS WE SHOULD INVITE THE TOWNSFOLK.
PEASANTS? AT A ROYAL WEDDING?
YES, AND ALLOW THEM TO SIT CLOSEST TO US AND BE SERVED FIRST.
YOU MUST BE MAD! WHY WOULD I DO THAT?
THOSE WITH PLENTY OF MONEY IN THEIR POCKETS WON'T APPRECIATE A MEAL AS MUCH AS THOSE WHO HAVE SO LITTLE TO START WITH. THEY WILL BE GRATEFUL TO YOU.

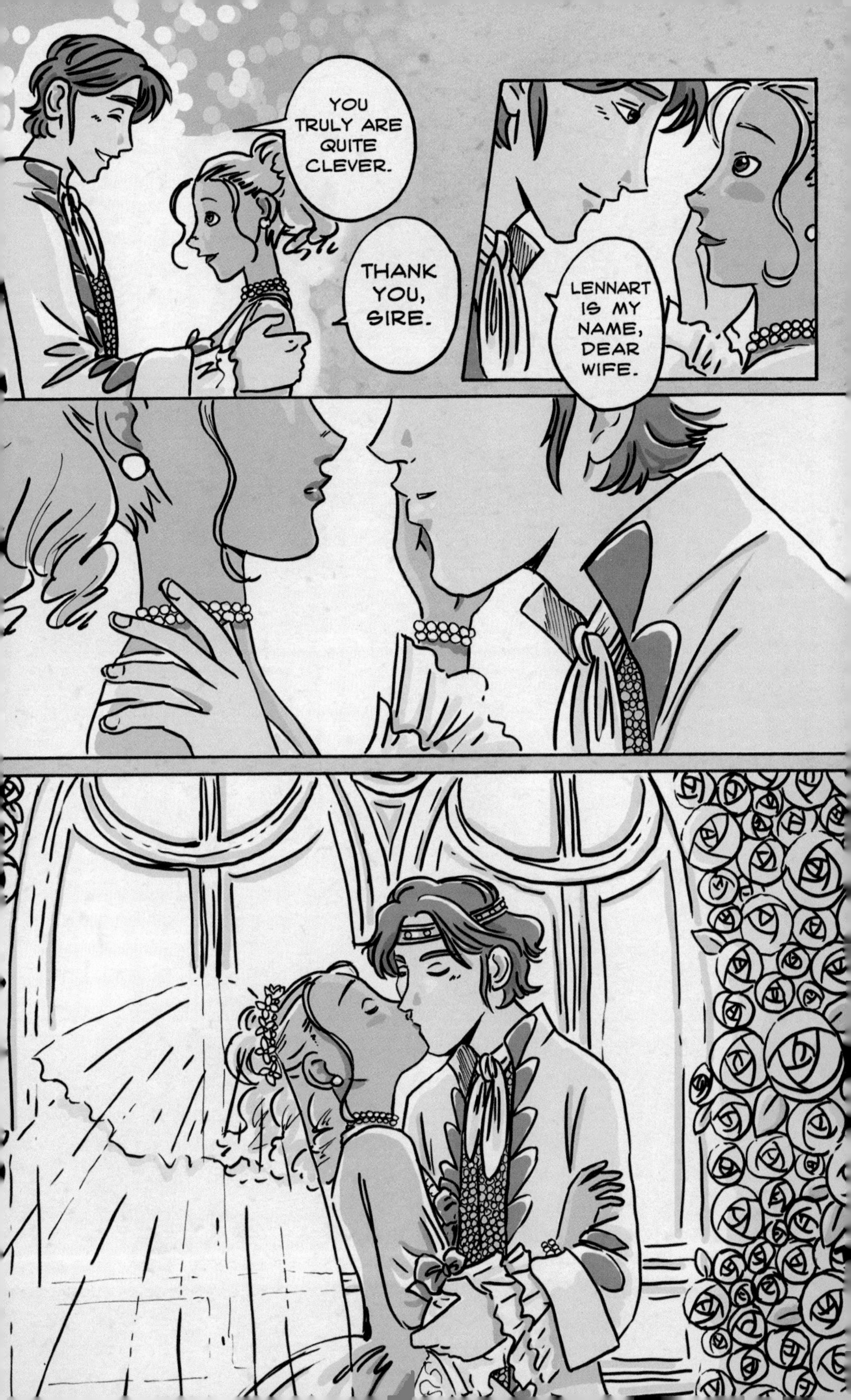
YOU TRULY ARE QUITE CLEVER.
THANK YOU, SIRE.
LENNART IS MY NAME, DEAR WIFE.

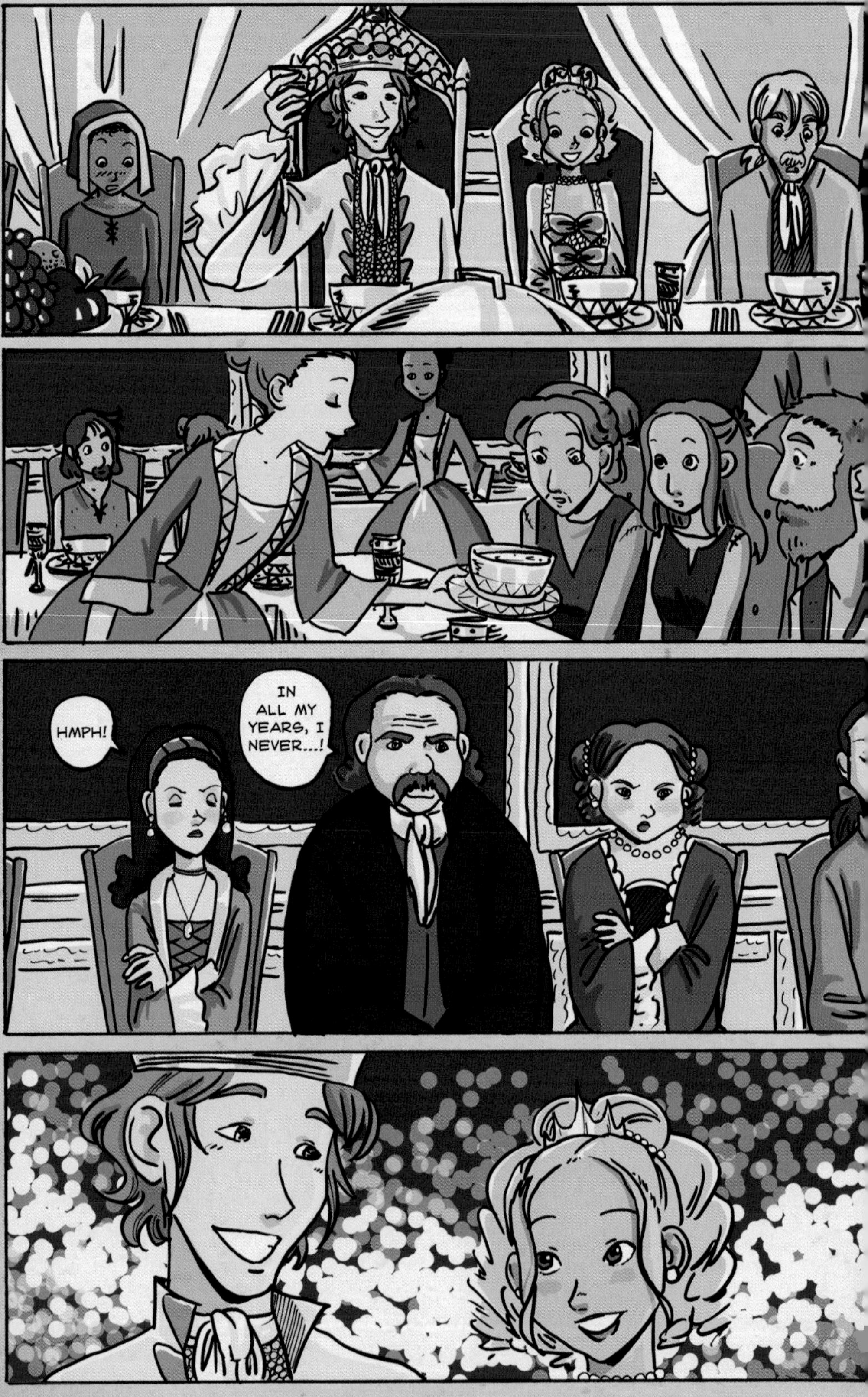
HMPH!
IN ALL MY YEARS, I NEVER...!

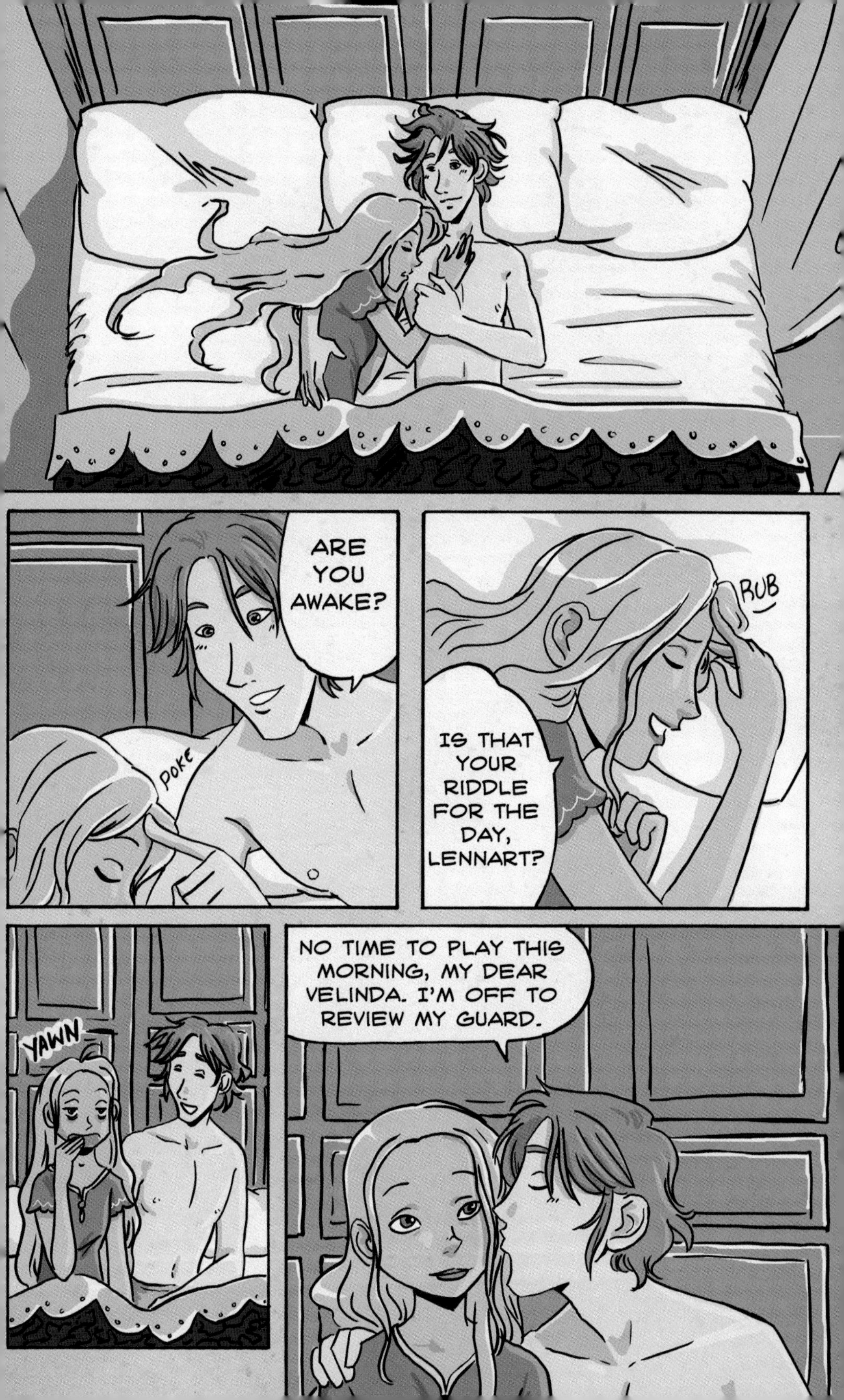
ARE YOU AWAKE?
POKE
RUB
IS THAT YOUR RIDDLE FOR THE DAY, LENNART?
YAWN
NO TIME TO PLAY THIS MORNING, MY DEAR VELINDA. I'M OFF TO REVIEW MY GUARD.

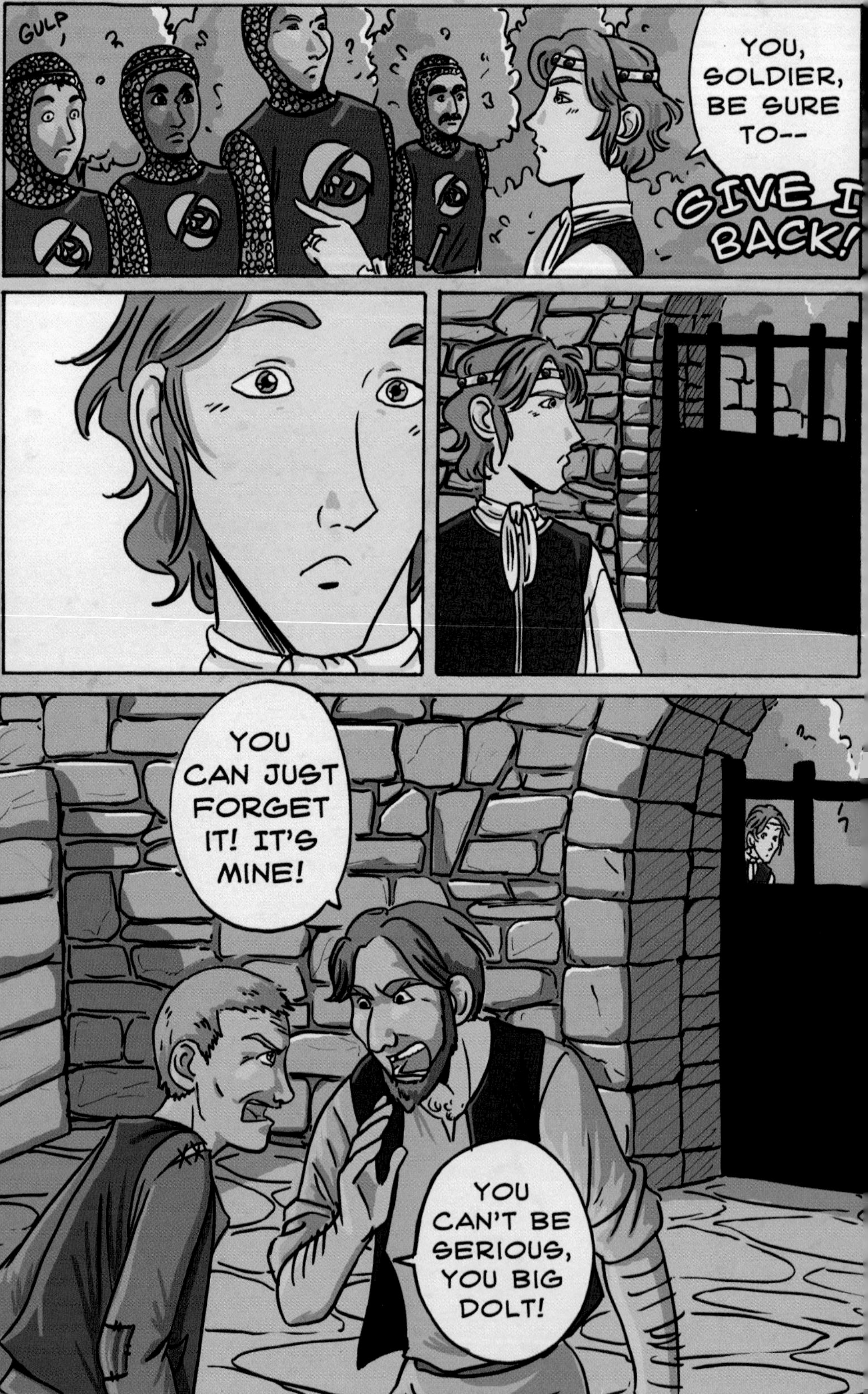
GULP
YOU, SOLDIER, BE SURE TO--
GIVE IT BACK!
YOU CAN JUST FORGET IT! IT'S MINE!
YOU CAN'T BE SERIOUS, YOU BIG DOLT!

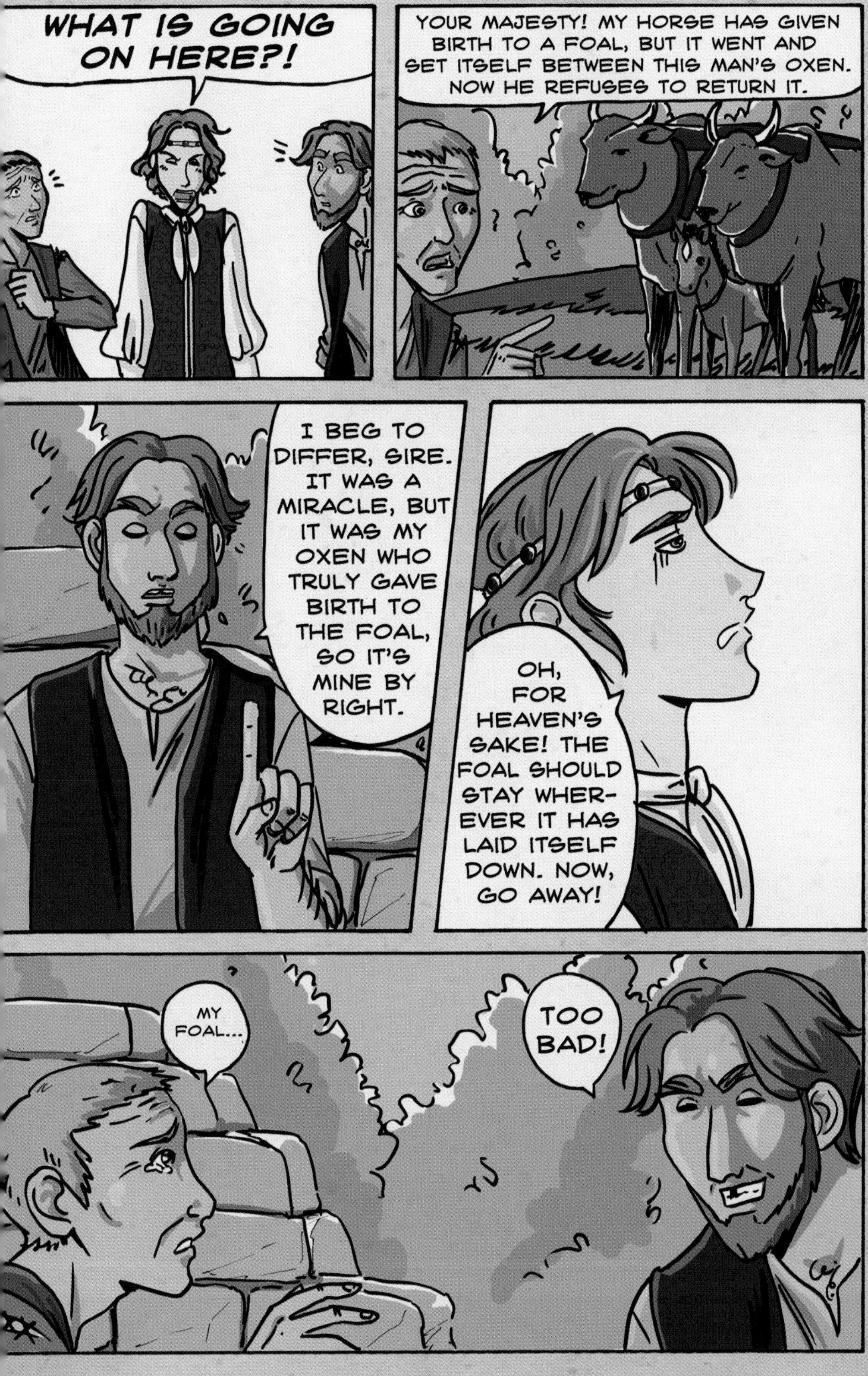
WHAT IS GOING ON HERE?!
YOUR MAJESTY! MY HORSE HAS GIVEN BIRTH TO A FOAL, BUT IT WENT AND SET ITSELF BETWEEN THIS MAN'S OXEN. NOW HE REFUSES TO RETURN IT.
I BEG TO DIFFER, SIRE. IT WAS A MIRACLE, BUT IT WAS MY OXEN WHO TRULY GAVE BIRTH TO THE FOAL, SO IT'S MINE BY RIGHT.
OH, FOR HEAVEN'S SAKE! THE FOAL SHOULD STAY WHER-EVER IT HAS LAID ITSELF DOWN. NOW, GO AWAY!
MY FOAL...
TOO BAD!

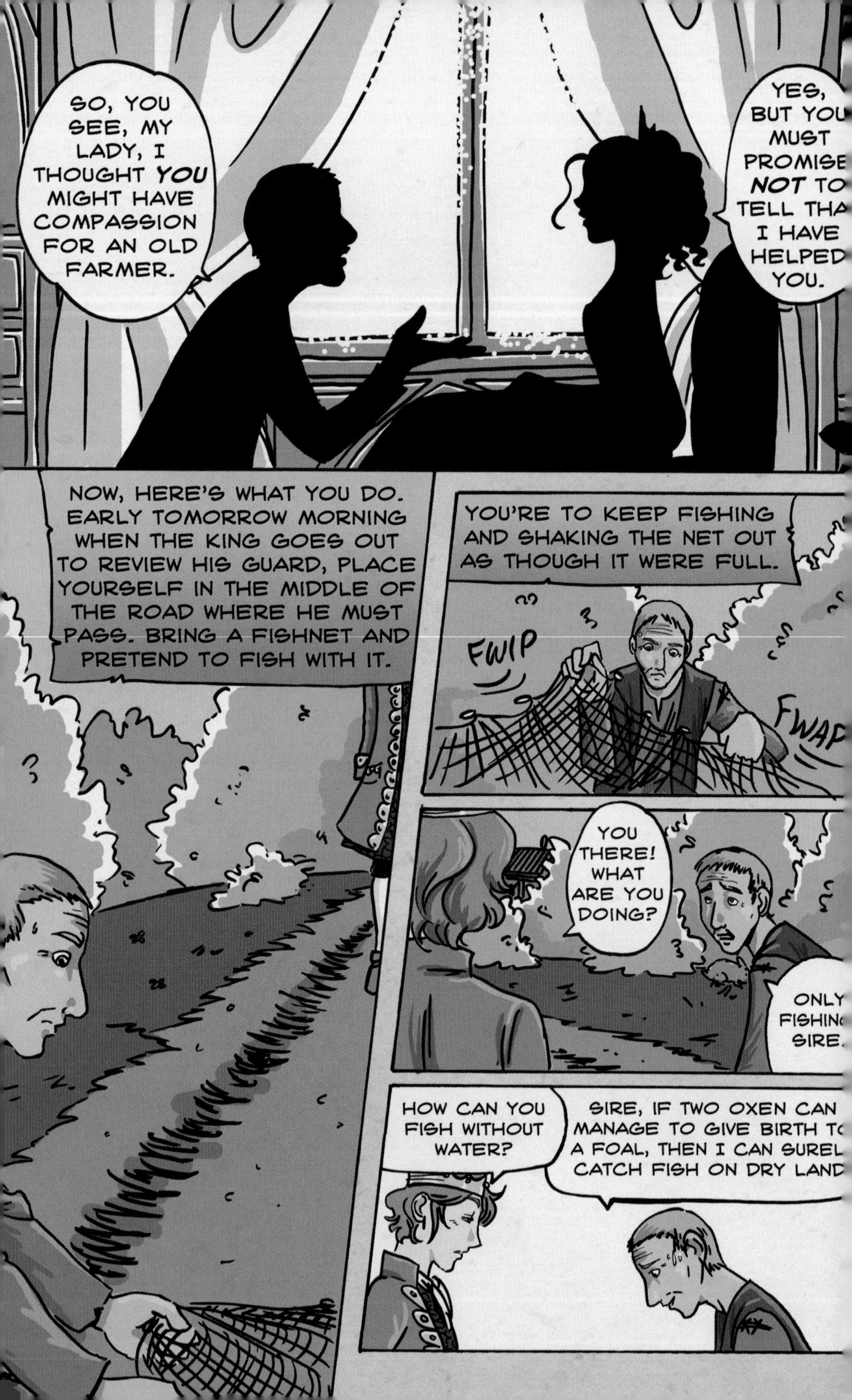
SO, YOU SEE, MY LADY, I THOUGHT *YOU* MIGHT HAVE COMPASSION FOR AN OLD FARMER.
YES, BUT YOU MUST PROMISE *NOT* TO TELL THA I HAVE HELPED YOU.
NOW, HERE'S WHAT YOU DO. EARLY TOMORROW MORNING WHEN THE KING GOES OUT TO REVIEW HIS GUARD, PLACE YOURSELF IN THE MIDDLE OF THE ROAD WHERE HE MUST PASS. BRING A FISHNET AND PRETEND TO FISH WITH IT.
YOU'RE TO KEEP FISHING AND SHAKING THE NET OUT AS THOUGH IT WERE FULL.
FWIP
FWAP
YOU THERE! WHAT ARE YOU DOING?
ONLY FISHIN SIRE.
HOW CAN YOU FISH WITHOUT WATER?
SIRE, IF TWO OXEN CAN MANAGE TO GIVE BIRTH TO A FOAL, THEN I CAN SUREL CATCH FISH ON DRY LAND

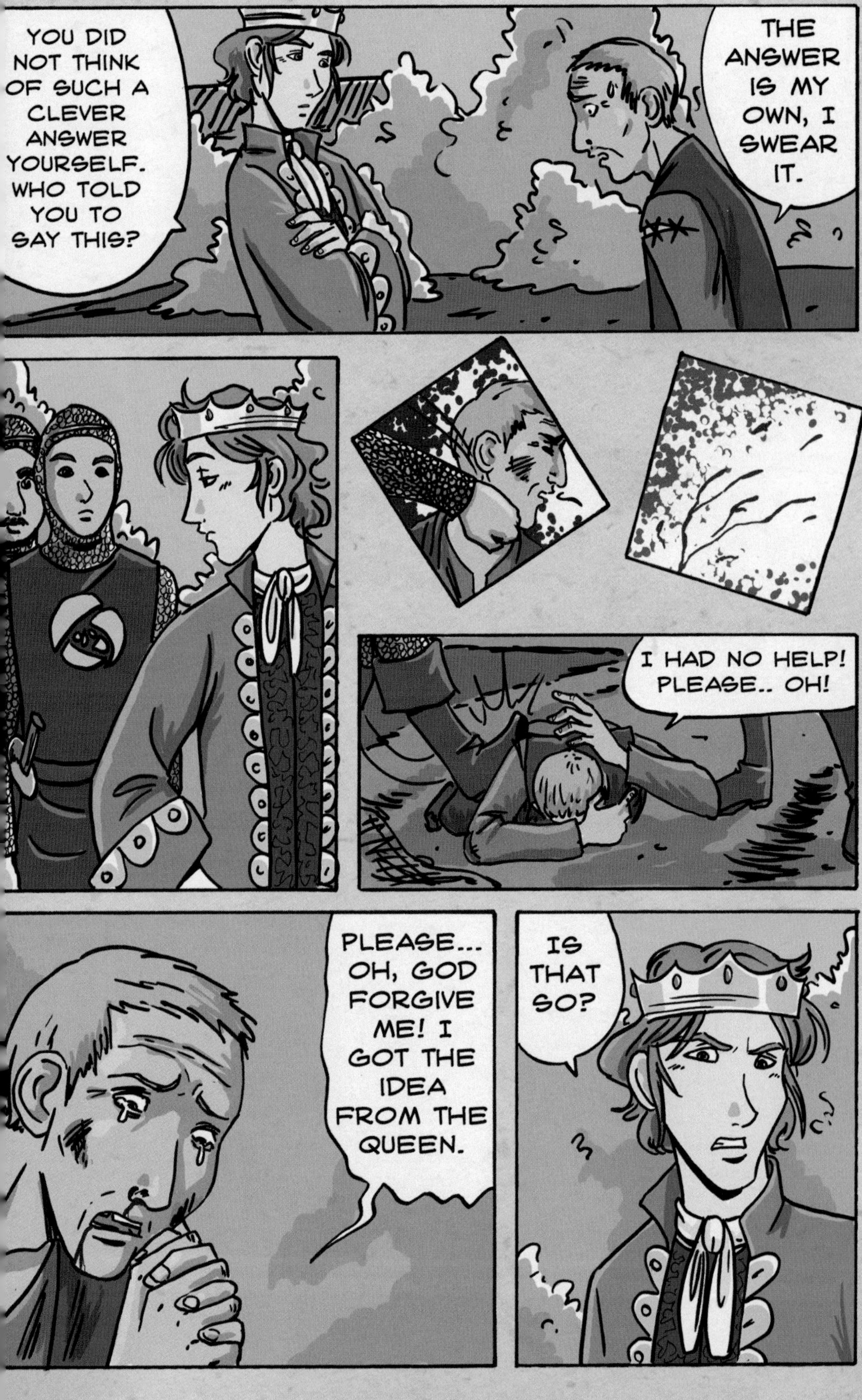
YOU DID NOT THINK OF SUCH A CLEVER ANSWER YOURSELF. WHO TOLD YOU TO SAY THIS?
THE ANSWER IS MY OWN, I SWEAR IT.
I HAD NO HELP! PLEASE.. OH!
PLEASE... OH, GOD FORGIVE ME! I GOT THE IDEA FROM THE QUEEN.
IS THAT SO?

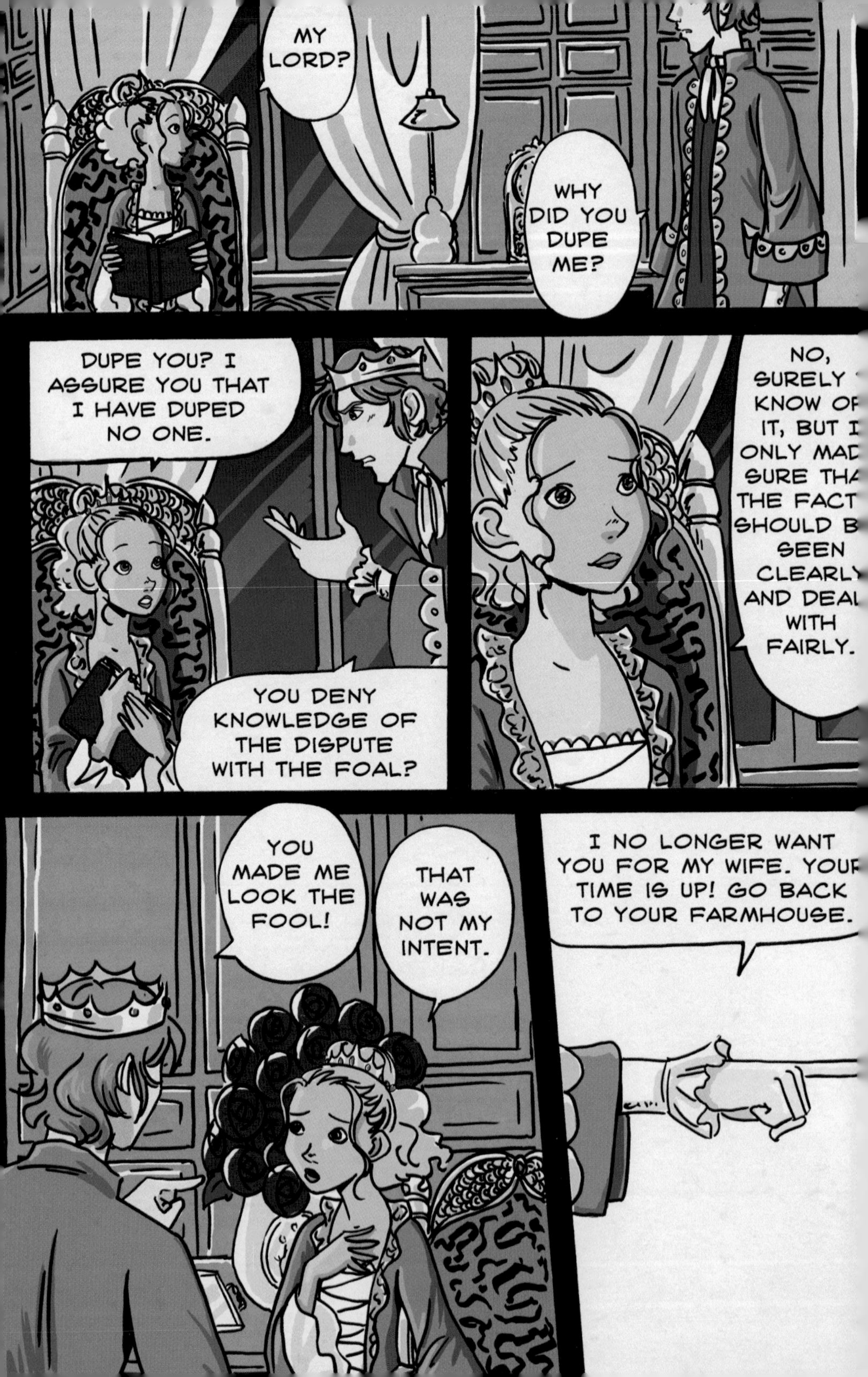

MY LORD?
WHY DID YOU DUPE ME?
DUPE YOU? I ASSURE YOU THAT I HAVE DUPED NO ONE.
YOU DENY KNOWLEDGE OF THE DISPUTE WITH THE FOAL?
NO, SURELY KNOW OF IT, BUT I ONLY MAD SURE TH THE FACT SHOULD B SEEN CLEARL AND DEA WITH FAIRLY.
YOU MADE ME LOOK THE FOOL!
THAT WAS NOT MY INTENT.
I NO LONGER WANT YOU FOR MY WIFE. YOU TIME IS UP! GO BACK TO YOUR FARMHOUSE.

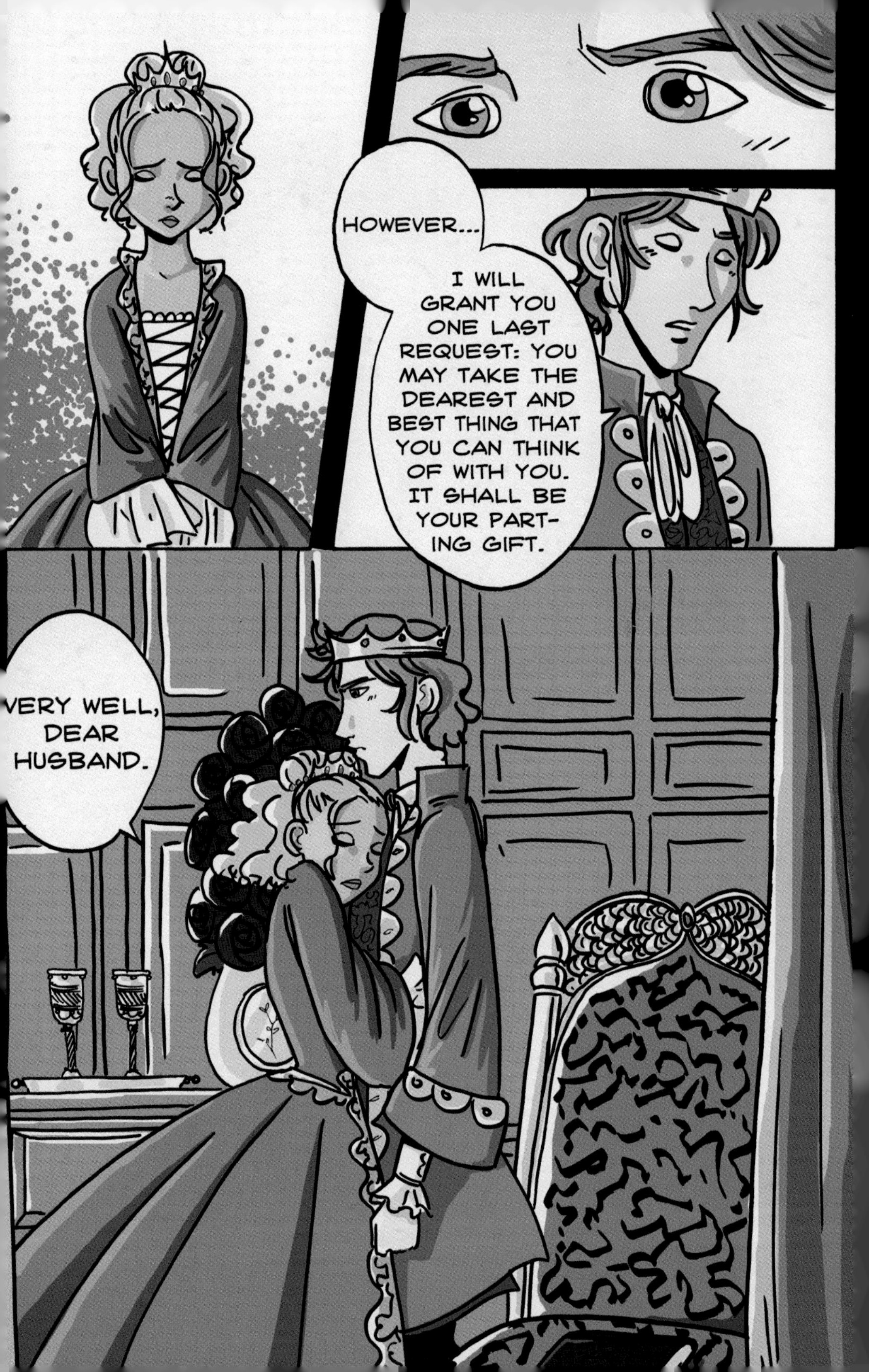
HOWEVER...
I WILL GRANT YOU ONE LAST REQUEST: YOU MAY TAKE THE DEAREST AND BEST THING THAT YOU CAN THINK OF WITH YOU. IT SHALL BE YOUR PART-ING GIFT.
VERY WELL, DEAR HUSBAND.

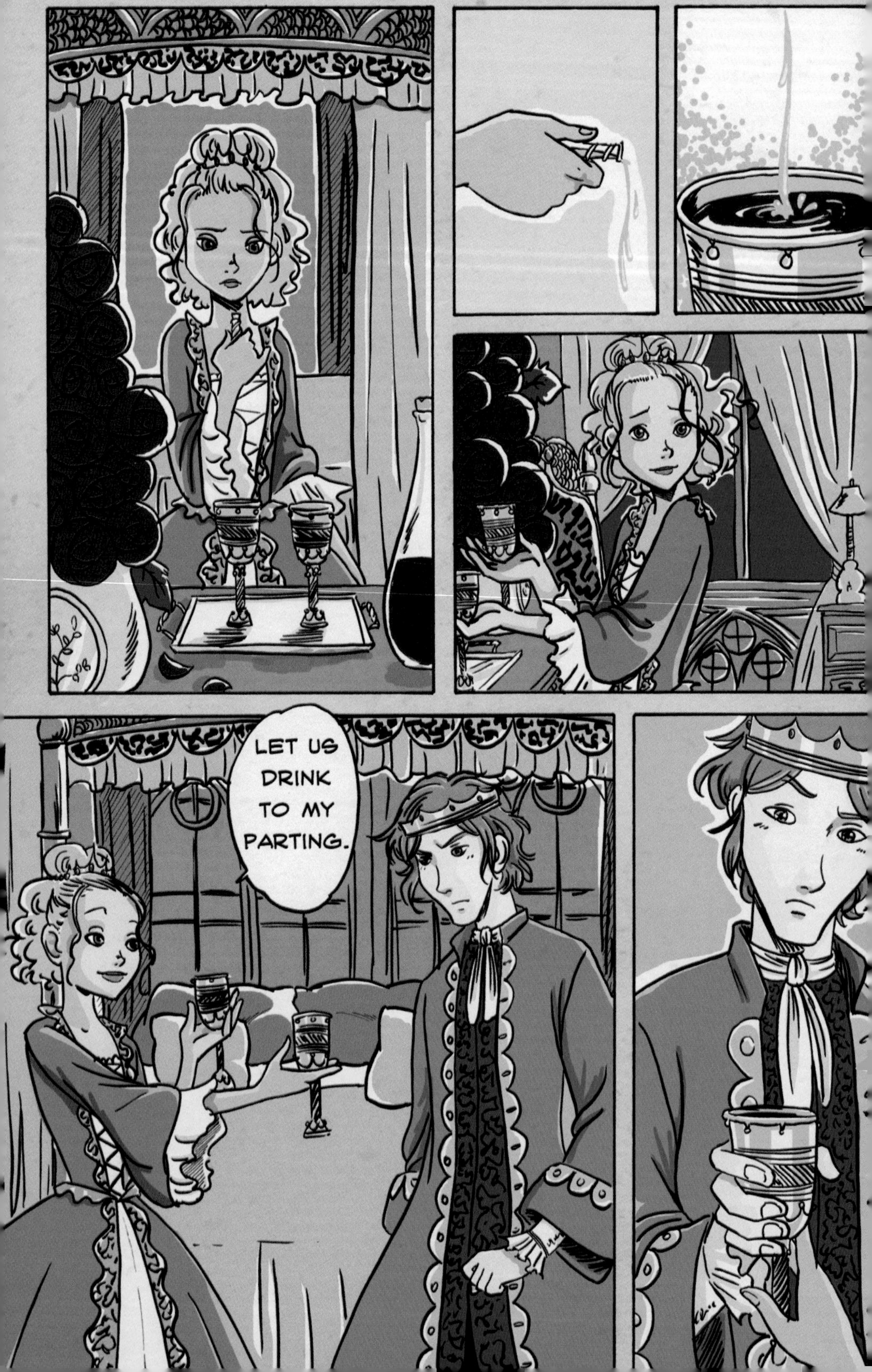
LET US DRINK TO MY PARTING.

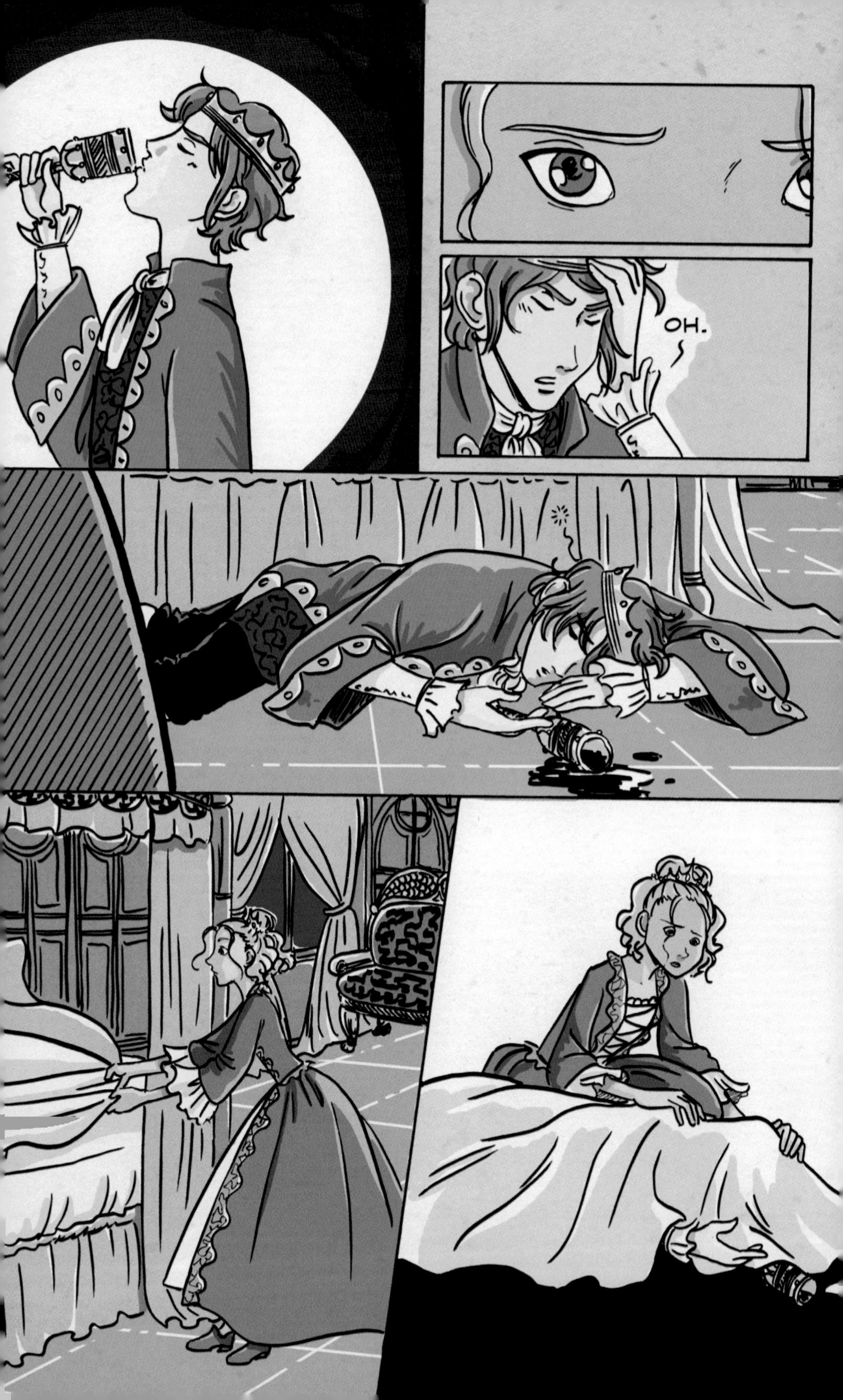
OH.

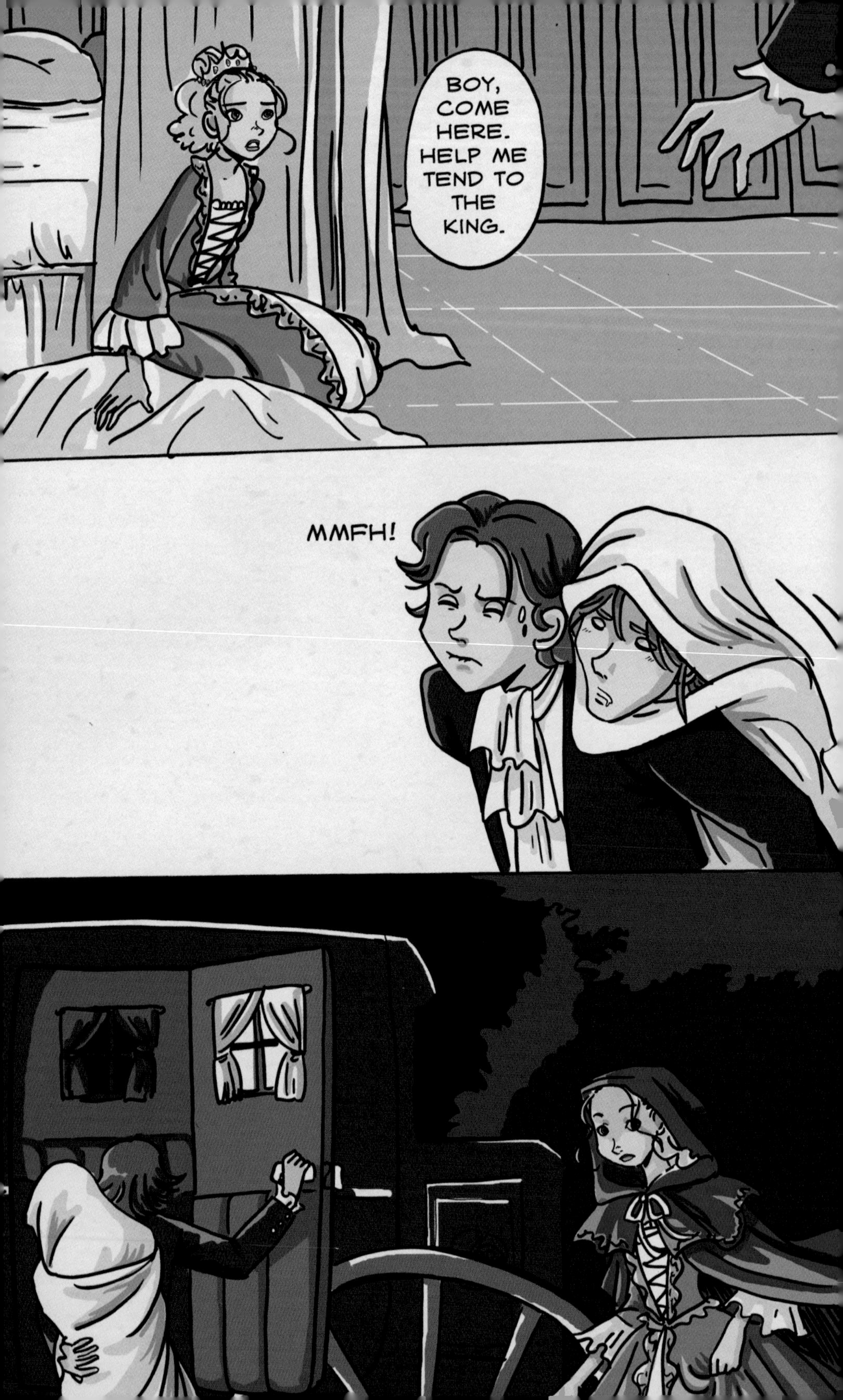
BOY, COME HERE. HELP ME TEND TO THE KING.
MMFH!

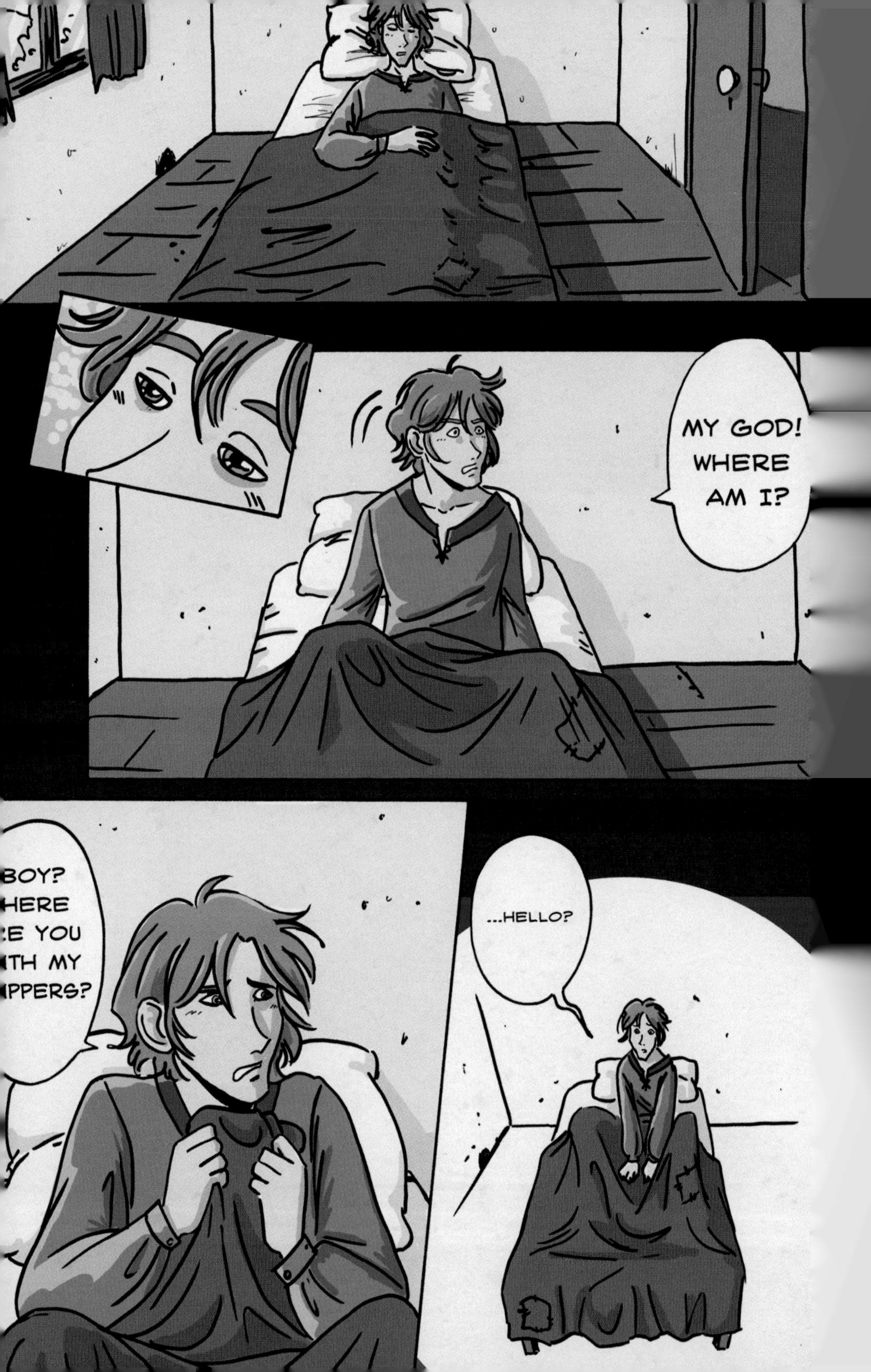
MY GOD! WHERE AM I?
BOY? HERE E YOU ITH MY IPPERS?
...HELLO?

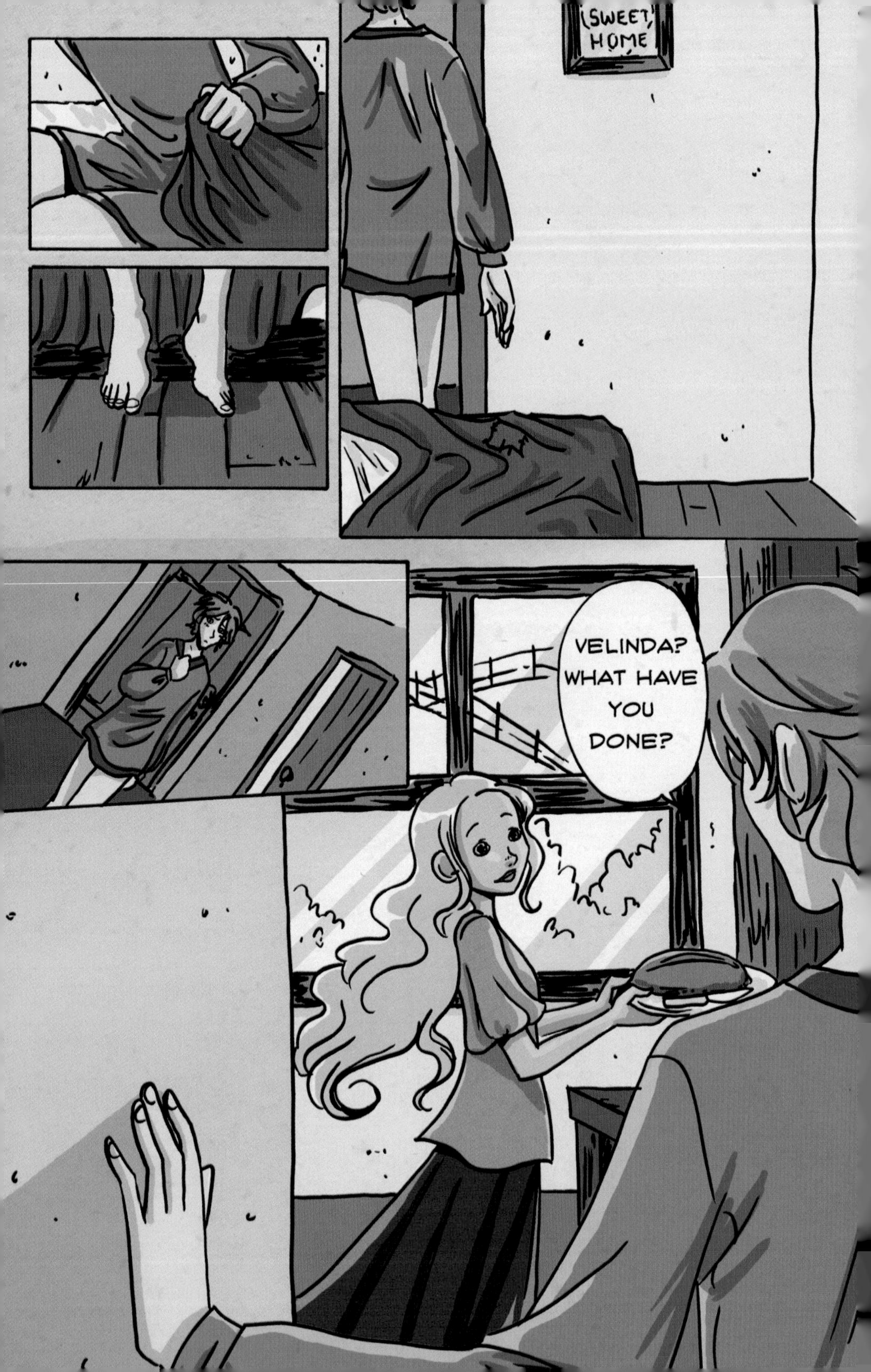
SWEET HOME
VELINDA? WHAT HAVE YOU DONE?

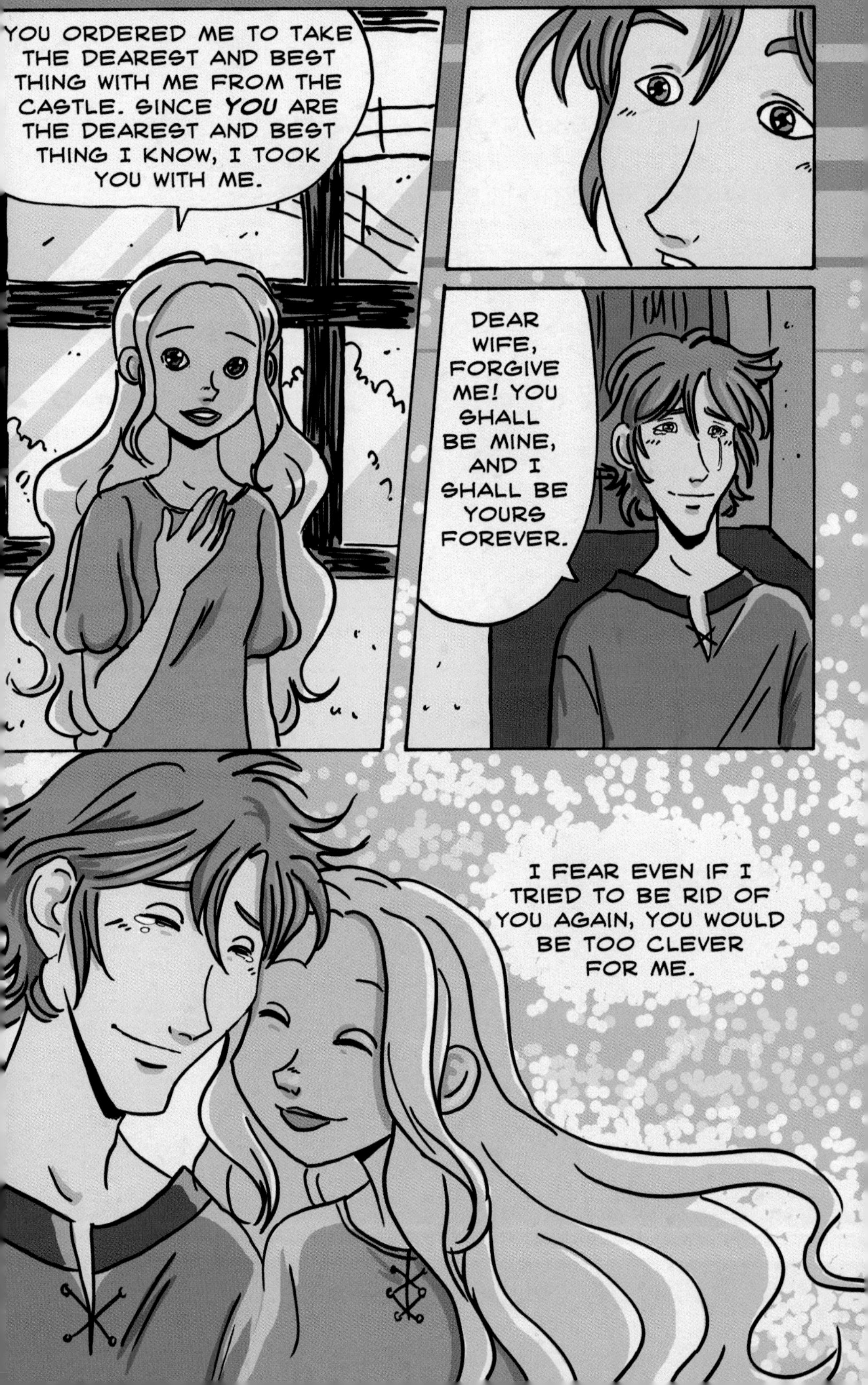
YOU ORDERED ME TO TAKE THE DEAREST AND BEST THING WITH ME FROM THE CASTLE. SINCE *YOU* ARE THE DEAREST AND BEST THING I KNOW, I TOOK YOU WITH ME.
DEAR WIFE, FORGIVE ME! YOU SHALL BE MINE, AND I SHALL BE YOURS FOREVER.
I FEAR EVEN IF I TRIED TO BE RID OF YOU AGAIN, YOU WOULD BE TOO CLEVER FOR ME.

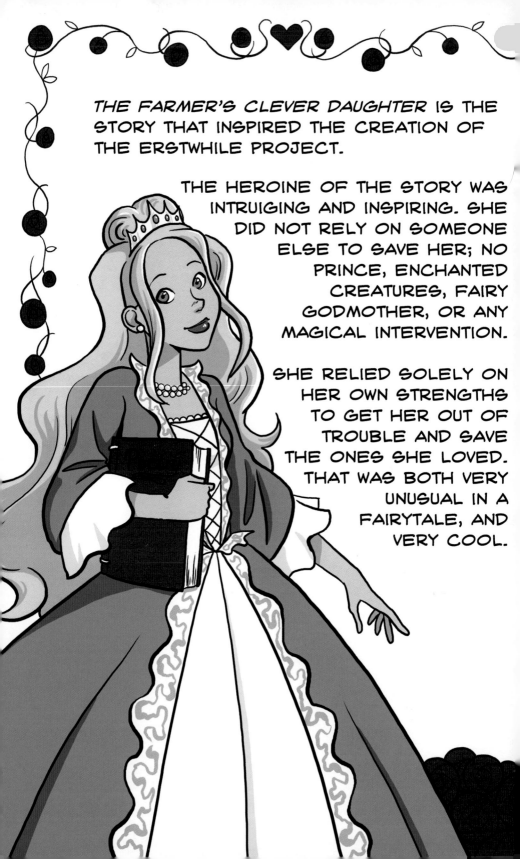

THE FARMER'S CLEVER DAUGHTER IS THE STORY THAT INSPIRED THE CREATION OF THE ERSTWHILE PROJECT.

THE HEROINE OF THE STORY WAS INTRUIGING AND INSPIRING. SHE DID NOT RELY ON SOMEONE ELSE TO SAVE HER; NO PRINCE, ENCHANTED CREATURES, FAIRY GODMOTHER, OR ANY MAGICAL INTERVENTION.

SHE RELIED SOLELY ON HER OWN STRENGTHS TO GET HER OUT OF TROUBLE AND SAVE THE ONES SHE LOVED. THAT WAS BOTH VERY UNUSUAL IN A FAIRYTALE, AND VERY COOL.

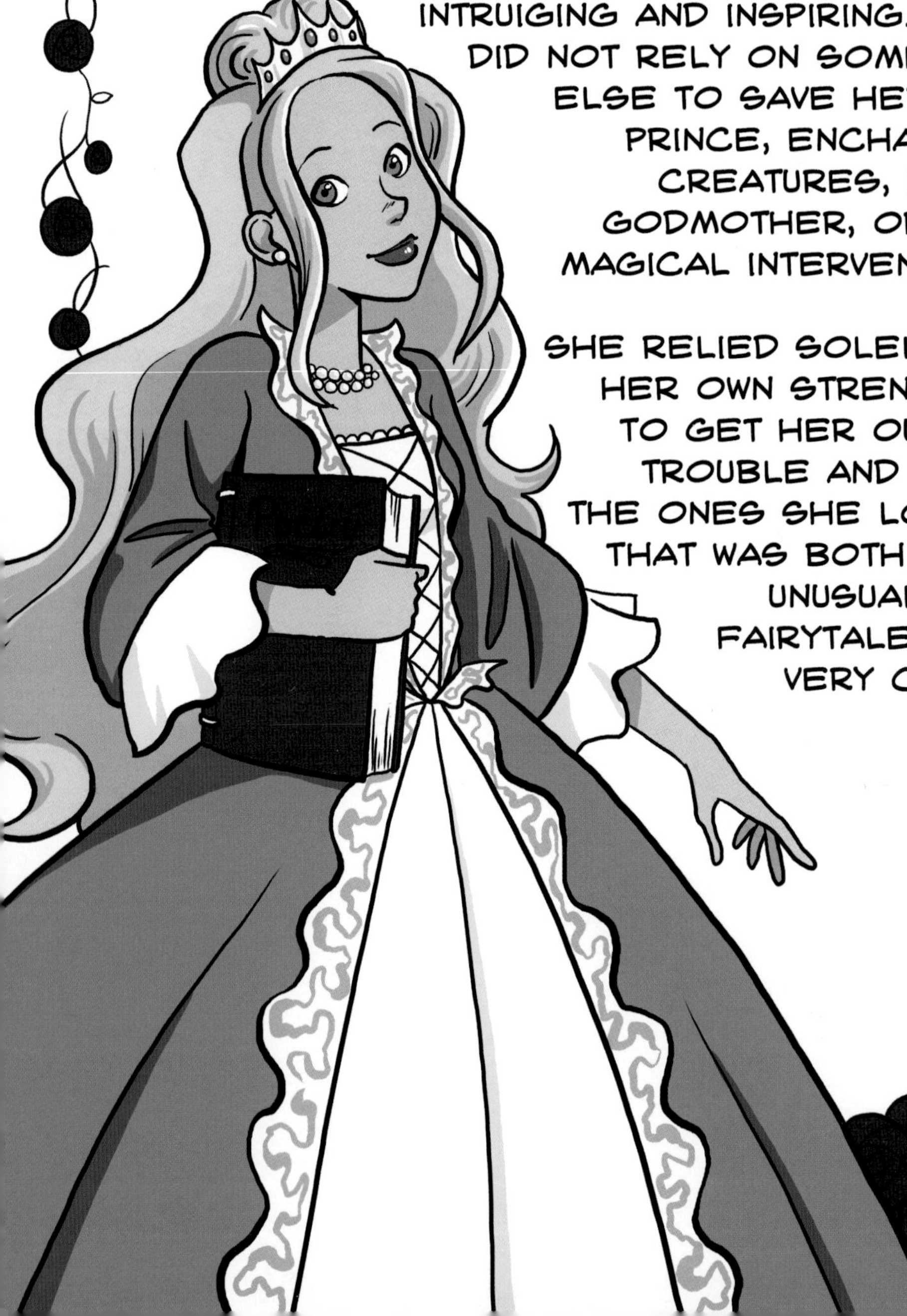

THE OLD MAN & HIS GRANDSON

STORY ADAPTED BY
GINA BIGGS

ILLUSTRATED BY
LOUISA ROY

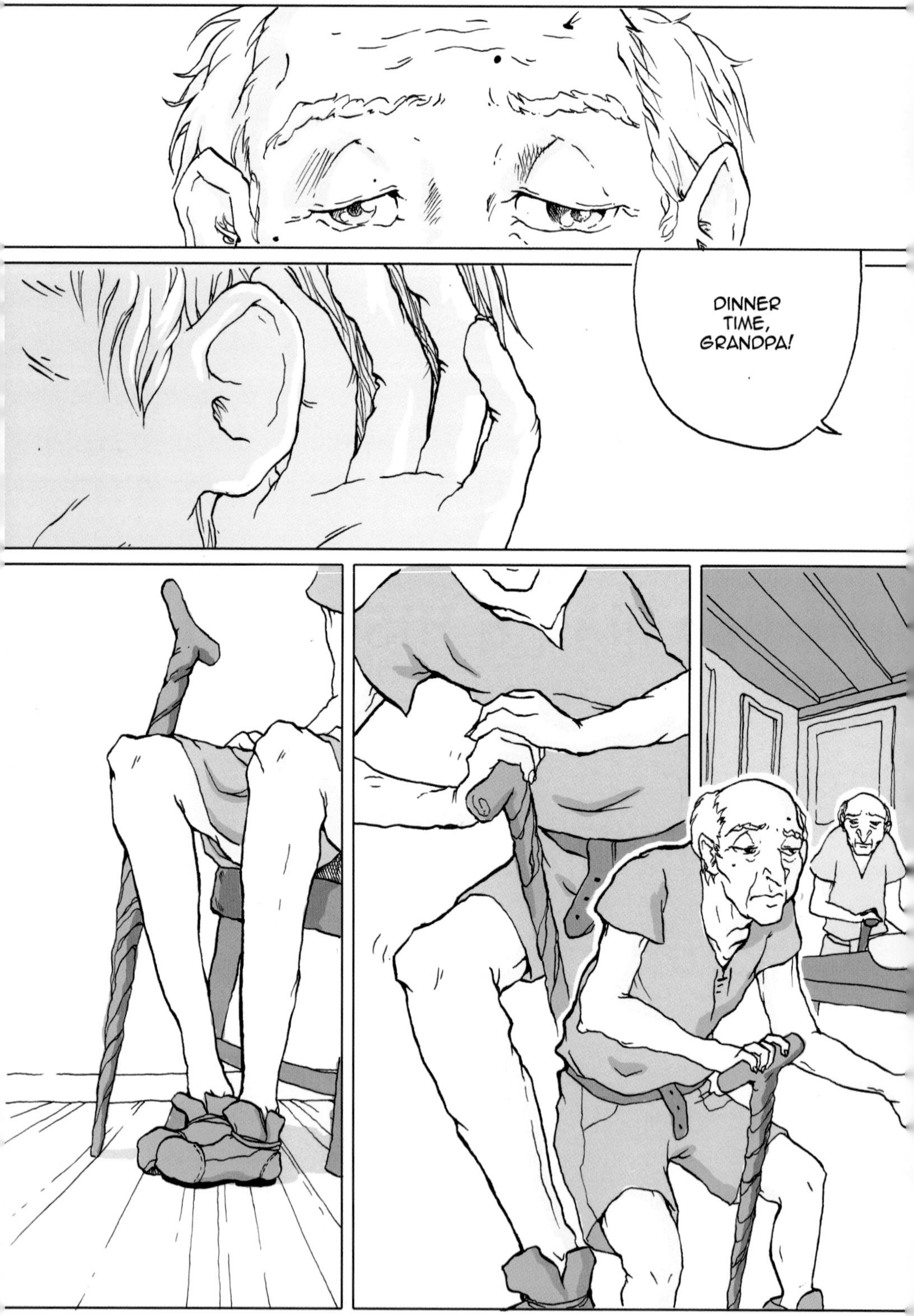
DINNER TIME, GRANDPA!

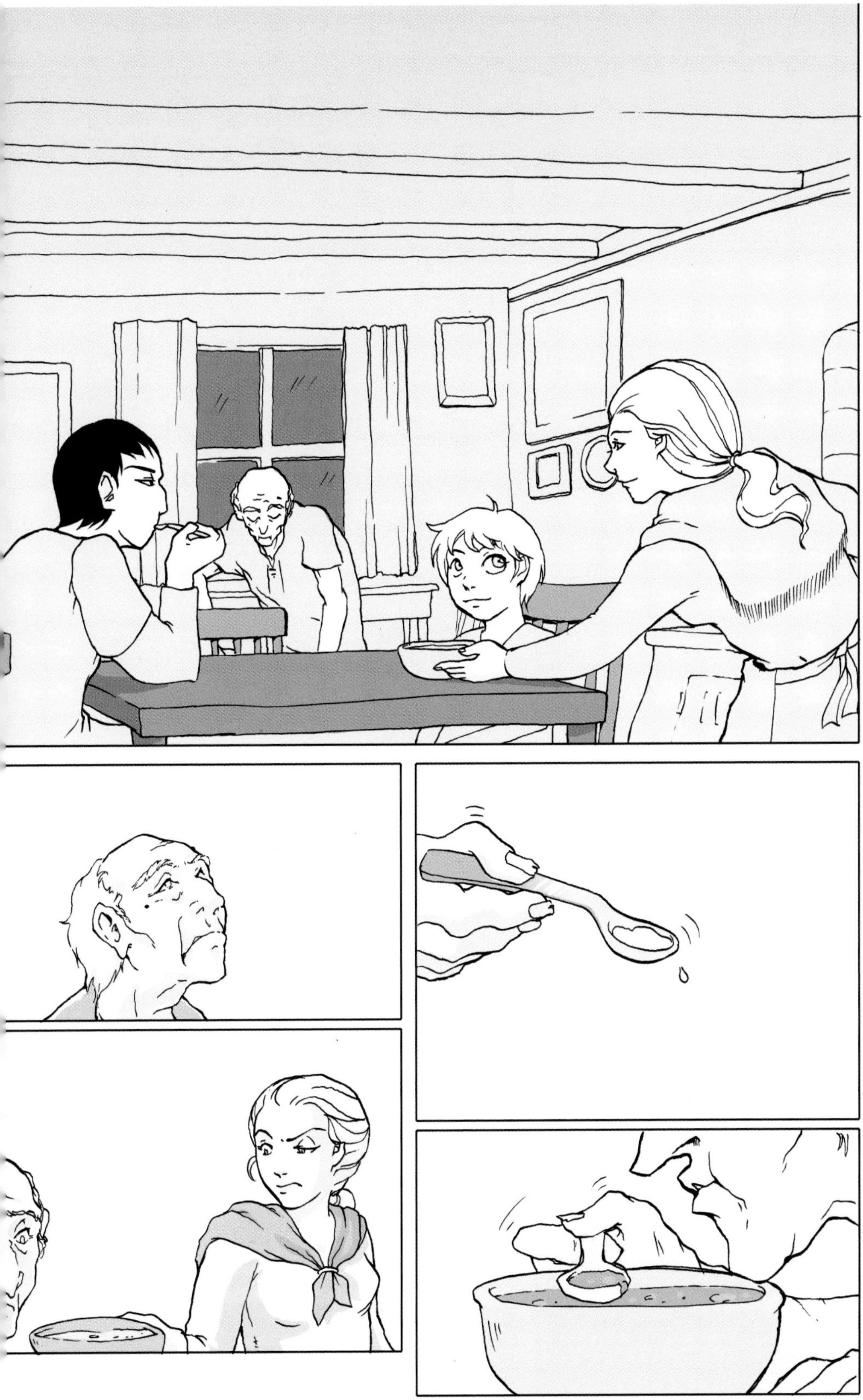

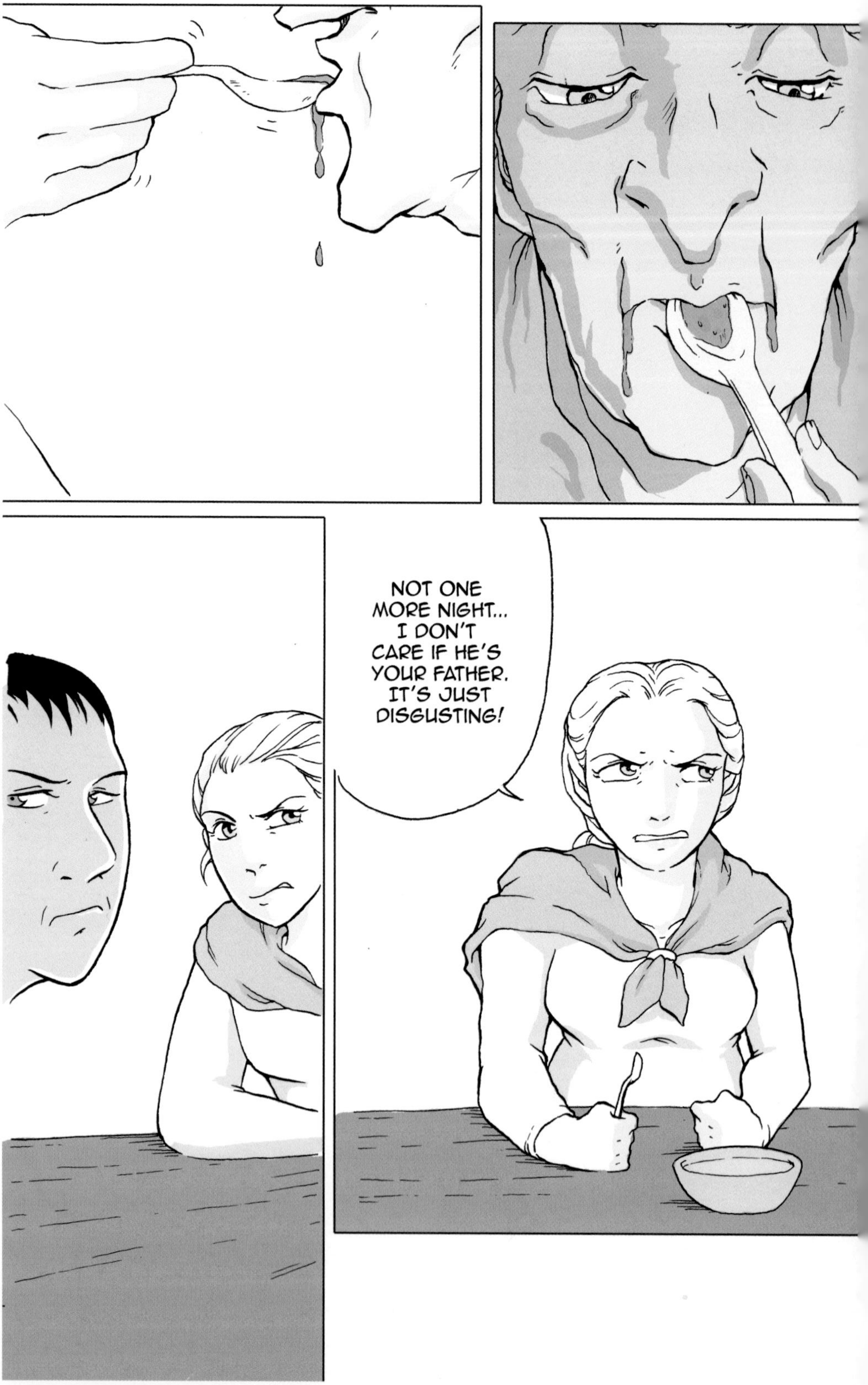
NOT ONE MORE NIGHT... I DON'T CARE IF HE'S YOUR FATHER. IT'S JUST DISGUSTING!

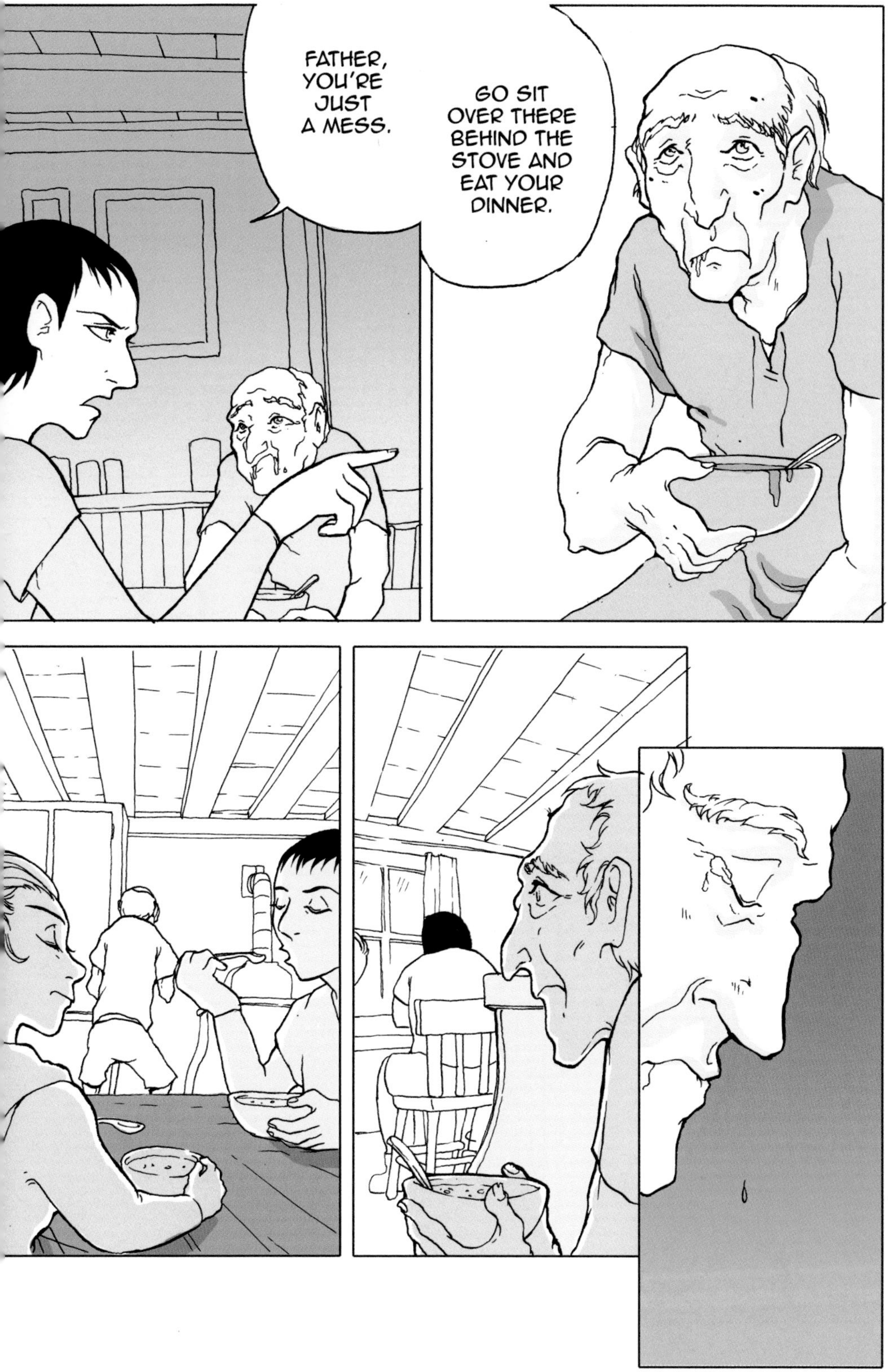
FATHER, YOU'RE JUST A MESS.
GO SIT OVER THERE BEHIND THE STOVE AND EAT YOUR DINNER.

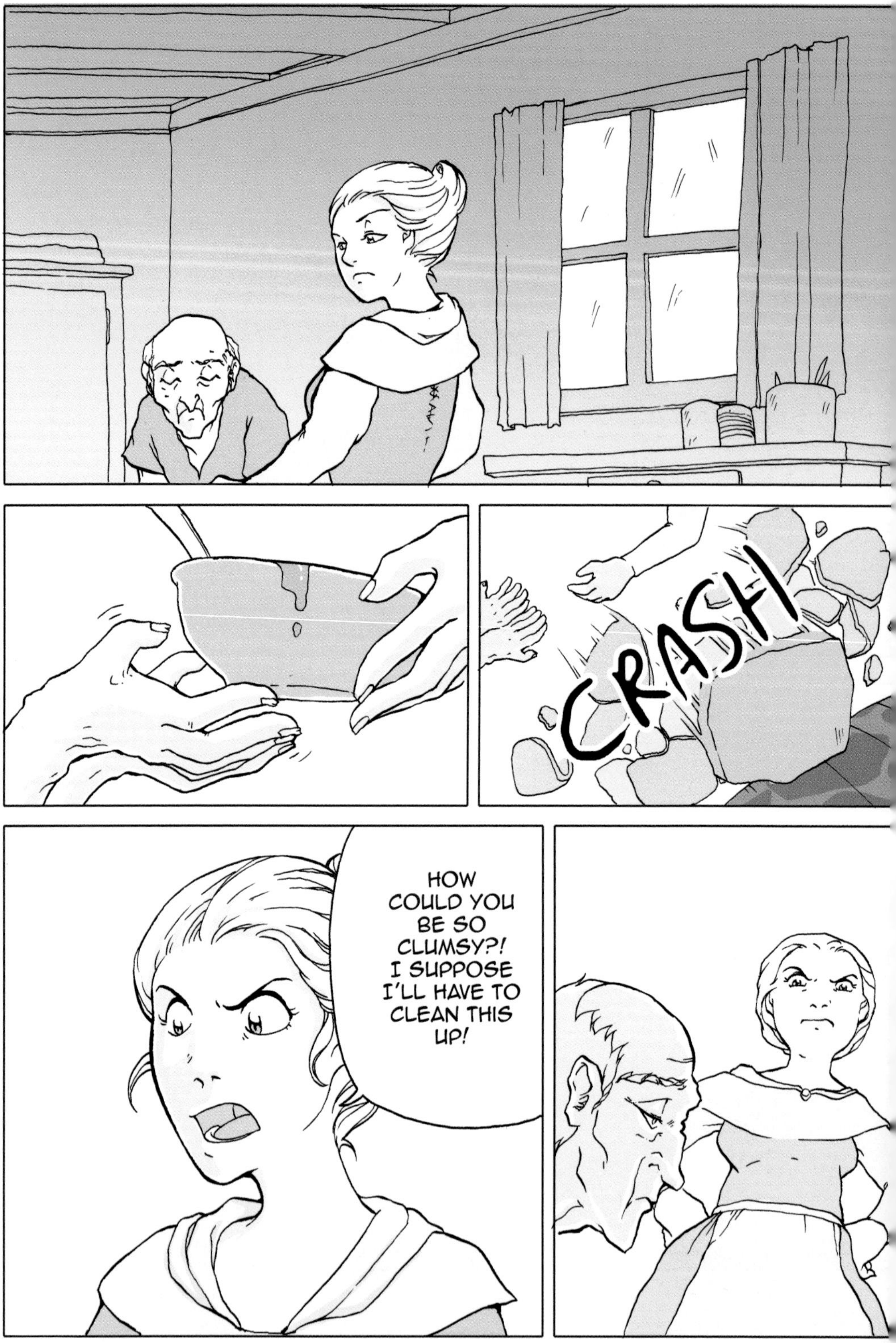
CRASH
HOW COULD YOU BE SO CLUMSY?! I SUPPOSE I'LL HAVE TO CLEAN THIS UP!

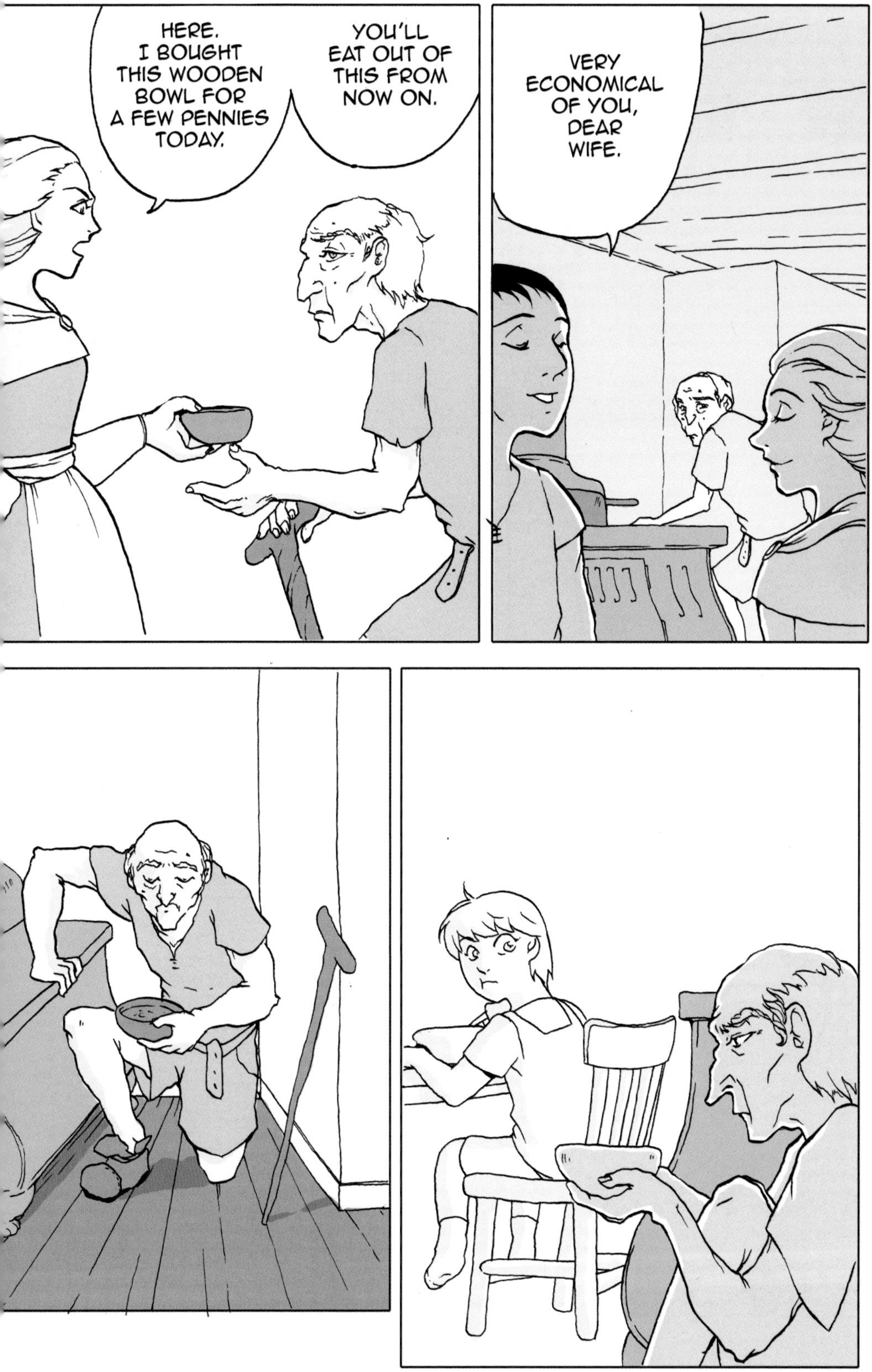
HERE. I BOUGHT THIS WOODEN BOWL FOR A FEW PENNIES TODAY.
YOU'LL EAT OUT OF THIS FROM NOW ON.
VERY ECONOMICAL OF YOU, DEAR WIFE.

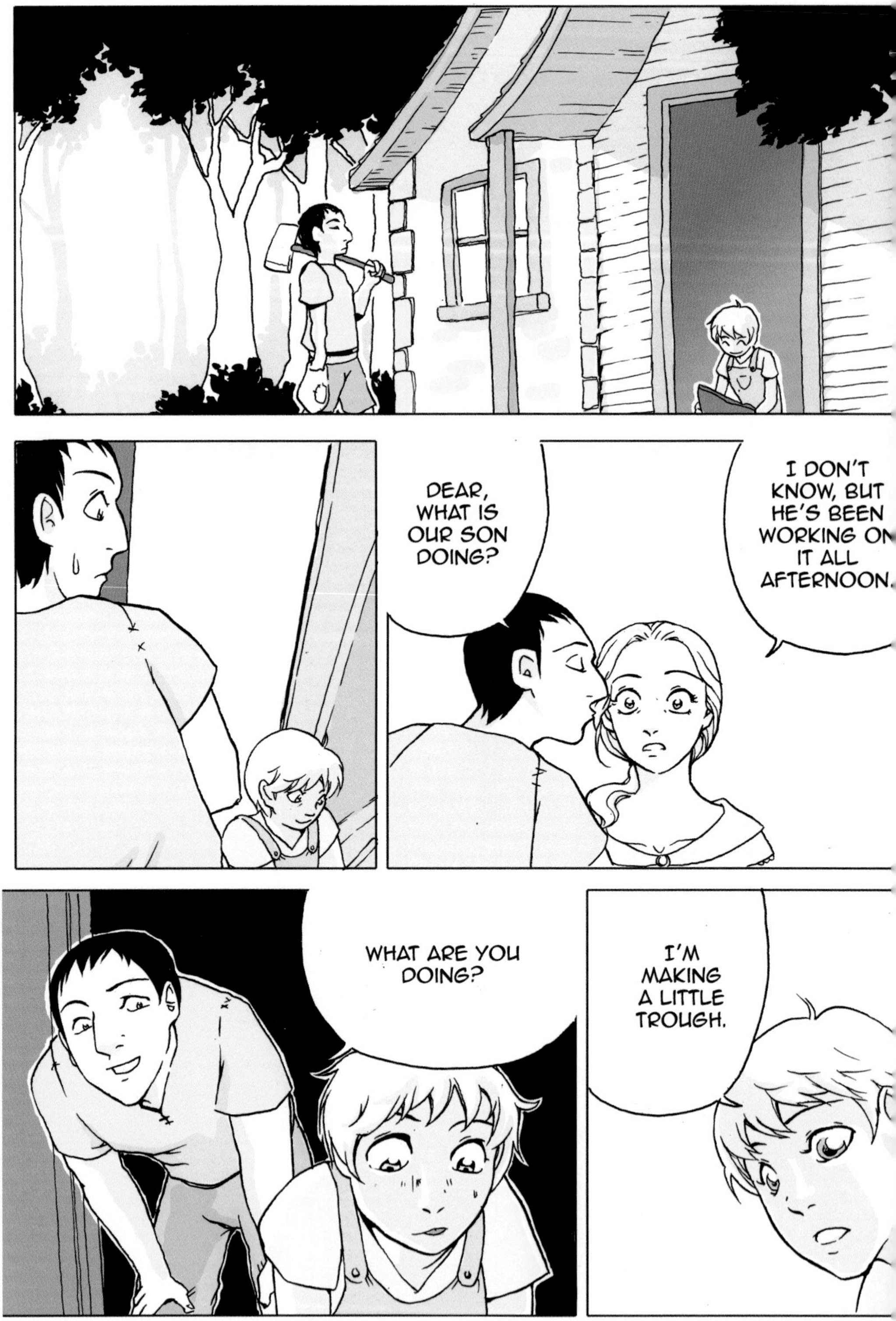
DEAR, WHAT IS OUR SON DOING?
I DON'T KNOW, BUT HE'S BEEN WORKING ON IT ALL AFTERNOON.
WHAT ARE YOU DOING?
I'M MAKING A LITTLE TROUGH.

MY MOTHER AND FATHER SHALL EAT OUT OF IT WHEN I GROW UP.

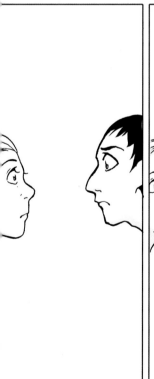

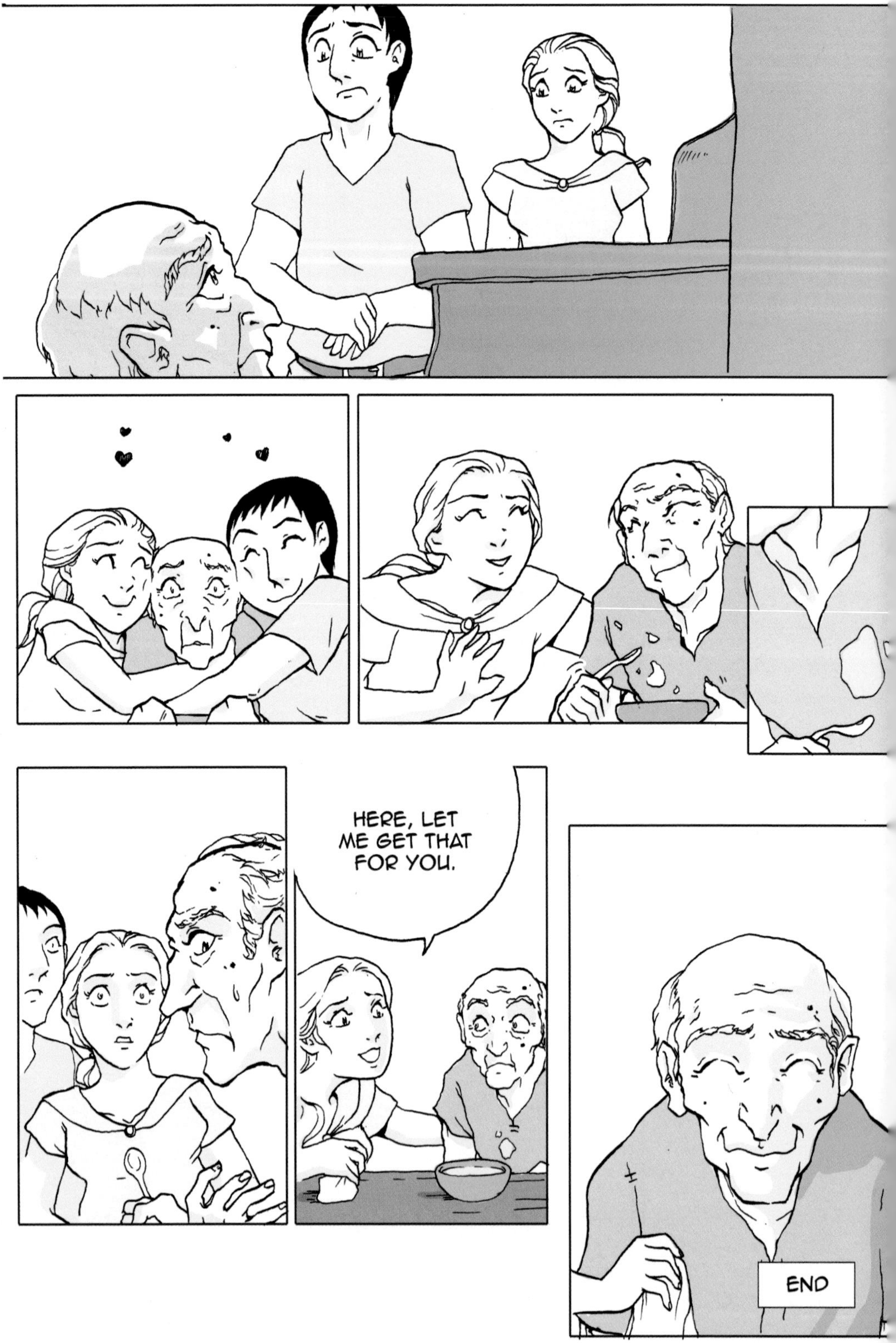
HERE, LET ME GET THAT FOR YOU.
END

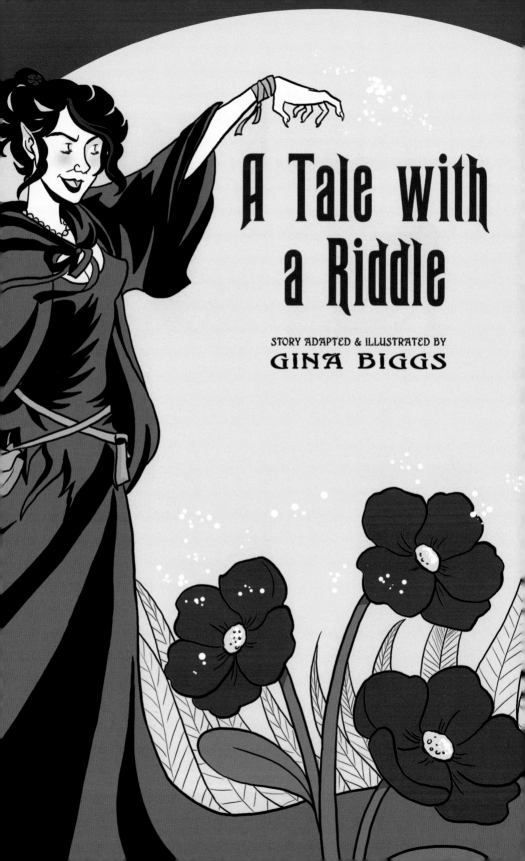

A Tale with a Riddle

STORY ADAPTED & ILLUSTRATED BY
GINA BIGGS

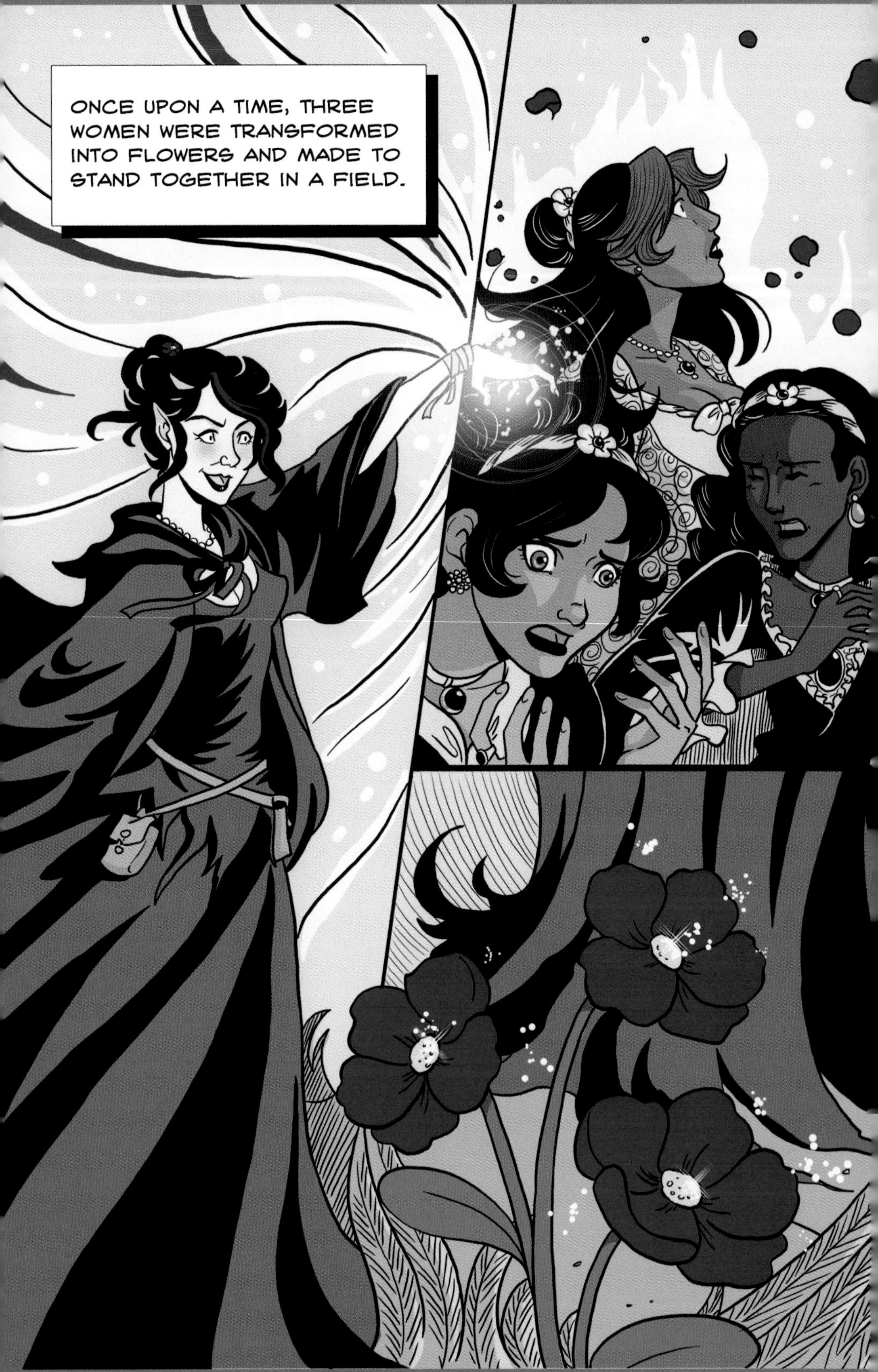
ONCE UPON A TIME, THREE WOMEN WERE TRANSFORMED INTO FLOWERS AND MADE TO STAND TOGETHER IN A FIELD.

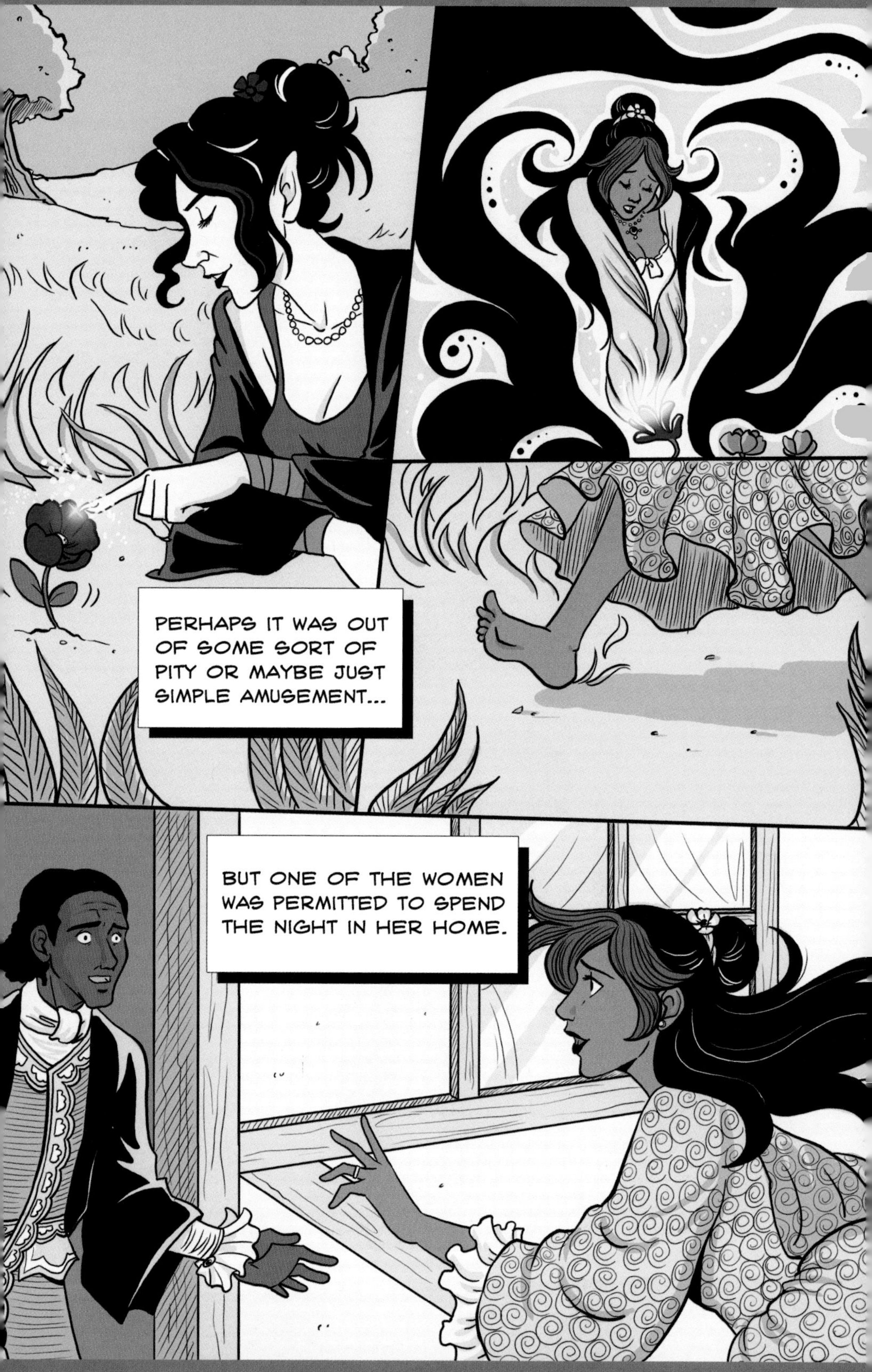
PERHAPS IT WAS OUT OF SOME SORT OF PITY OR MAYBE JUST SIMPLE AMUSEMENT...
BUT ONE OF THE WOMEN WAS PERMITTED TO SPEND THE NIGHT IN HER HOME.

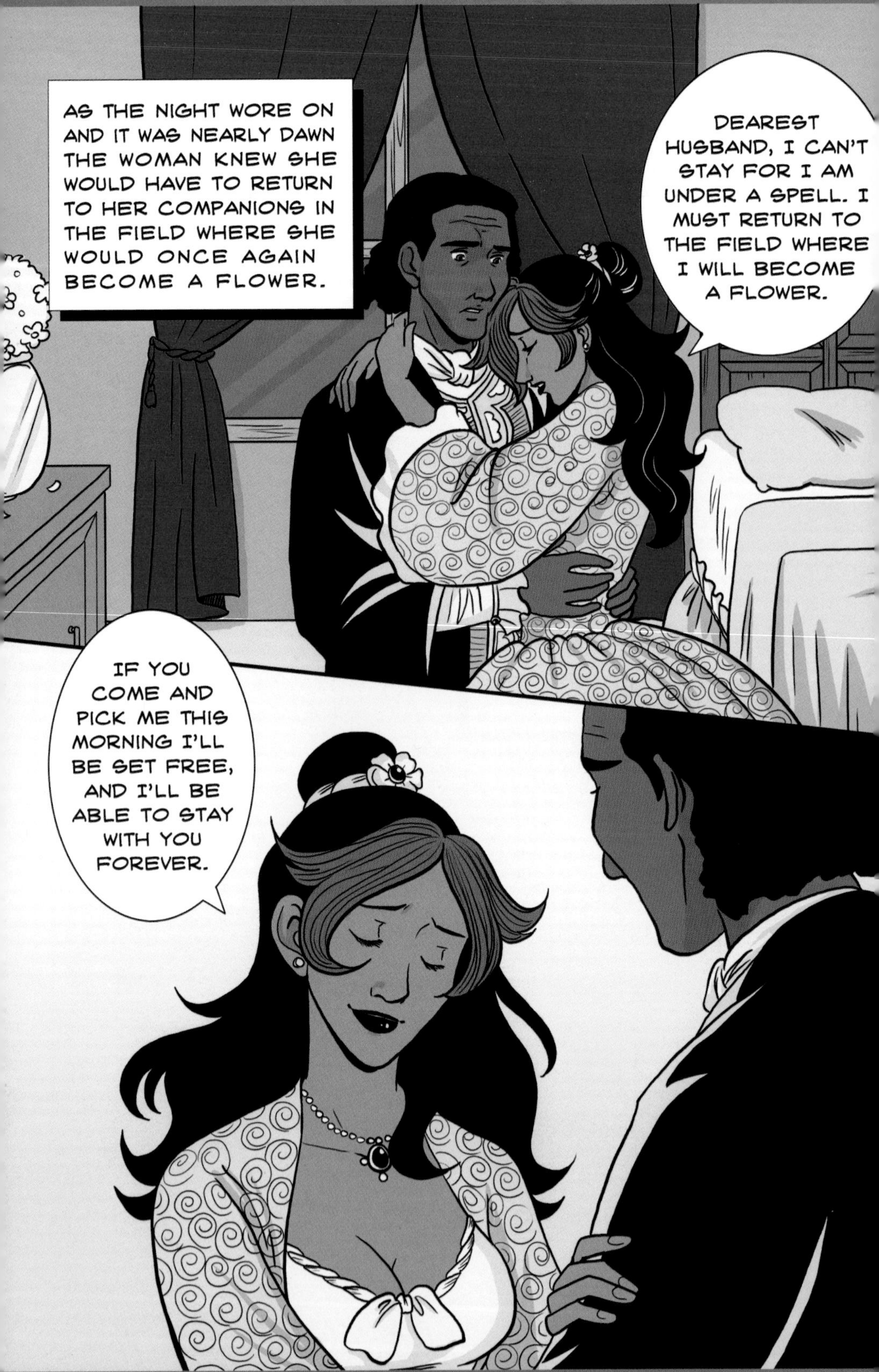
AS THE NIGHT WORE ON AND IT WAS NEARLY DAWN THE WOMAN KNEW SHE WOULD HAVE TO RETURN TO HER COMPANIONS IN THE FIELD WHERE SHE WOULD ONCE AGAIN BECOME A FLOWER.
DEAREST HUSBAND, I CAN'T STAY FOR I AM UNDER A SPELL. I MUST RETURN TO THE FIELD WHERE I WILL BECOME A FLOWER.
IF YOU COME AND PICK ME THIS MORNING I'LL BE SET FREE, AND I'LL BE ABLE TO STAY WITH YOU FOREVER.

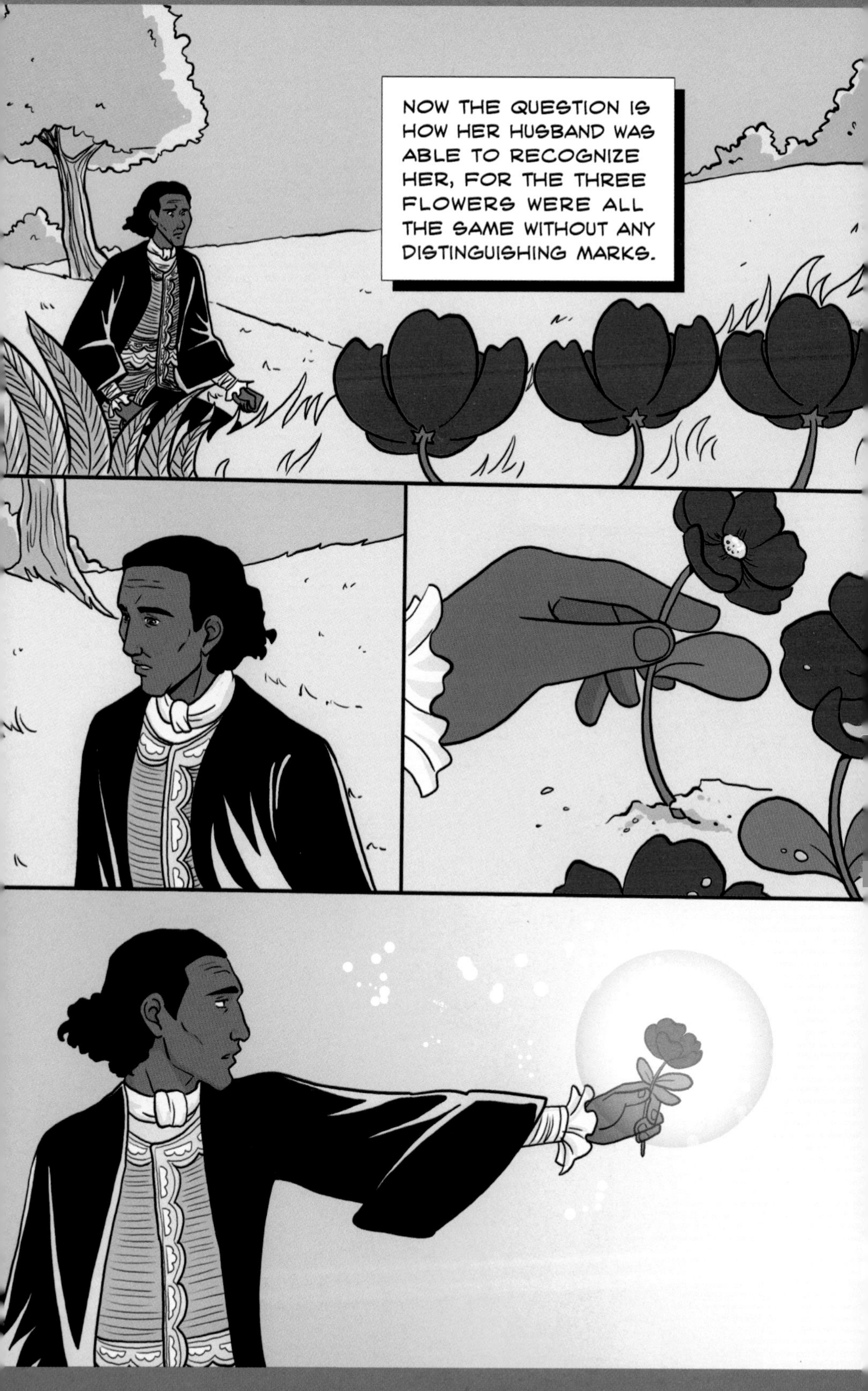
NOW THE QUESTION IS HOW HER HUSBAND WAS ABLE TO RECOGNIZE HER, FOR THE THREE FLOWERS WERE ALL THE SAME WITHOUT ANY DISTINGUISHING MARKS.

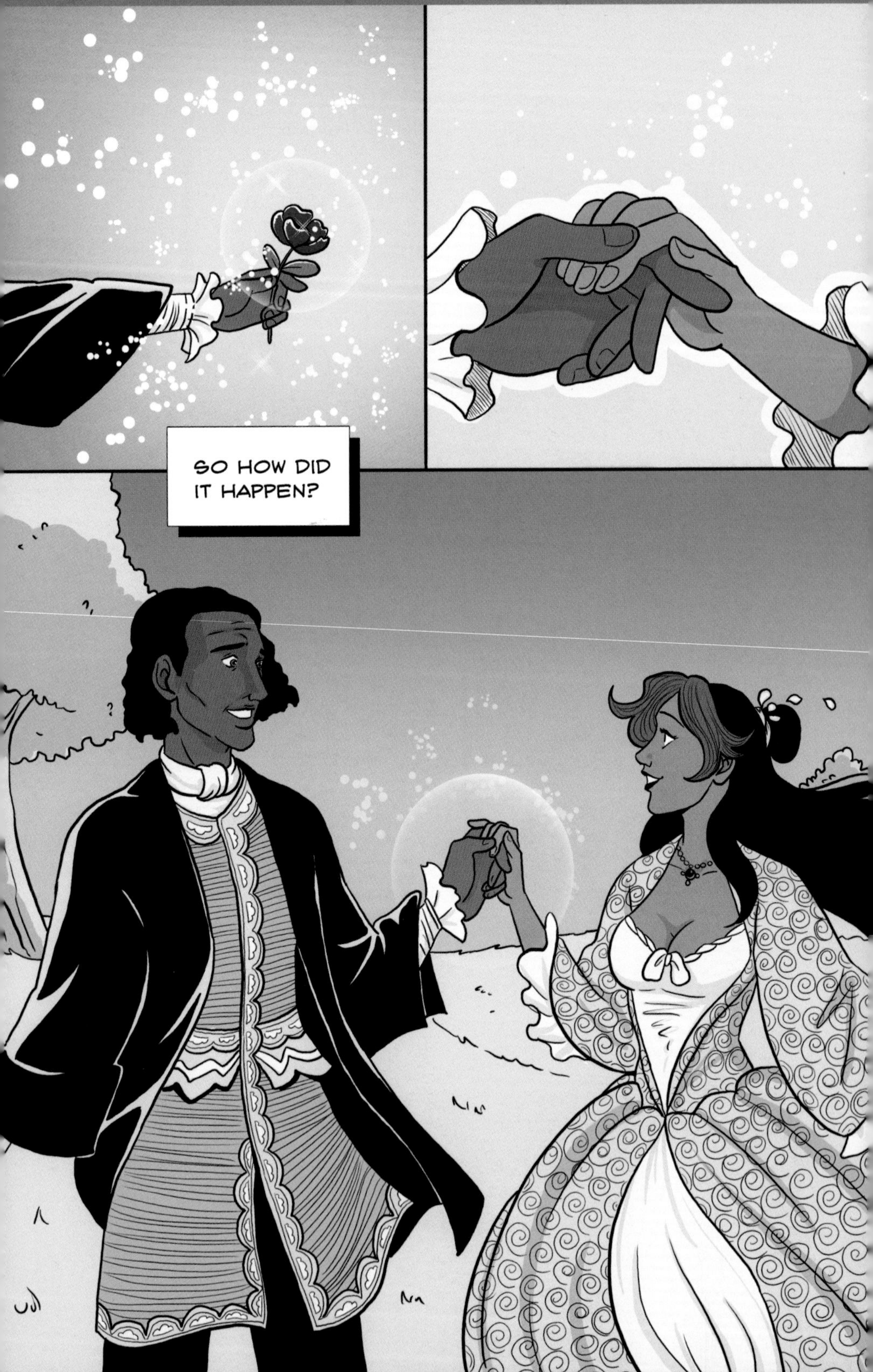
SO HOW DID
IT HAPPEN?

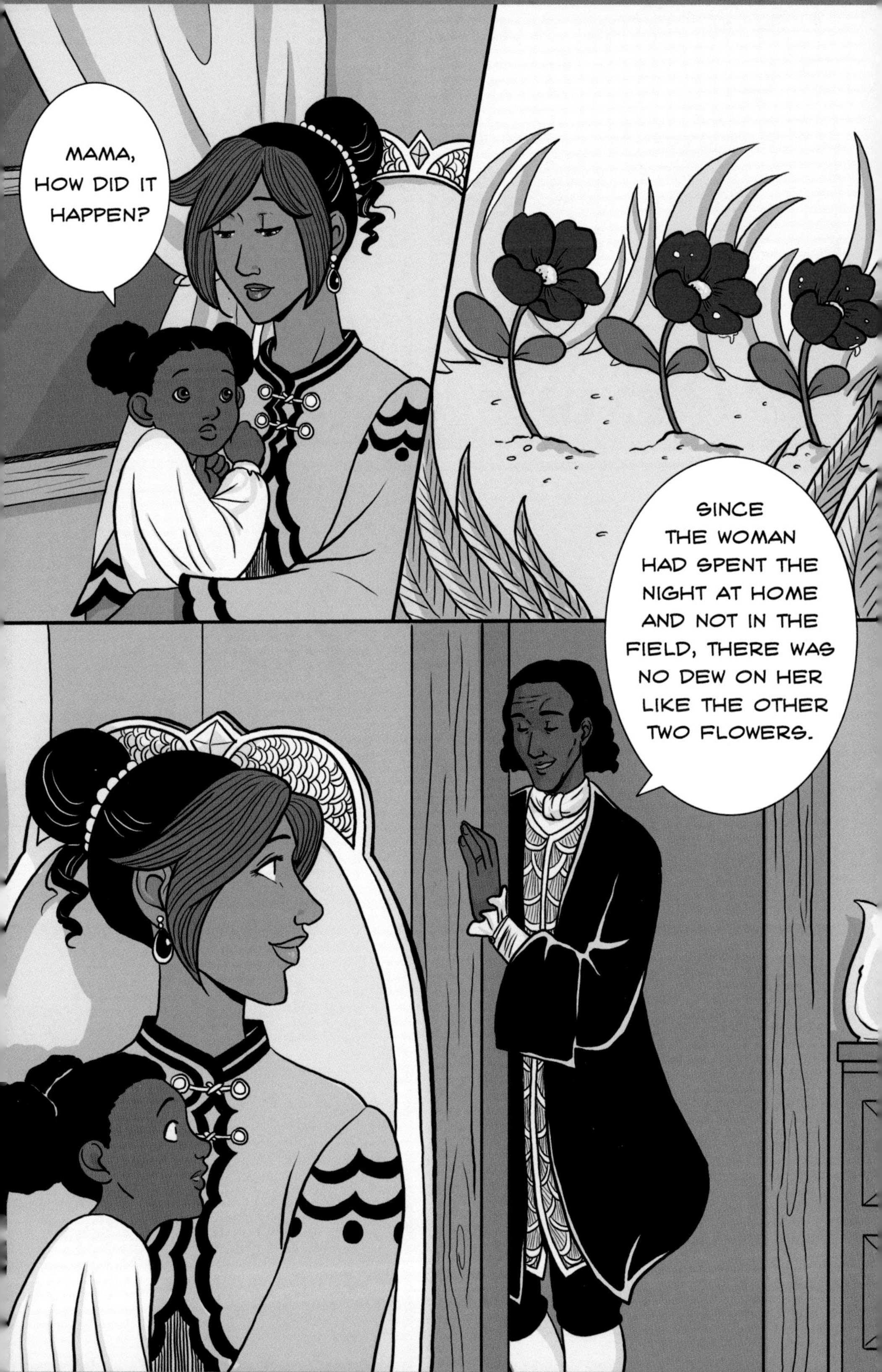
MAMA, HOW DID IT HAPPEN?
SINCE THE WOMAN HAD SPENT THE NIGHT AT HOME AND NOT IN THE FIELD, THERE WAS NO DEW ON HER LIKE THE OTHER TWO FLOWERS.

The Sweet PORRIDGE

STORY ADAPTED & ILLUSTRATED BY GINA BIGGS

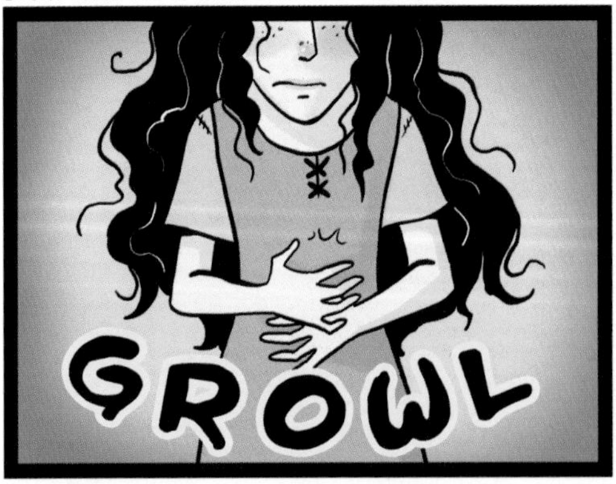
GROWL

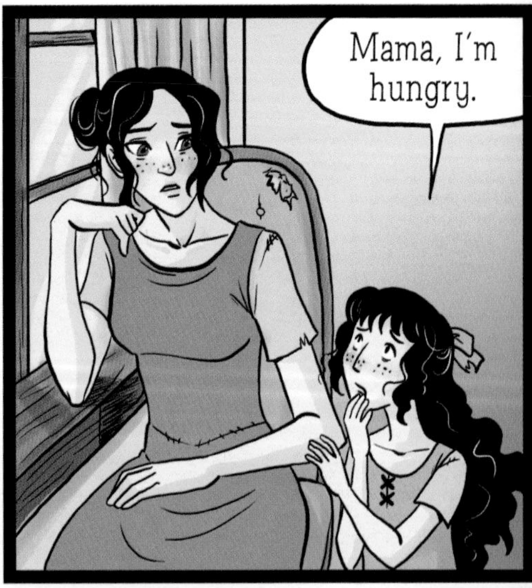
Mama, I'm hungry.

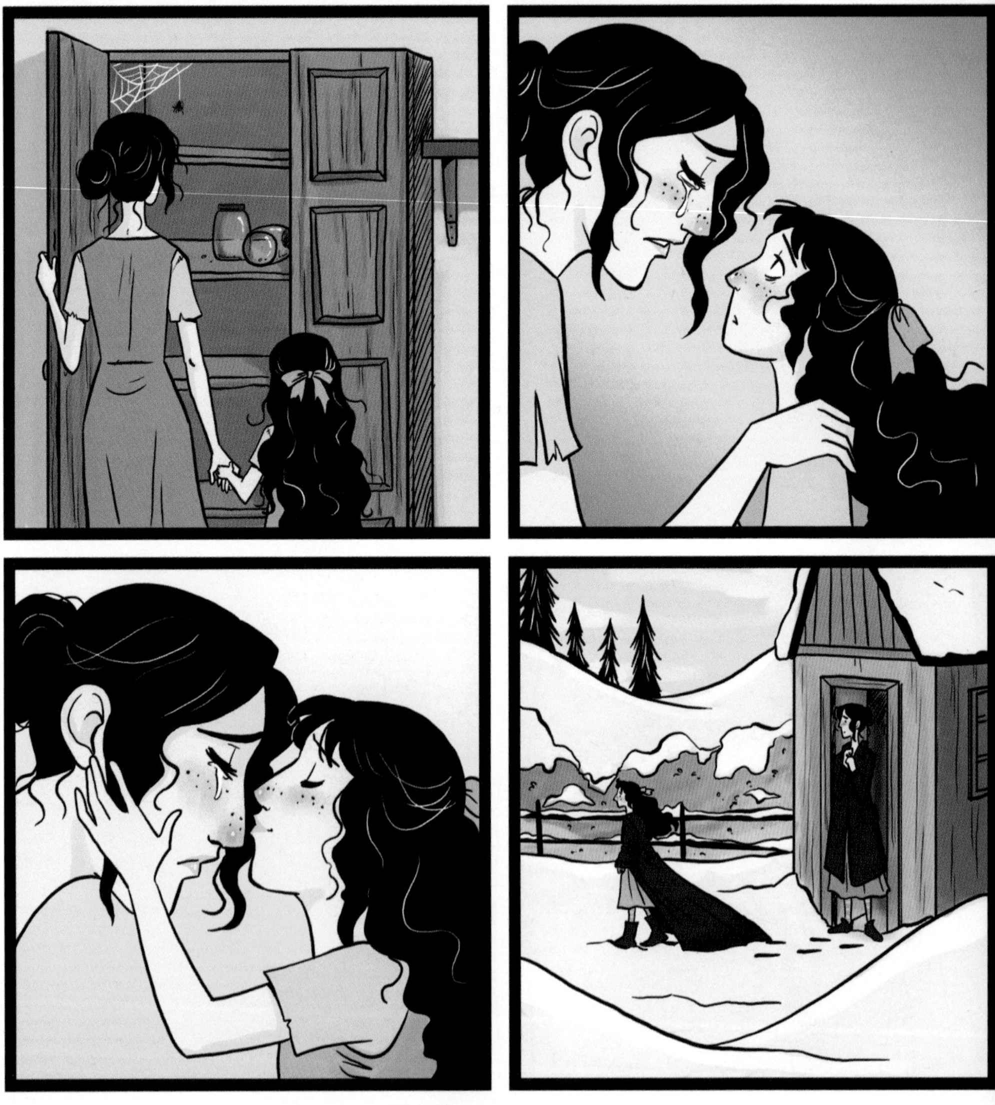

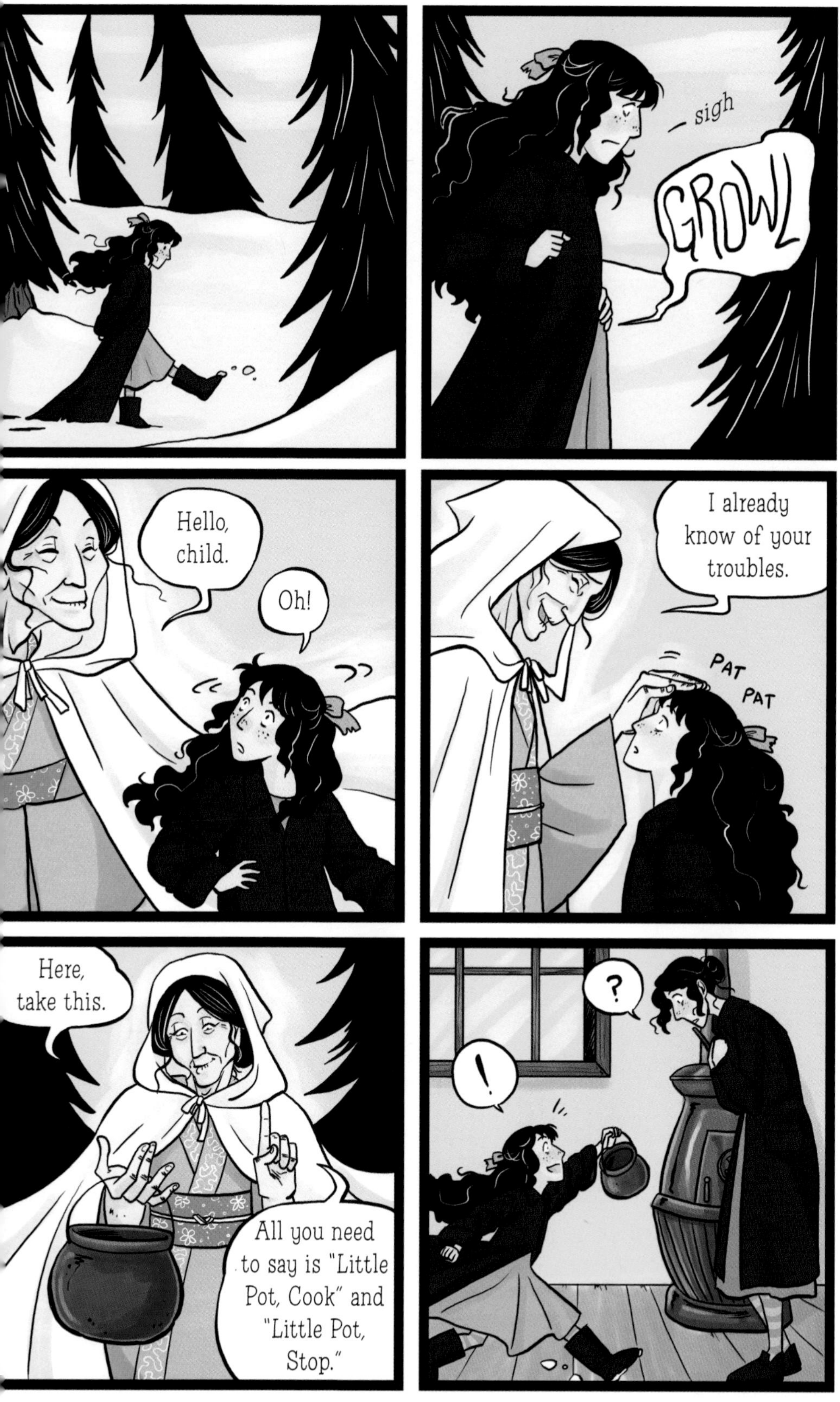
sigh
GROWL
Hello, child.
Oh!
I already know of your troubles.
PAT PAT
Here, take this.
All you need to say is "Little Pot, Cook" and "Little Pot, Stop."
?
!

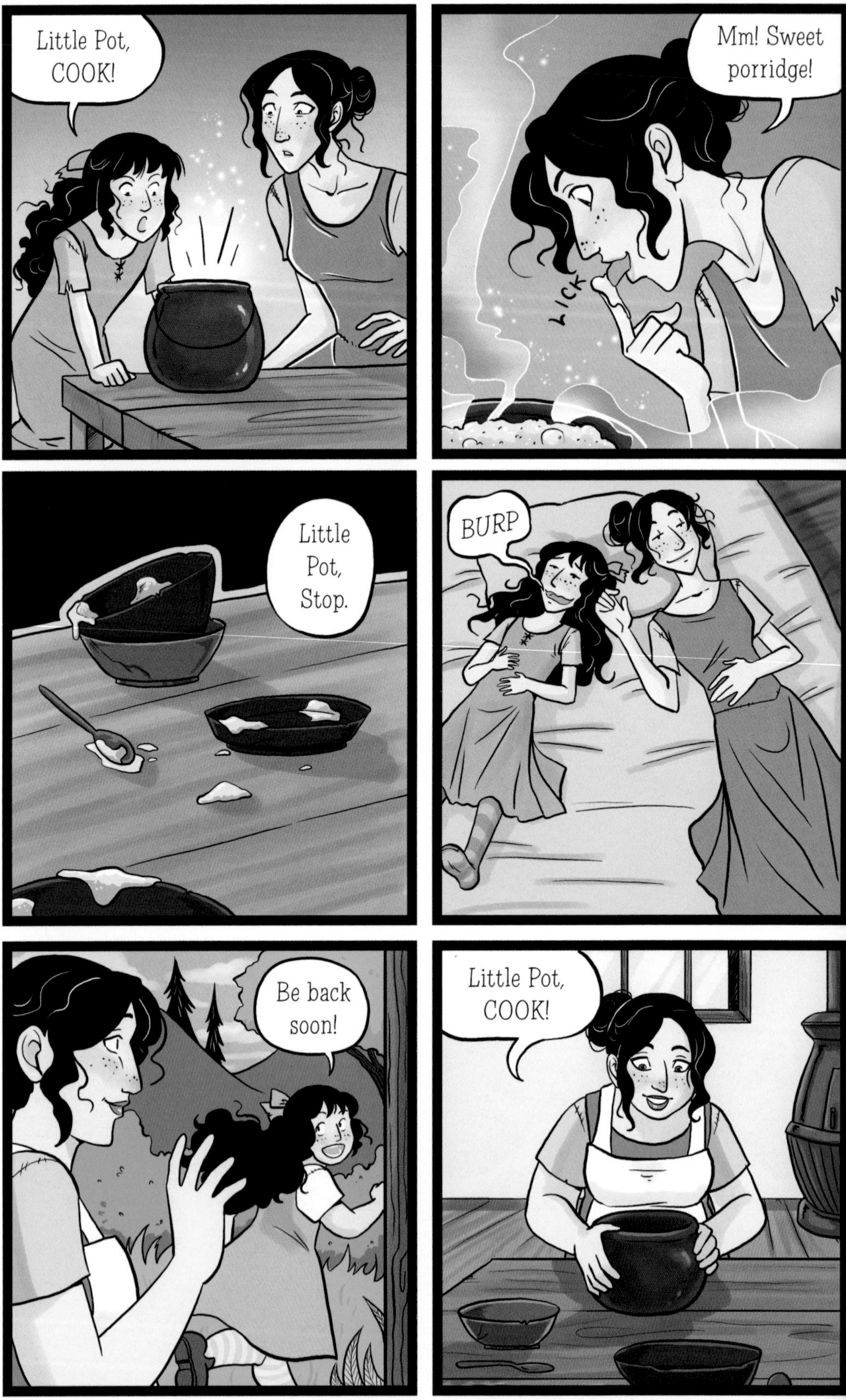
Little Pot, COOK!
Mm! Sweet porridge!
LICK
Little Pot, Stop.
BURP
Be back soon!
Little Pot, COOK!

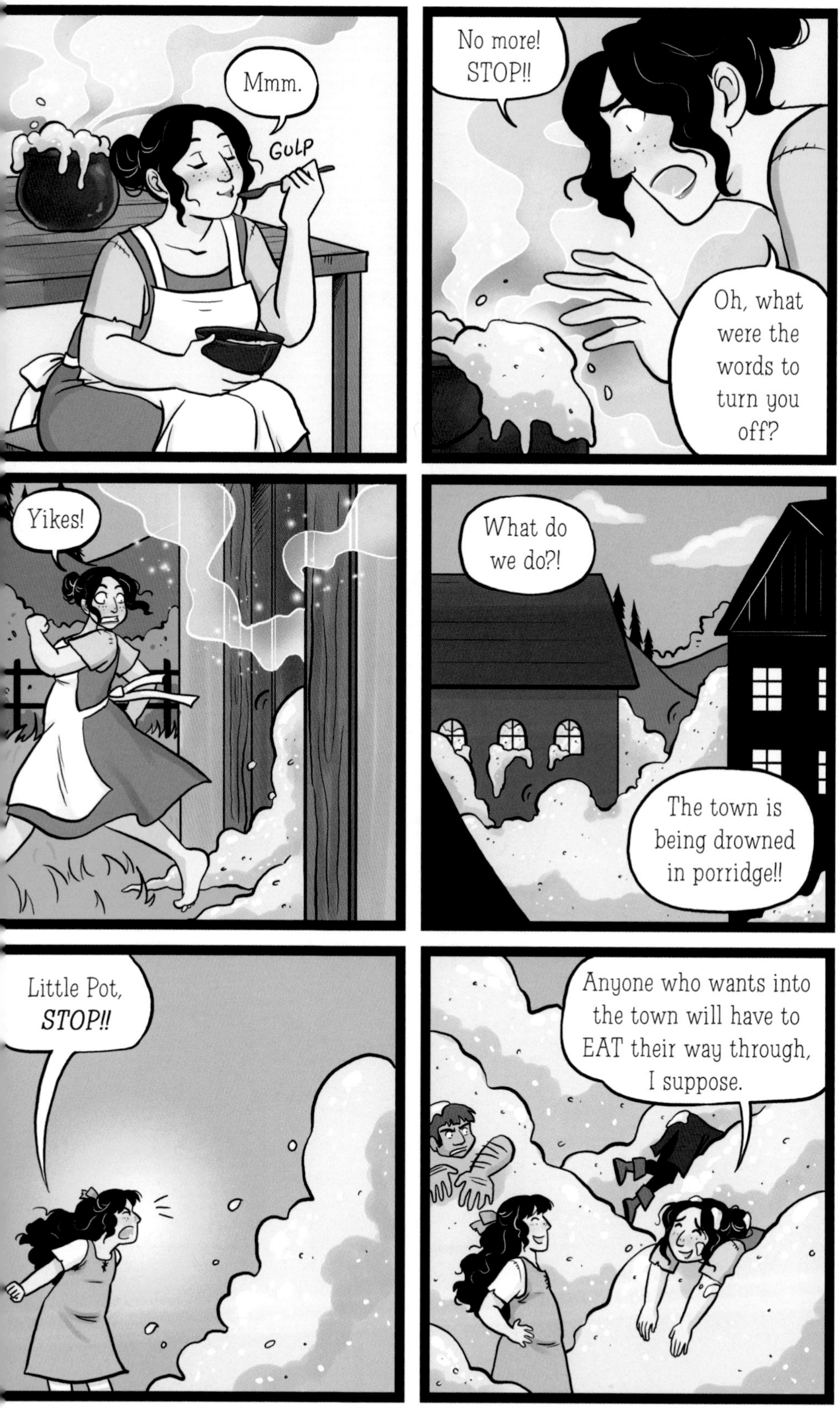

Mmm.
GULP
No more! STOP!!
Oh, what were the words to turn you off?
Yikes!
What do we do?!
The town is being drowned in porridge!!
Little Pot, *STOP!!*
Anyone who wants into the town will have to EAT their way through, I suppose.

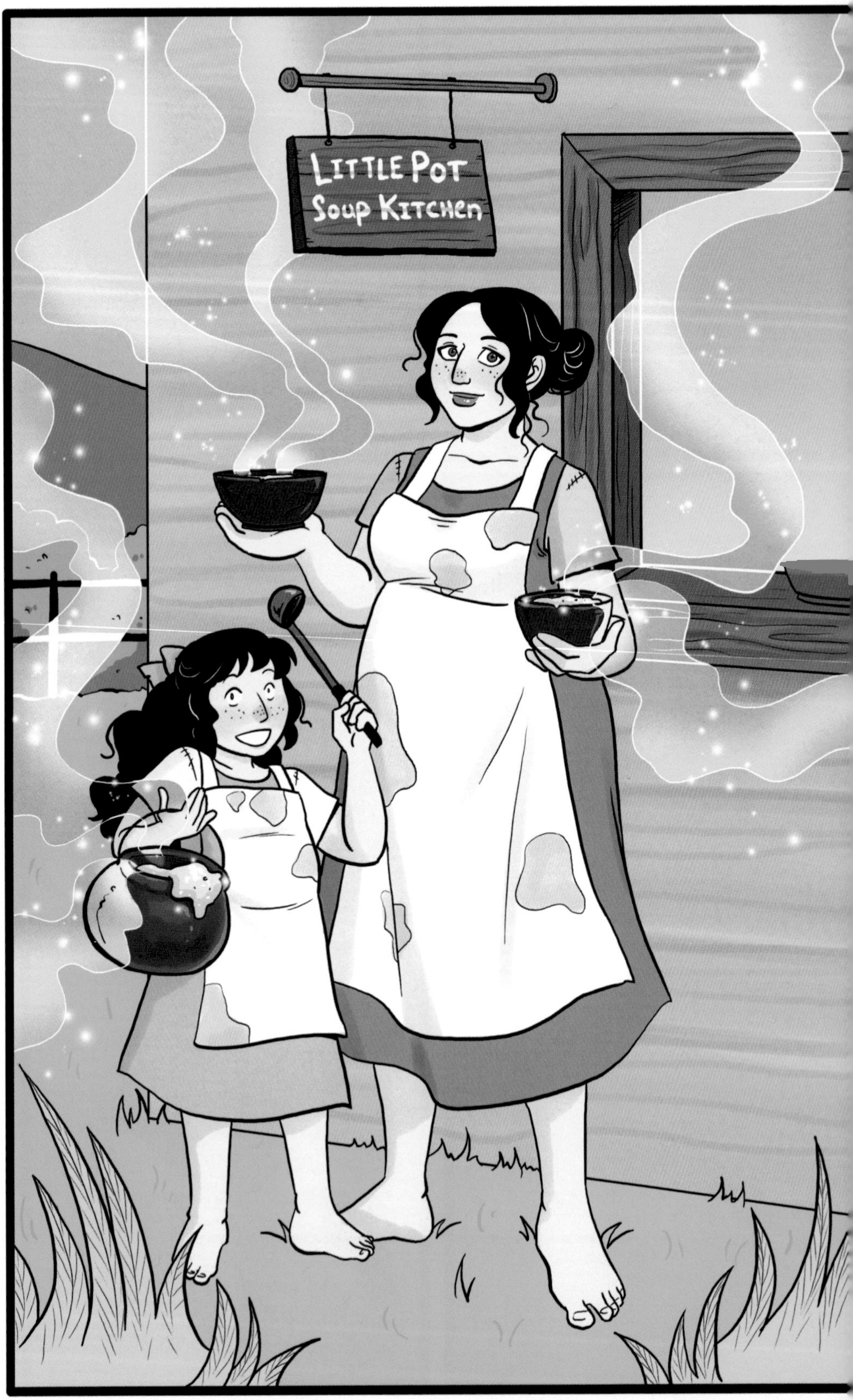
LITTLE POT
Soup KITCHEN

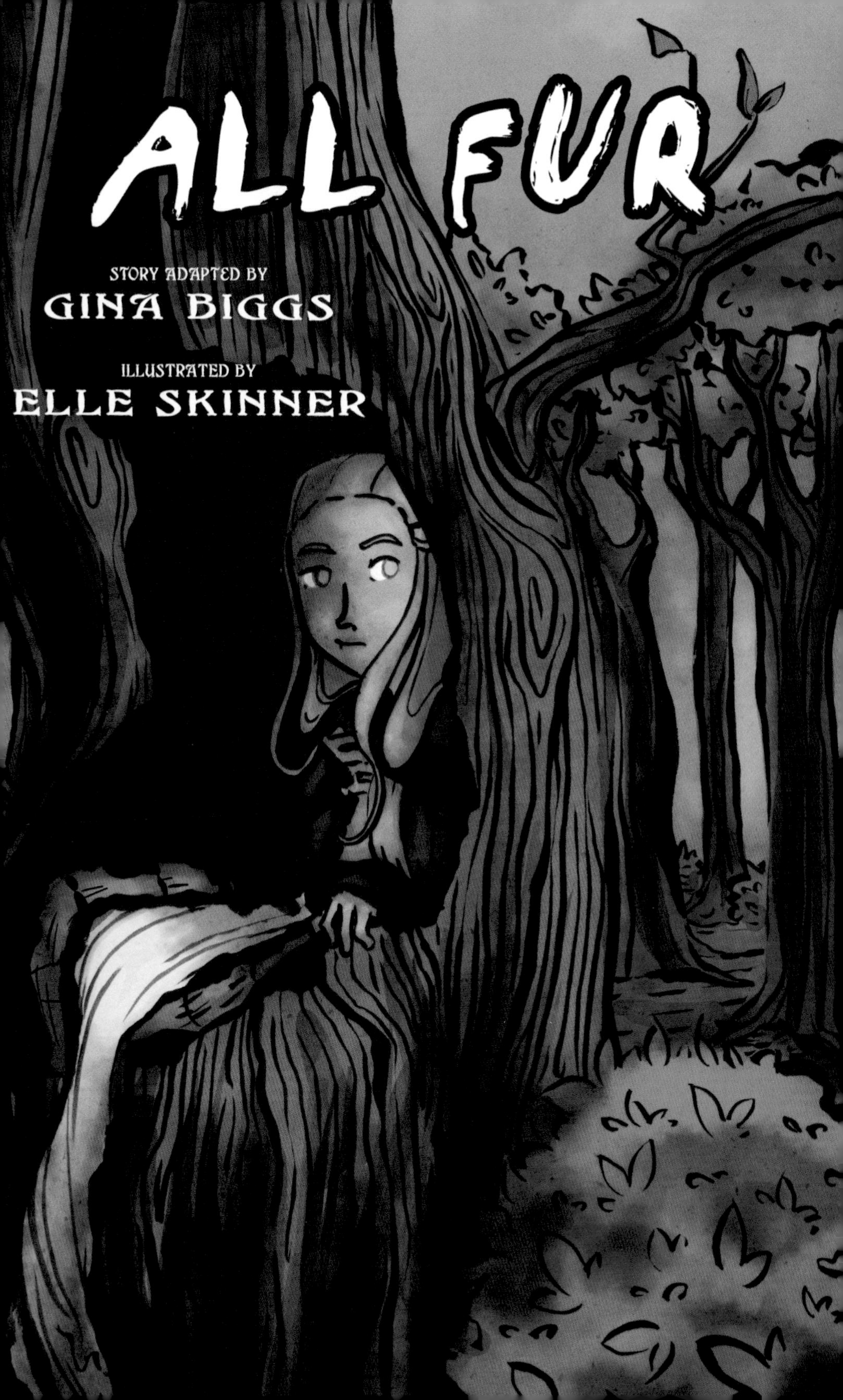
ALL FUR
STORY ADAPTED BY
GINA BIGGS
ILLUSTRATED BY
ELLE SKINNER

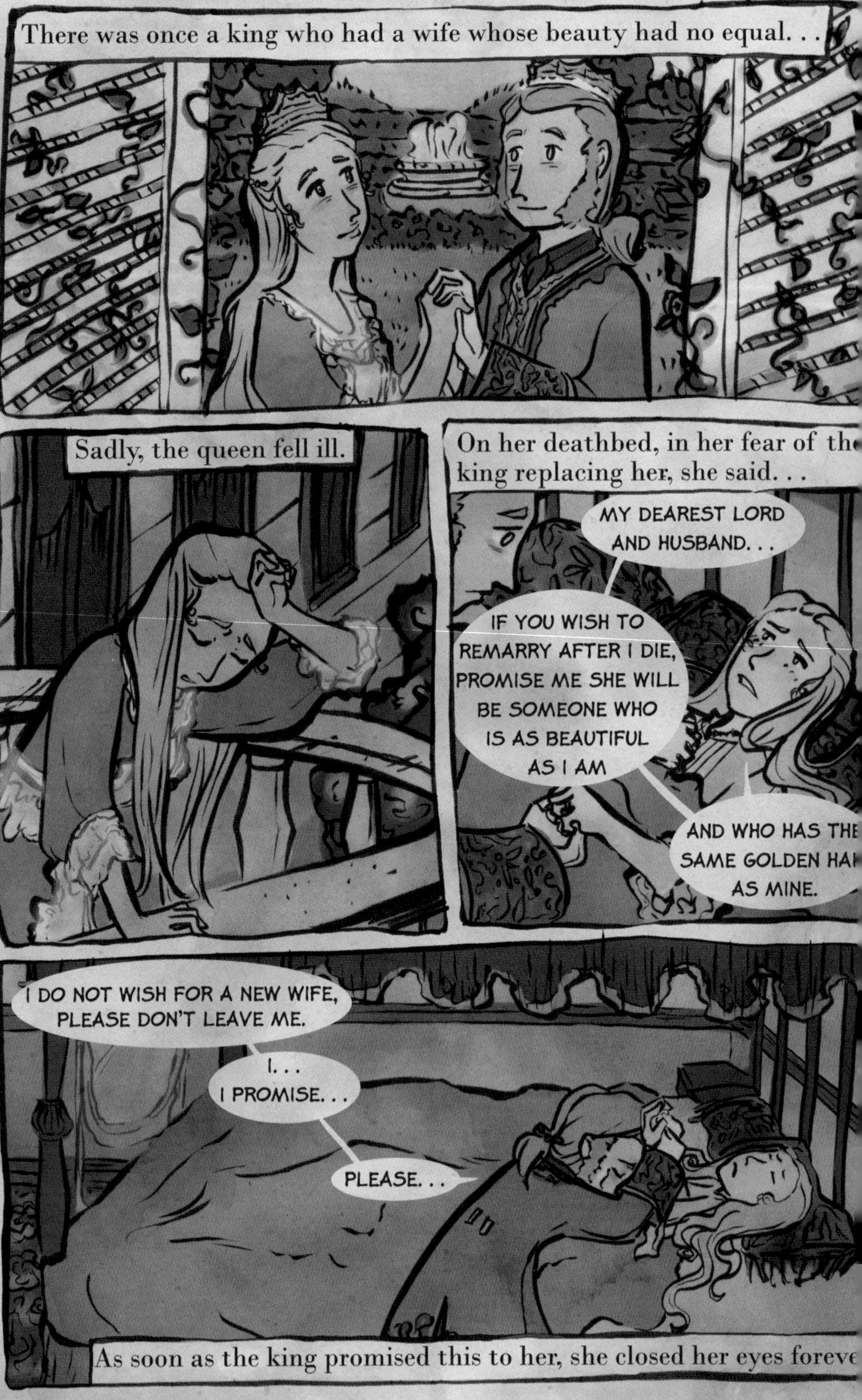
There was once a king who had a wife whose beauty had no equal. . .
Sadly, the queen fell ill.
On her deathbed, in her fear of th
king replacing her, she said. . .
MY DEAREST LORD AND HUSBAND. . .
IF YOU WISH TO REMARRY AFTER I DIE, PROMISE ME SHE WILL BE SOMEONE WHO IS AS BEAUTIFUL AS I AM
AND WHO HAS THE SAME GOLDEN HA AS MINE.
I DO NOT WISH FOR A NEW WIFE, PLEASE DON'T LEAVE ME.
I. . . I PROMISE. . .
PLEASE. . .
As soon as the king promised this to her, she closed her eyes foreve

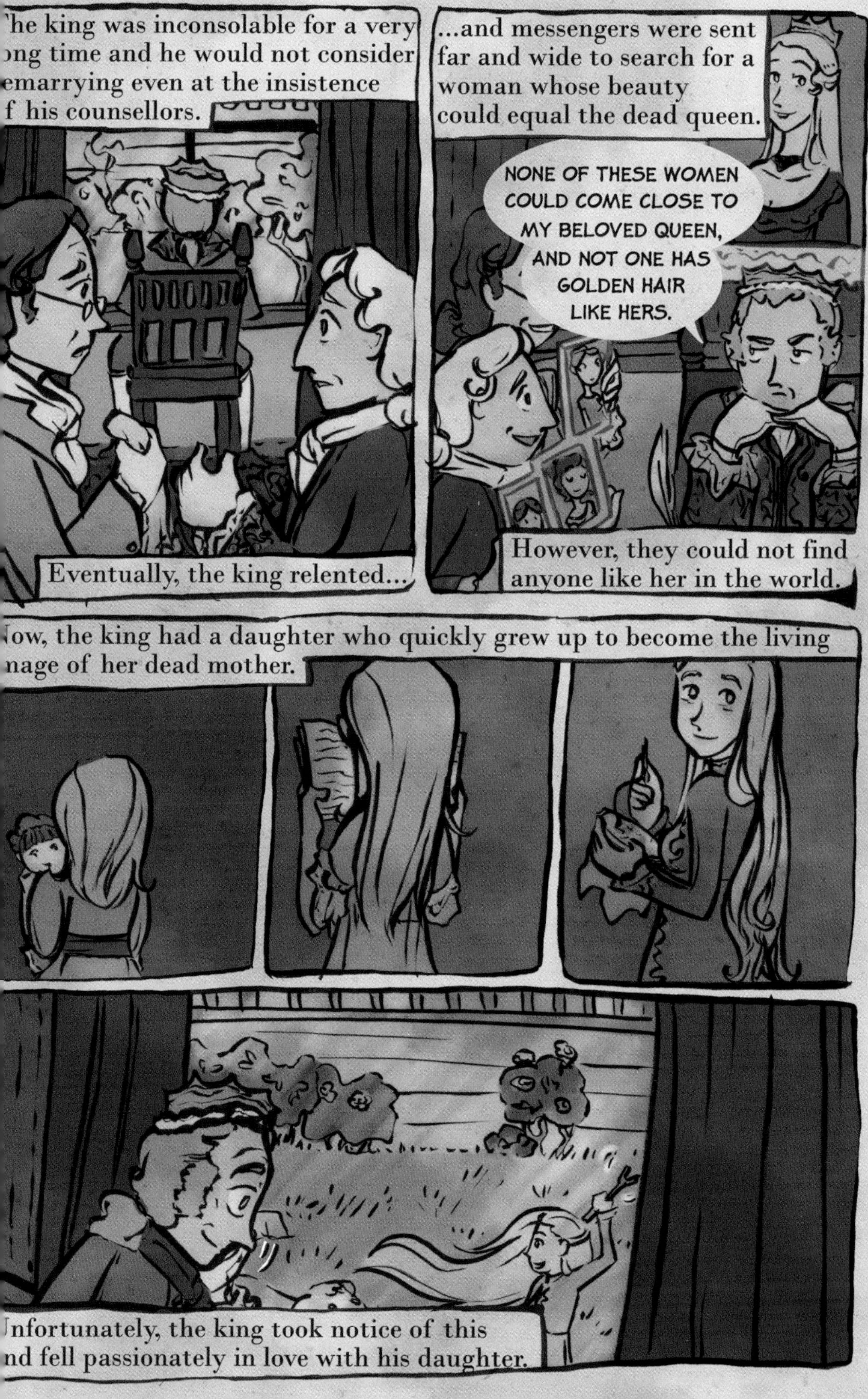
he king was inconsolable for a very
ong time and he would not consider
emarrying even at the insistence
f his counsellors.
Eventually, the king relented...
...and messengers were sent
far and wide to search for a
woman whose beauty
could equal the dead queen.
NONE OF THESE WOMEN COULD COME CLOSE TO MY BELOVED QUEEN, AND NOT ONE HAS GOLDEN HAIR LIKE HERS.
However, they could not find
anyone like her in the world.
ow, the king had a daughter who quickly grew up to become the living
nage of her dead mother.
nfortunately, the king took notice of this
nd fell passionately in love with his daughter.

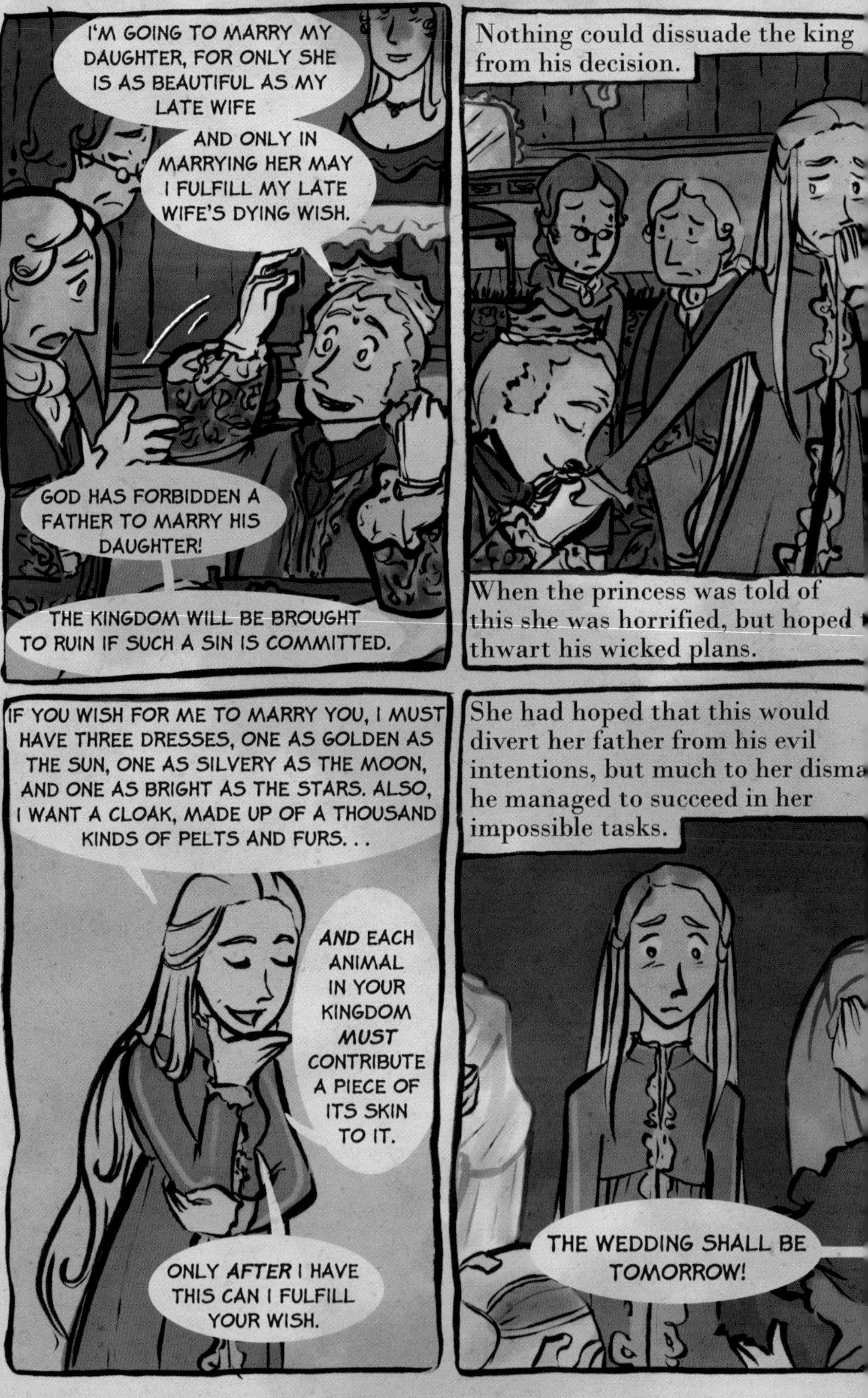
I'M GOING TO MARRY MY DAUGHTER, FOR ONLY SHE IS AS BEAUTIFUL AS MY LATE WIFE
AND ONLY IN MARRYING HER MAY I FULFILL MY LATE WIFE'S DYING WISH.
GOD HAS FORBIDDEN A FATHER TO MARRY HIS DAUGHTER!
THE KINGDOM WILL BE BROUGHT TO RUIN IF SUCH A SIN IS COMMITTED.
Nothing could dissuade the king from his decision.
When the princess was told of this she was horrified, but hoped thwart his wicked plans.
IF YOU WISH FOR ME TO MARRY YOU, I MUST HAVE THREE DRESSES, ONE AS GOLDEN AS THE SUN, ONE AS SILVERY AS THE MOON, AND ONE AS BRIGHT AS THE STARS. ALSO, I WANT A CLOAK, MADE UP OF A THOUSAND KINDS OF PELTS AND FURS. . .
AND EACH ANIMAL IN YOUR KINGDOM MUST CONTRIBUTE A PIECE OF ITS SKIN TO IT.
ONLY AFTER I HAVE THIS CAN I FULFILL YOUR WISH.
She had hoped that this would divert her father from his evil intentions, but much to her disma he managed to succeed in her impossible tasks.
THE WEDDING SHALL BE TOMORROW!

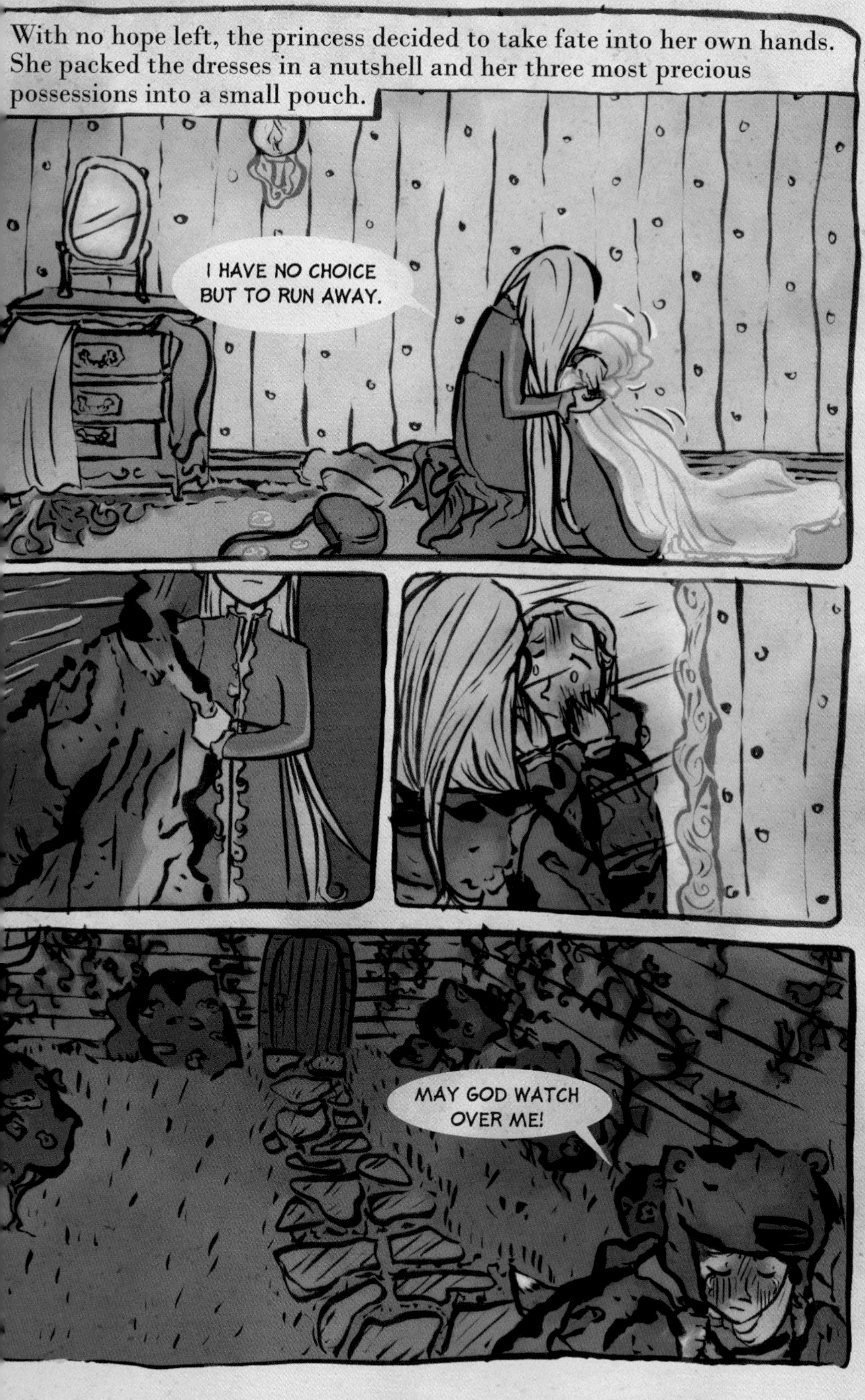
With no hope left, the princess decided to take fate into her own hands. She packed the dresses in a nutshell and her three most precious possessions into a small pouch.
I HAVE NO CHOICE BUT TO RUN AWAY.
MAY GOD WATCH OVER ME!

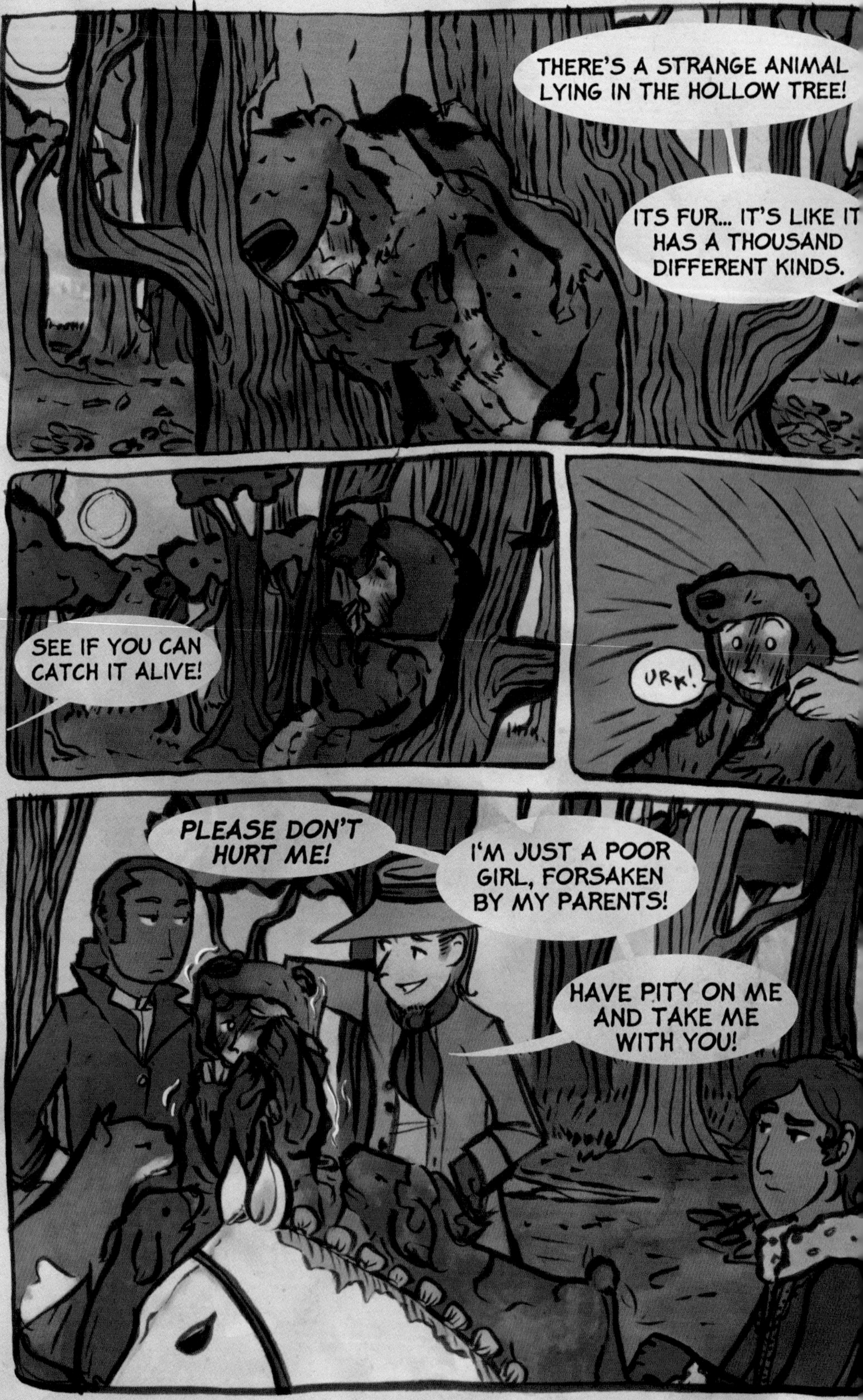
THERE'S A STRANGE ANIMAL LYING IN THE HOLLOW TREE!
ITS FUR... IT'S LIKE IT HAS A THOUSAND DIFFERENT KINDS.
SEE IF YOU CAN CATCH IT ALIVE!
URK!
PLEASE DON'T HURT ME!
I'M JUST A POOR GIRL, FORSAKEN BY MY PARENTS!
HAVE PITY ON ME AND TAKE ME WITH YOU!

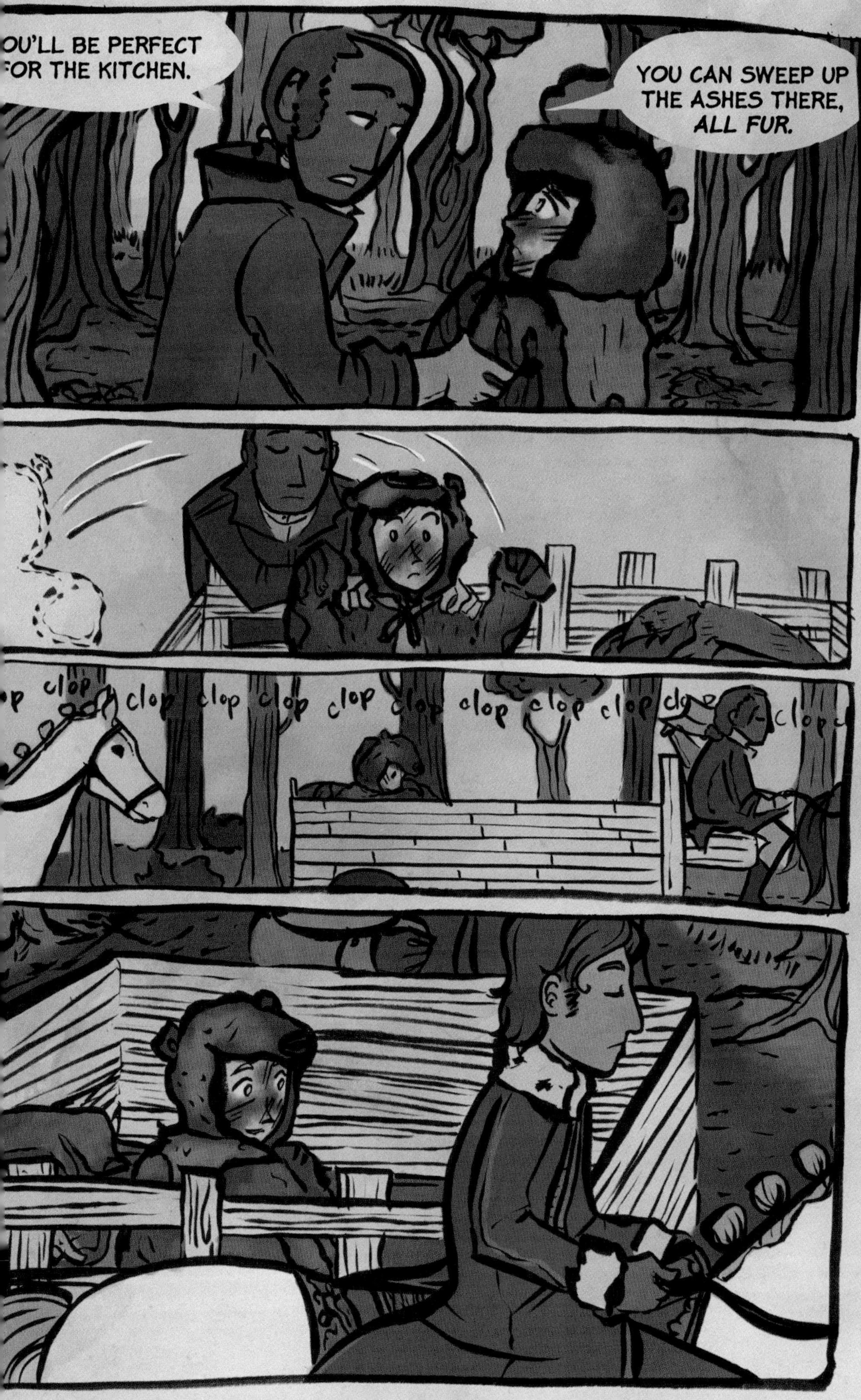
OU'LL BE PERFECT FOR THE KITCHEN.
YOU CAN SWEEP UP THE ASHES THERE, ALL FUR.
clop clop clop clop clop clop clop clop clop clop

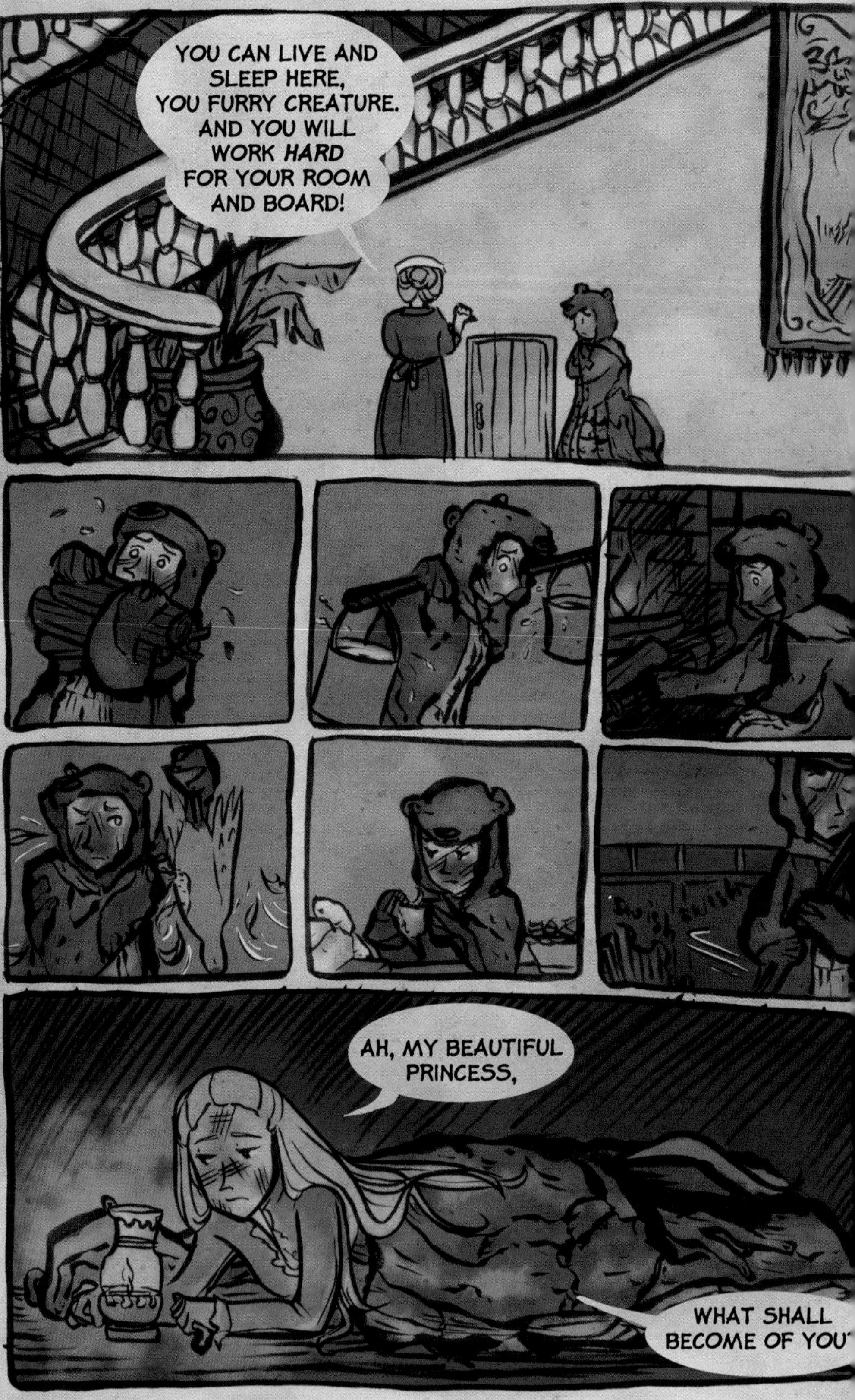
YOU CAN LIVE AND SLEEP HERE, YOU FURRY CREATURE. AND YOU WILL WORK *HARD* FOR YOUR ROOM AND BOARD!
AH, MY BEAUTIFUL PRINCESS,
WHAT SHALL BECOME OF YOU

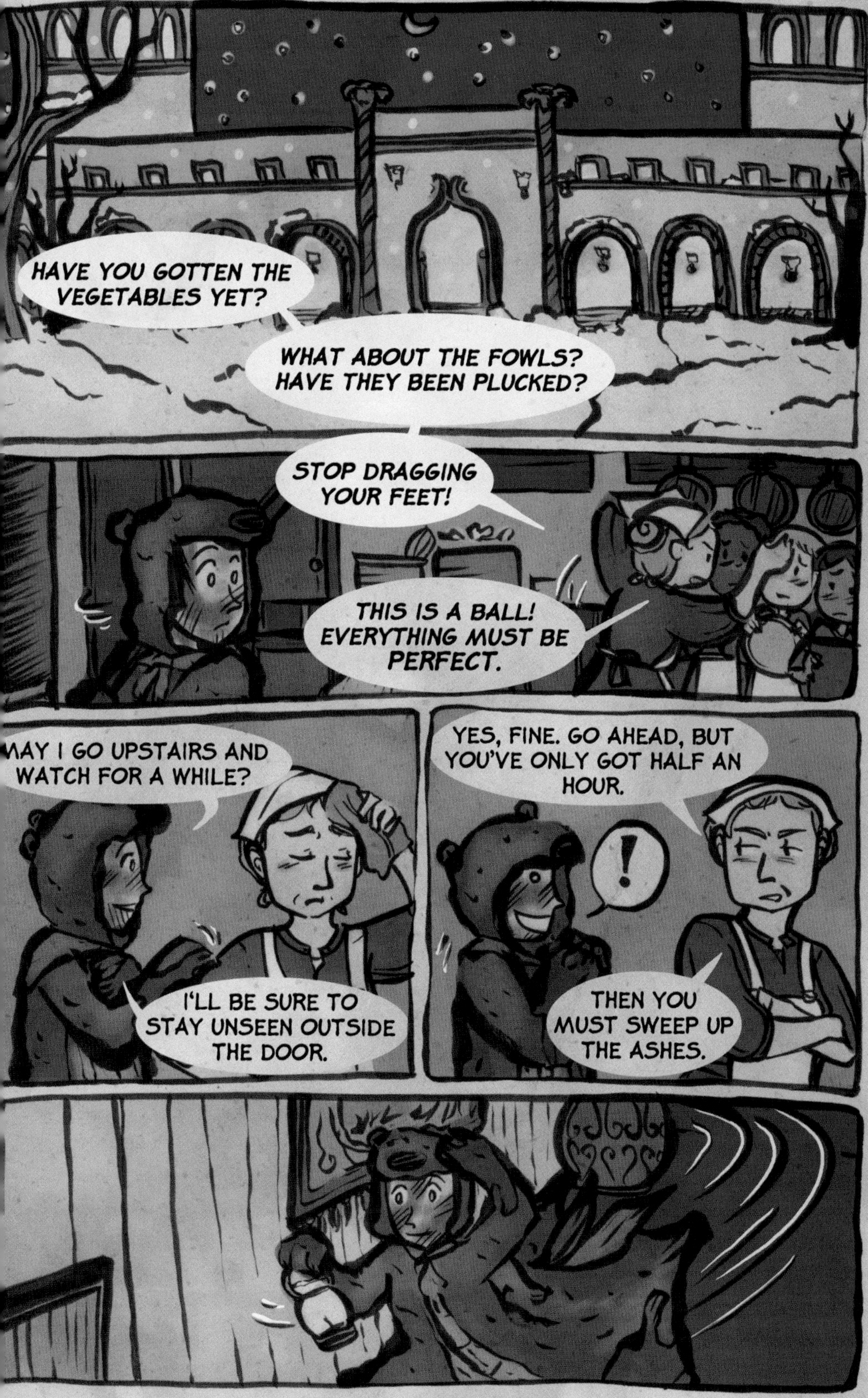
HAVE YOU GOTTEN THE VEGETABLES YET?
WHAT ABOUT THE FOWLS? HAVE THEY BEEN PLUCKED?
STOP DRAGGING YOUR FEET!
THIS IS A BALL! EVERYTHING MUST BE PERFECT.
MAY I GO UPSTAIRS AND WATCH FOR A WHILE?
I'LL BE SURE TO STAY UNSEEN OUTSIDE THE DOOR.
YES, FINE. GO AHEAD, BUT YOU'VE ONLY GOT HALF AN HOUR.
!
THEN YOU MUST SWEEP UP THE ASHES.

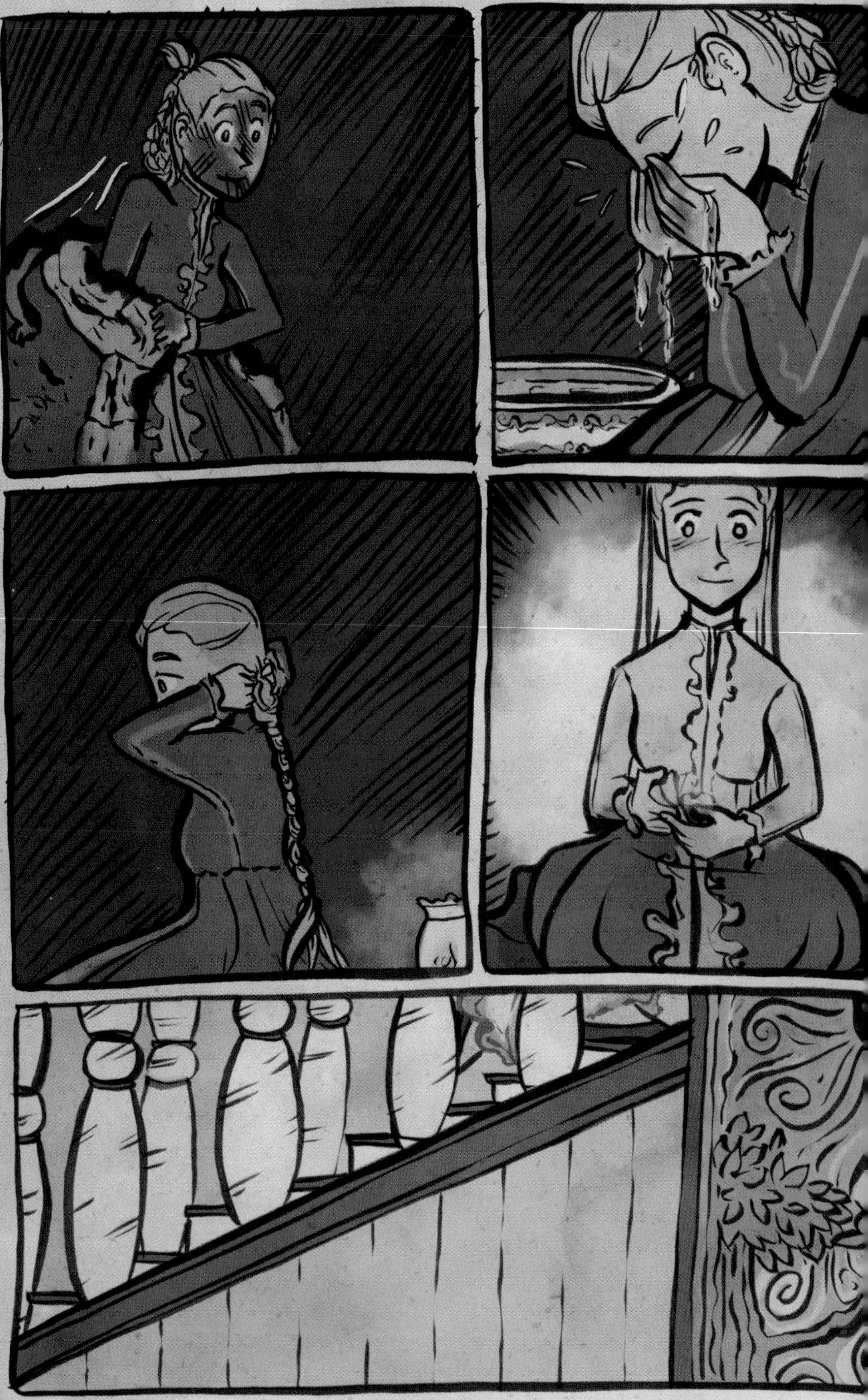

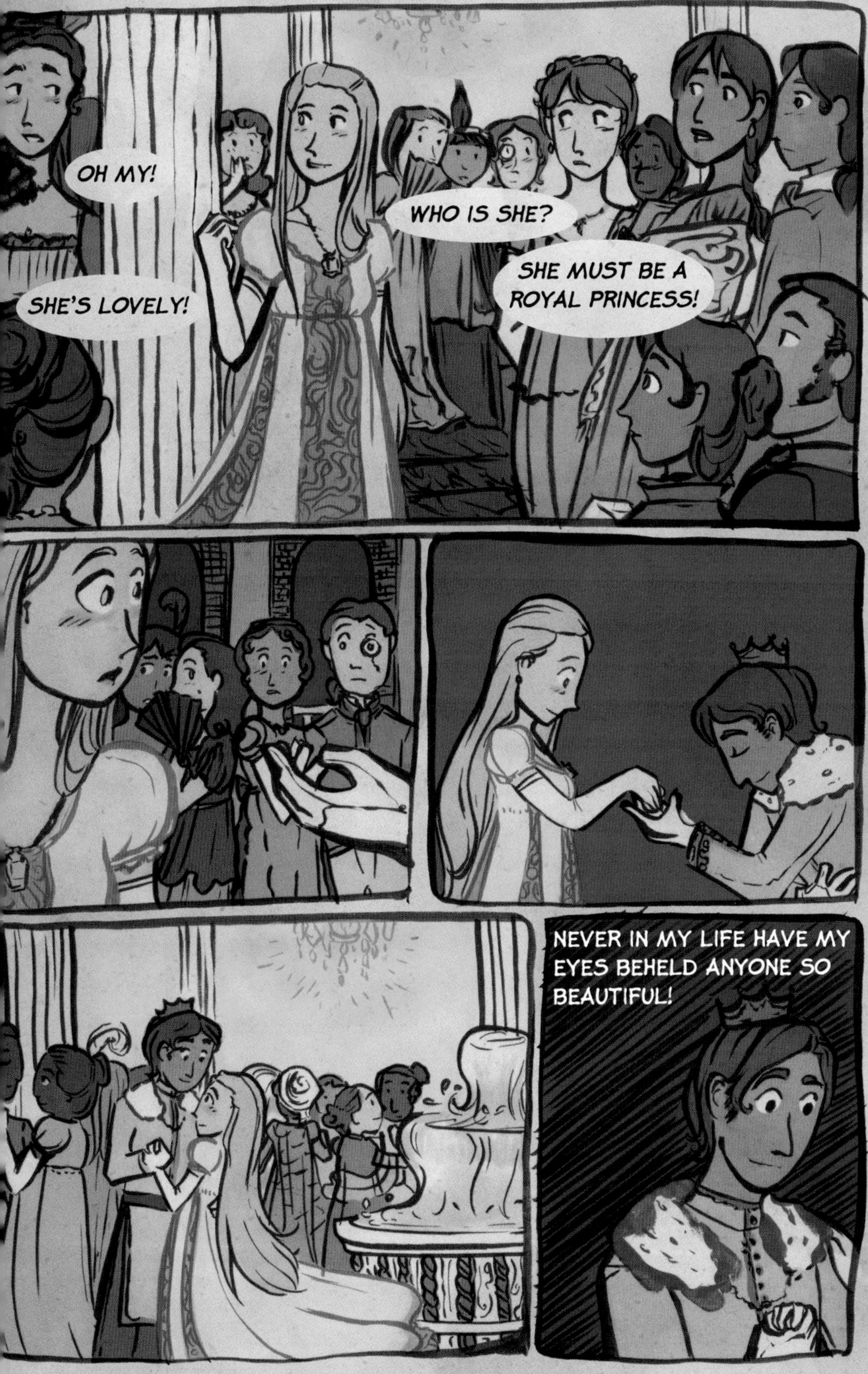
OH MY!
SHE'S LOVELY!
WHO IS SHE?
SHE MUST BE A ROYAL PRINCESS!
NEVER IN MY LIFE HAVE MY EYES BEHELD ANYONE SO BEAUTIFUL!

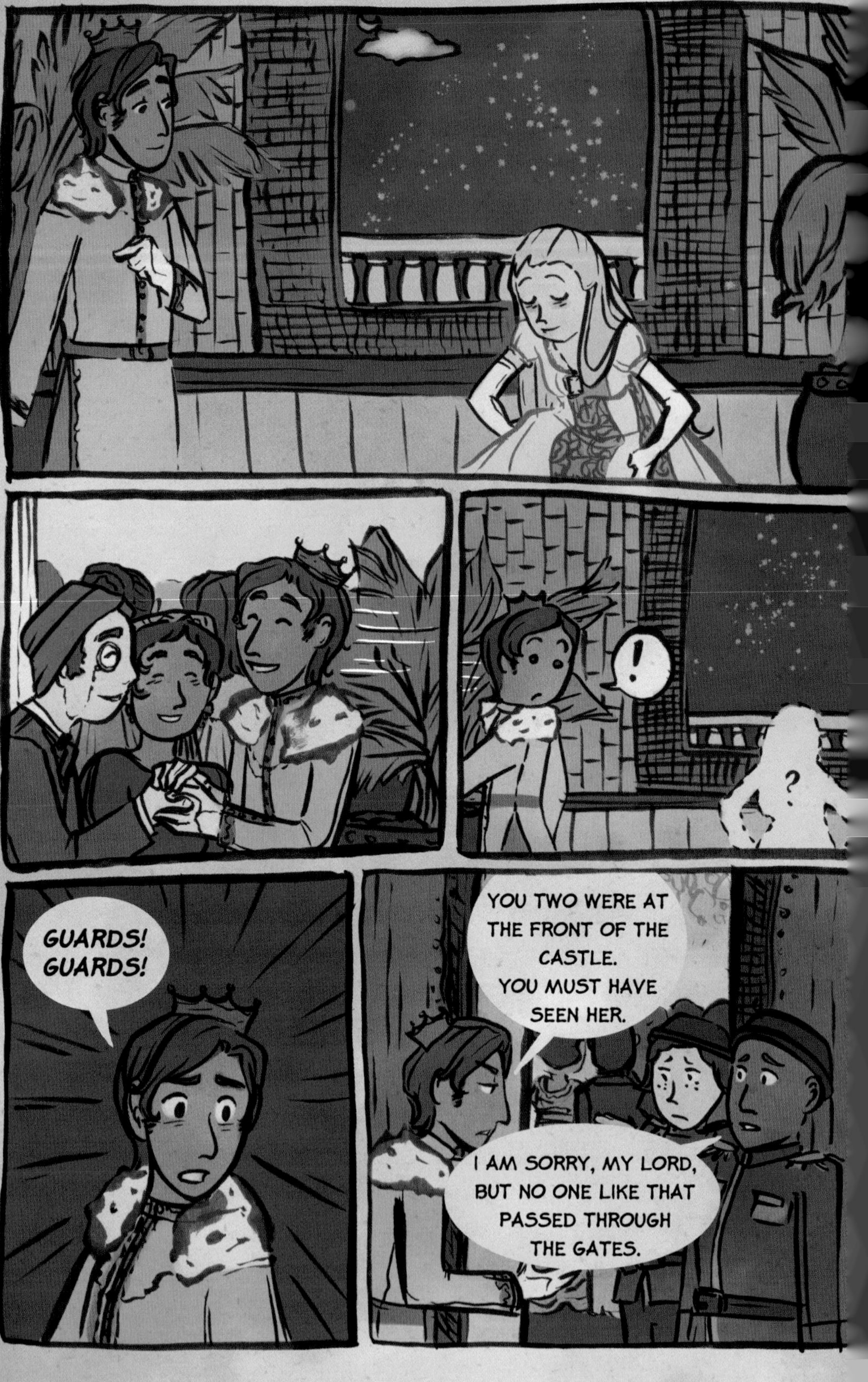
!
?
GUARDS! GUARDS!
YOU TWO WERE AT THE FRONT OF THE CASTLE. YOU MUST HAVE SEEN HER.
I AM SORRY, MY LORD, BUT NO ONE LIKE THAT PASSED THROUGH THE GATES.

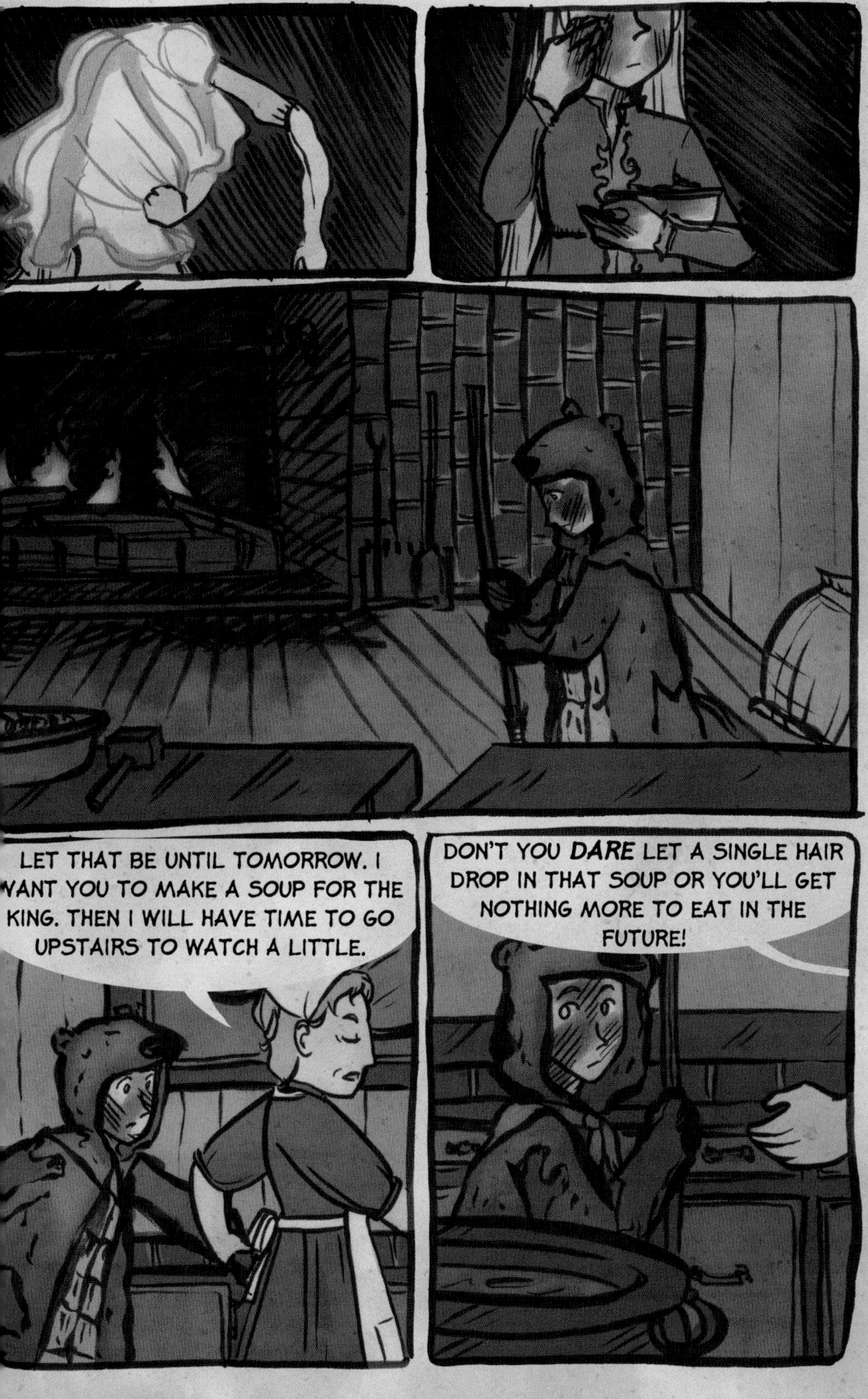
LET THAT BE UNTIL TOMORROW. I WANT YOU TO MAKE A SOUP FOR THE KING. THEN I WILL HAVE TIME TO GO UPSTAIRS TO WATCH A LITTLE.
DON'T YOU *DARE* LET A SINGLE HAIR DROP IN THAT SOUP OR YOU'LL GET NOTHING MORE TO EAT IN THE FUTURE!

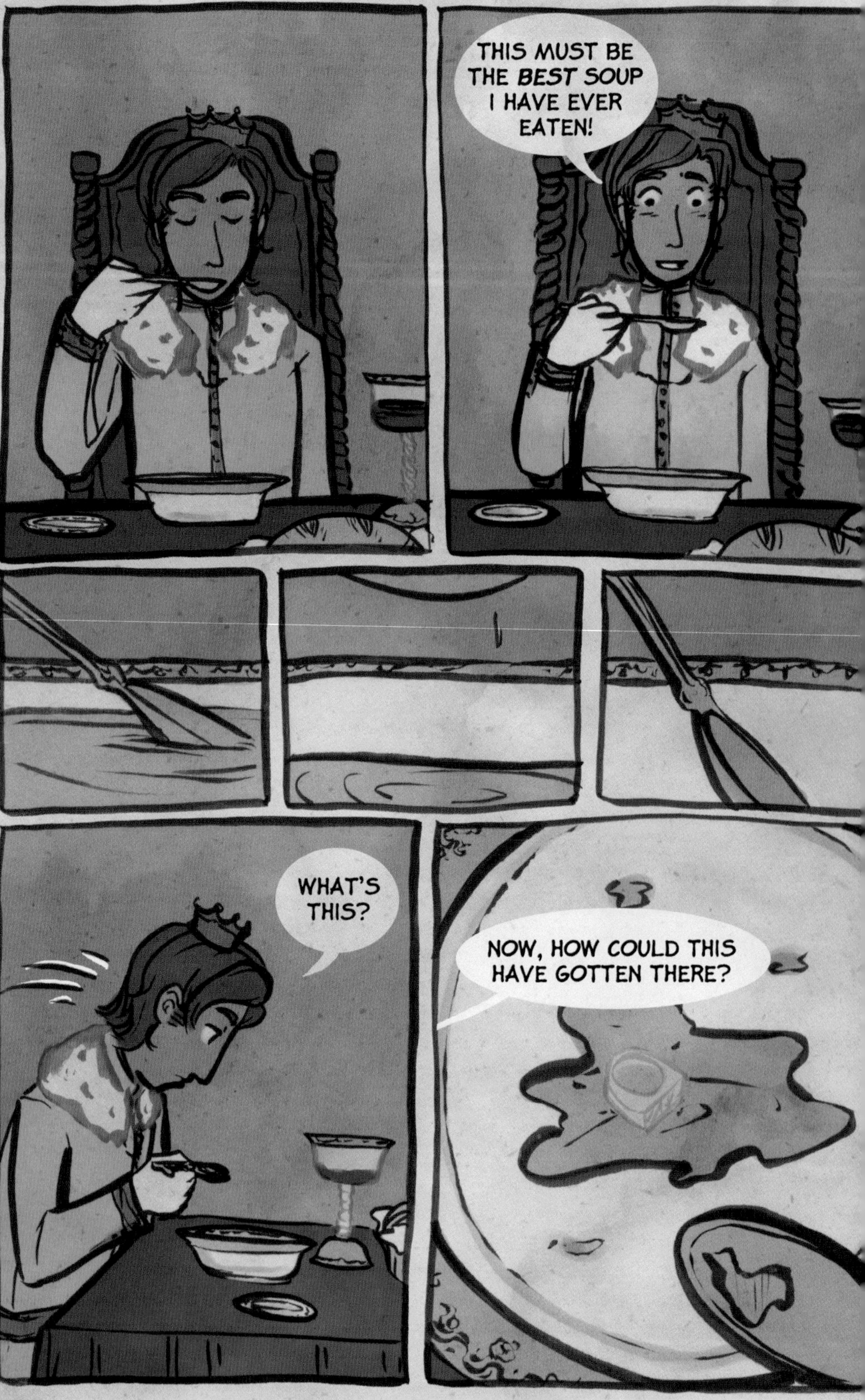
THIS MUST BE THE *BEST* SOUP I HAVE EVER EATEN!
WHAT'S THIS?
NOW, HOW COULD THIS HAVE GOTTEN THERE?

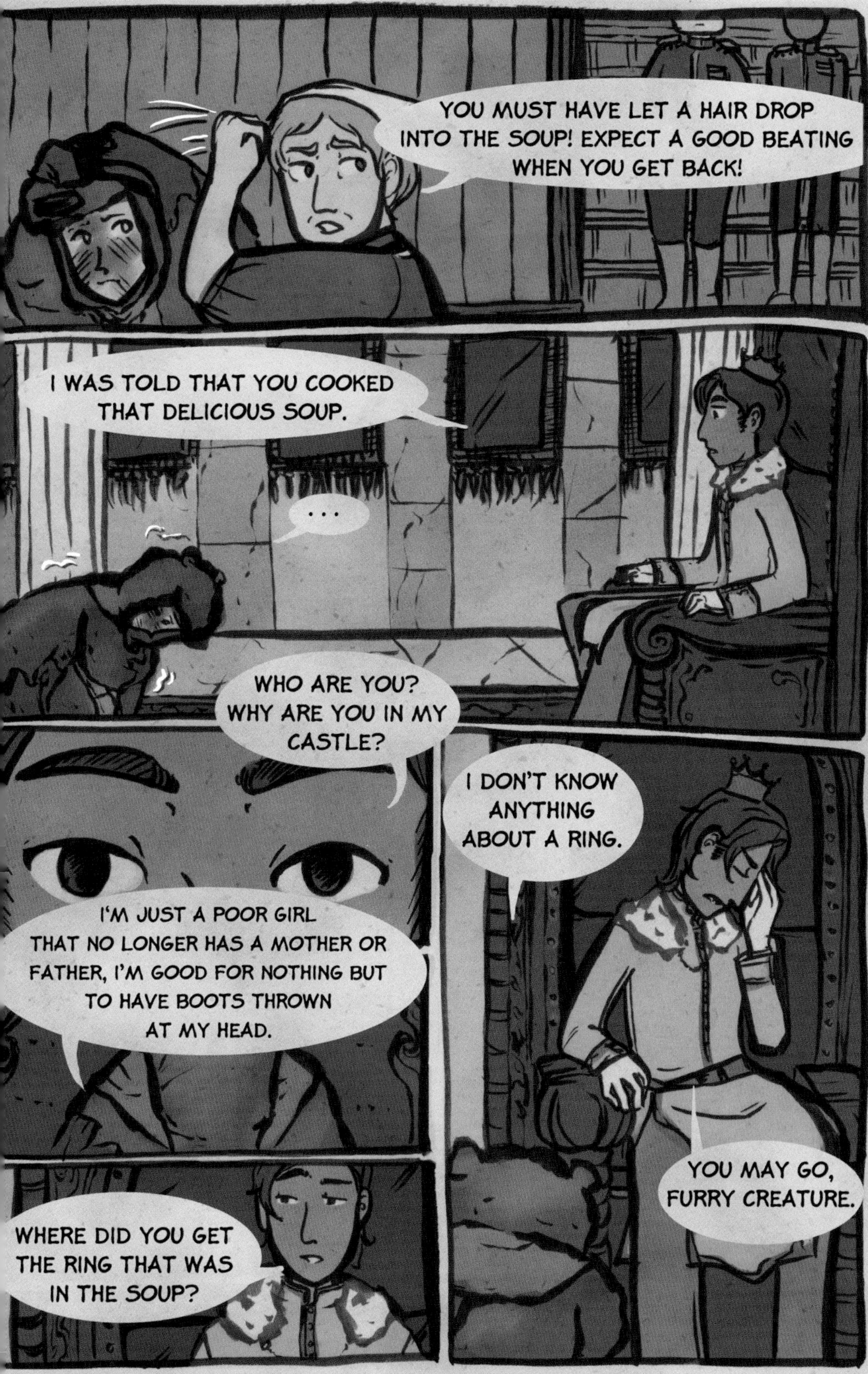
YOU MUST HAVE LET A HAIR DROP INTO THE SOUP! EXPECT A GOOD BEATING WHEN YOU GET BACK!
I WAS TOLD THAT YOU COOKED THAT DELICIOUS SOUP.
...
WHO ARE YOU? WHY ARE YOU IN MY CASTLE?
I'M JUST A POOR GIRL THAT NO LONGER HAS A MOTHER OR FATHER, I'M GOOD FOR NOTHING BUT TO HAVE BOOTS THROWN AT MY HEAD.
WHERE DID YOU GET THE RING THAT WAS IN THE SOUP?
I DON'T KNOW ANYTHING ABOUT A RING.
YOU MAY GO, FURRY CREATURE.

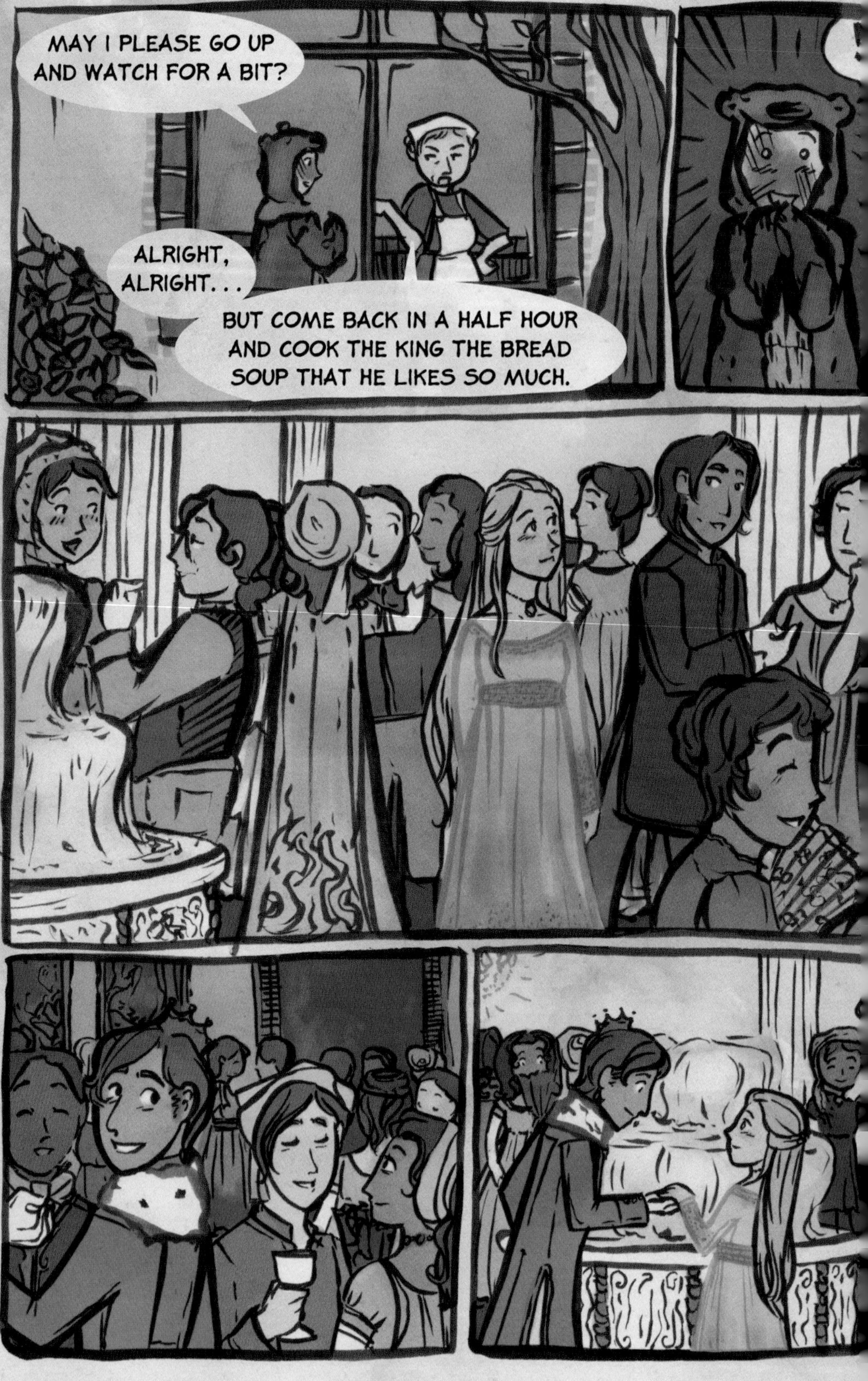
MAY I PLEASE GO UP AND WATCH FOR A BIT?
ALRIGHT, ALRIGHT. . .
BUT COME BACK IN A HALF HOUR AND COOK THE KING THE BREAD SOUP THAT HE LIKES SO MUCH.
!

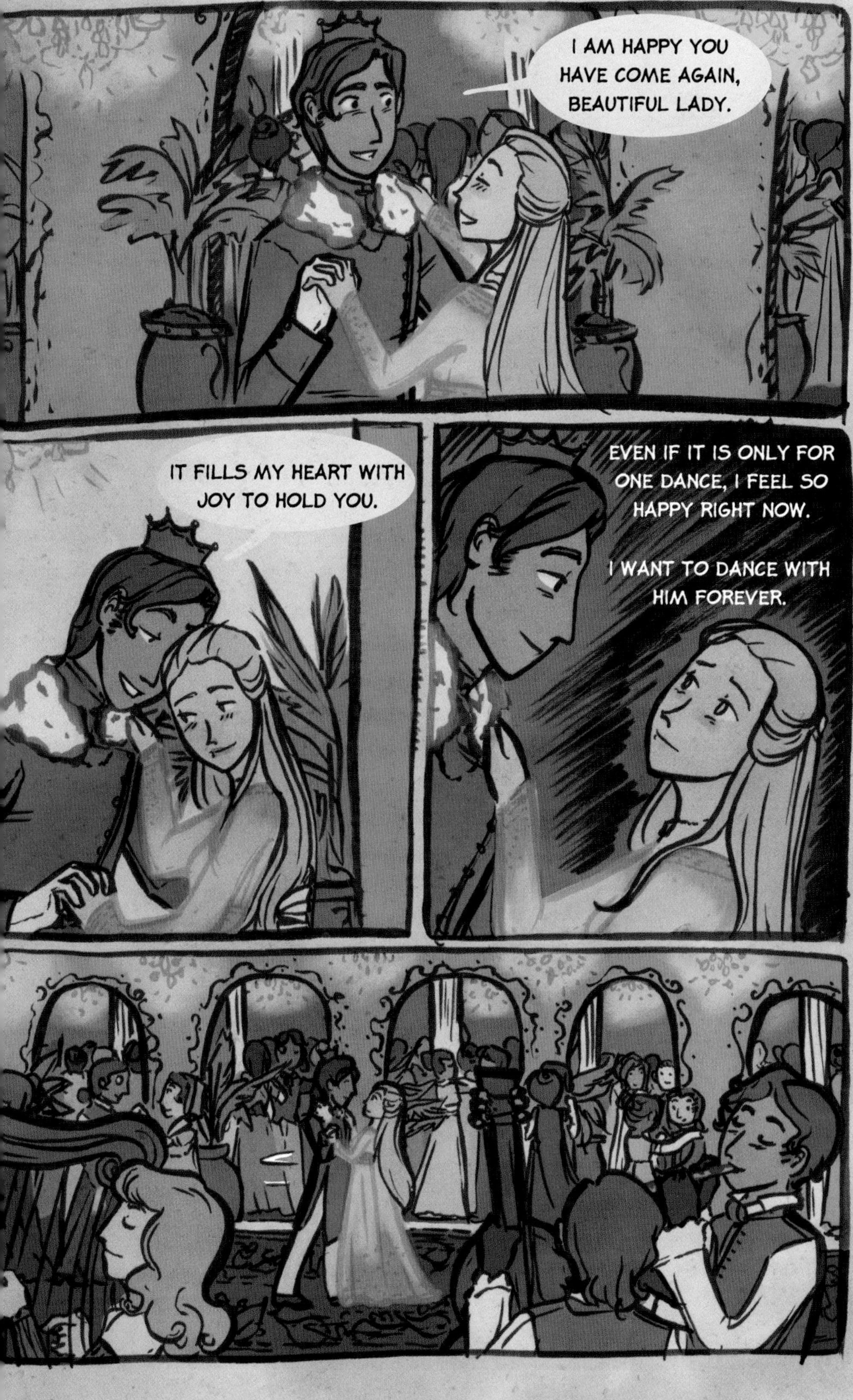
I AM HAPPY YOU HAVE COME AGAIN, BEAUTIFUL LADY.
IT FILLS MY HEART WITH JOY TO HOLD YOU.
EVEN IF IT IS ONLY FOR ONE DANCE, I FEEL SO HAPPY RIGHT NOW.
I WANT TO DANCE WITH HIM FOREVER.

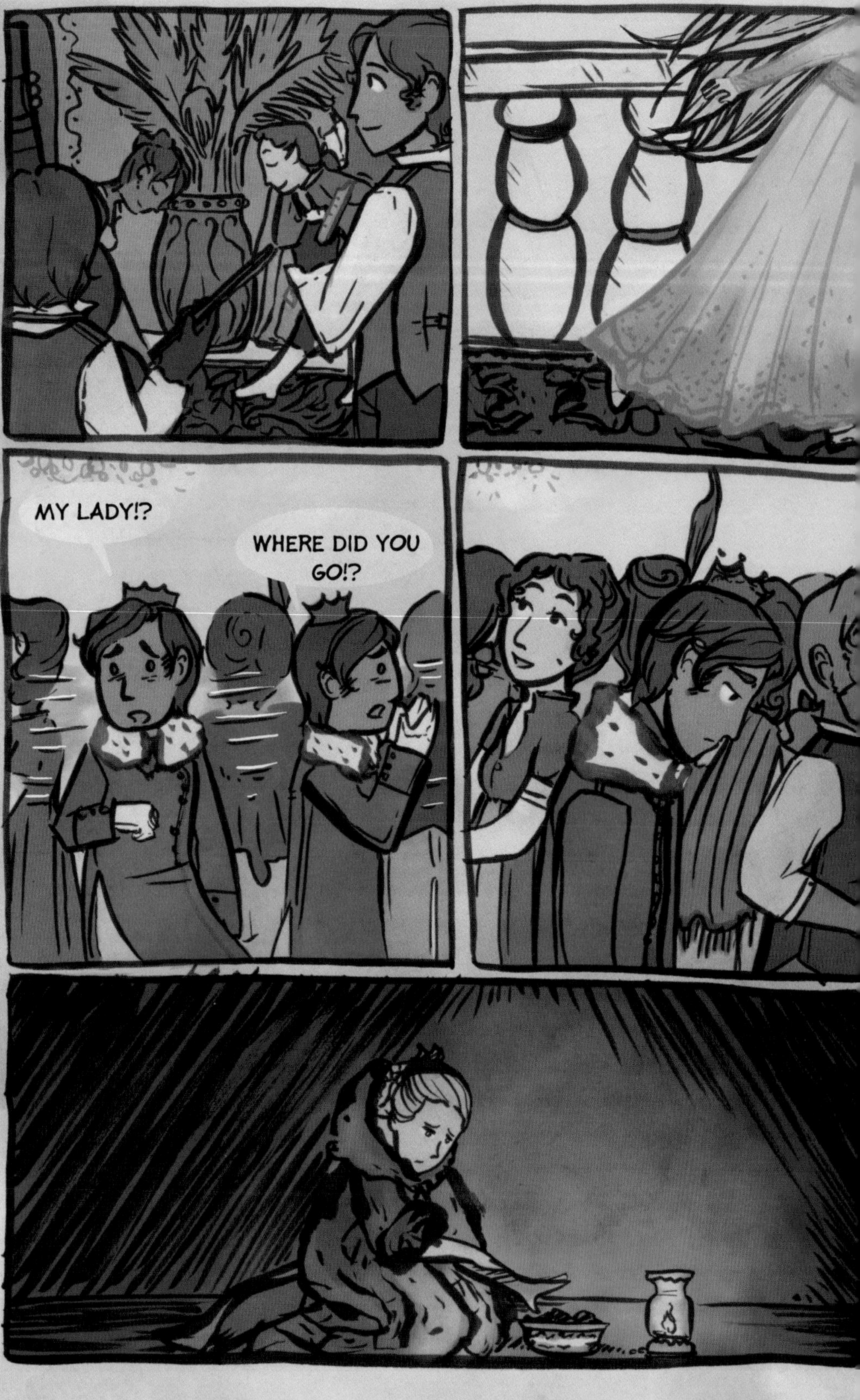
MY LADY!?
WHERE DID YOU GO!?

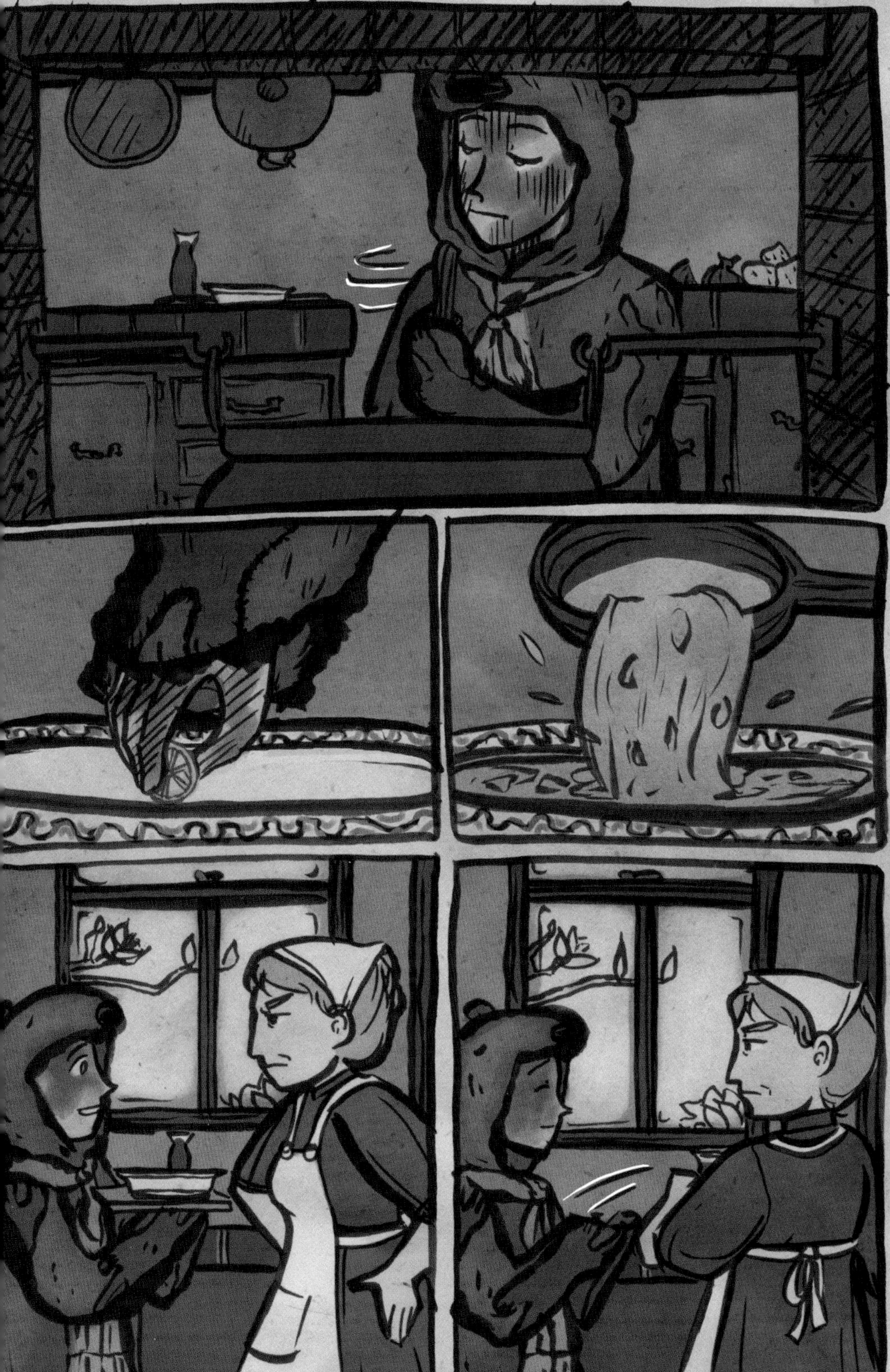

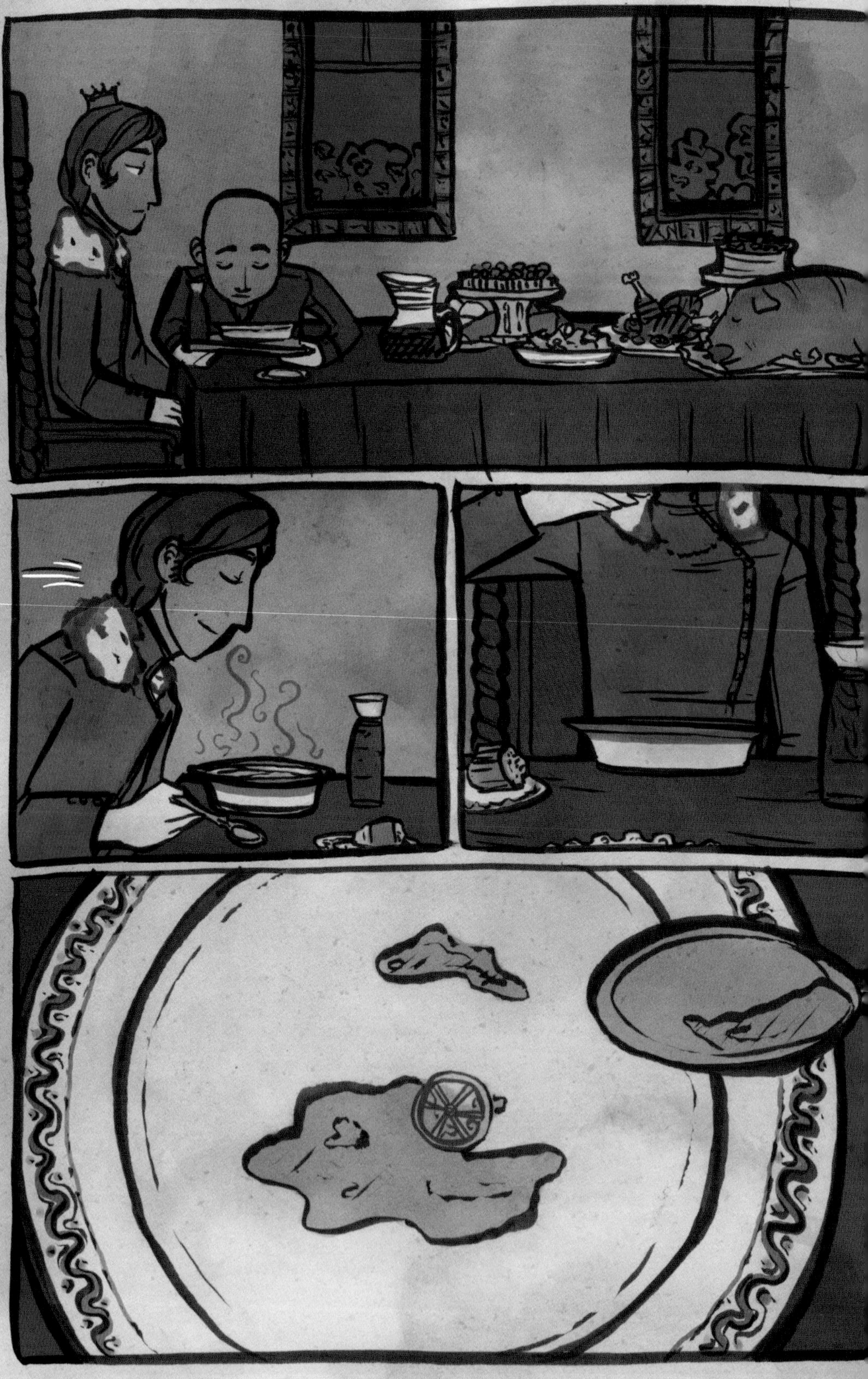

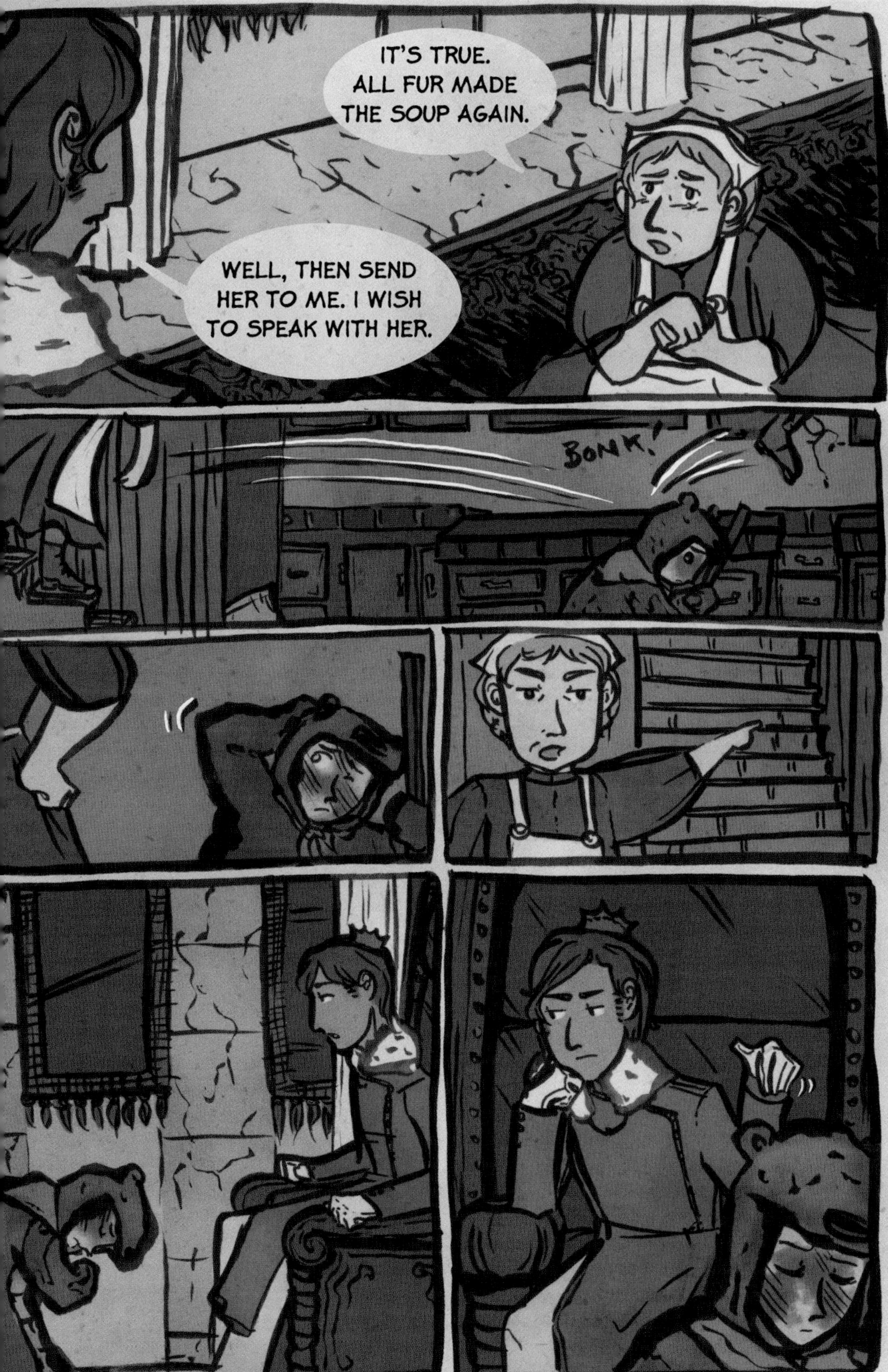
IT'S TRUE.
ALL FUR MADE
THE SOUP AGAIN.
WELL, THEN SEND
HER TO ME. I WISH
TO SPEAK WITH HER.
BONK!

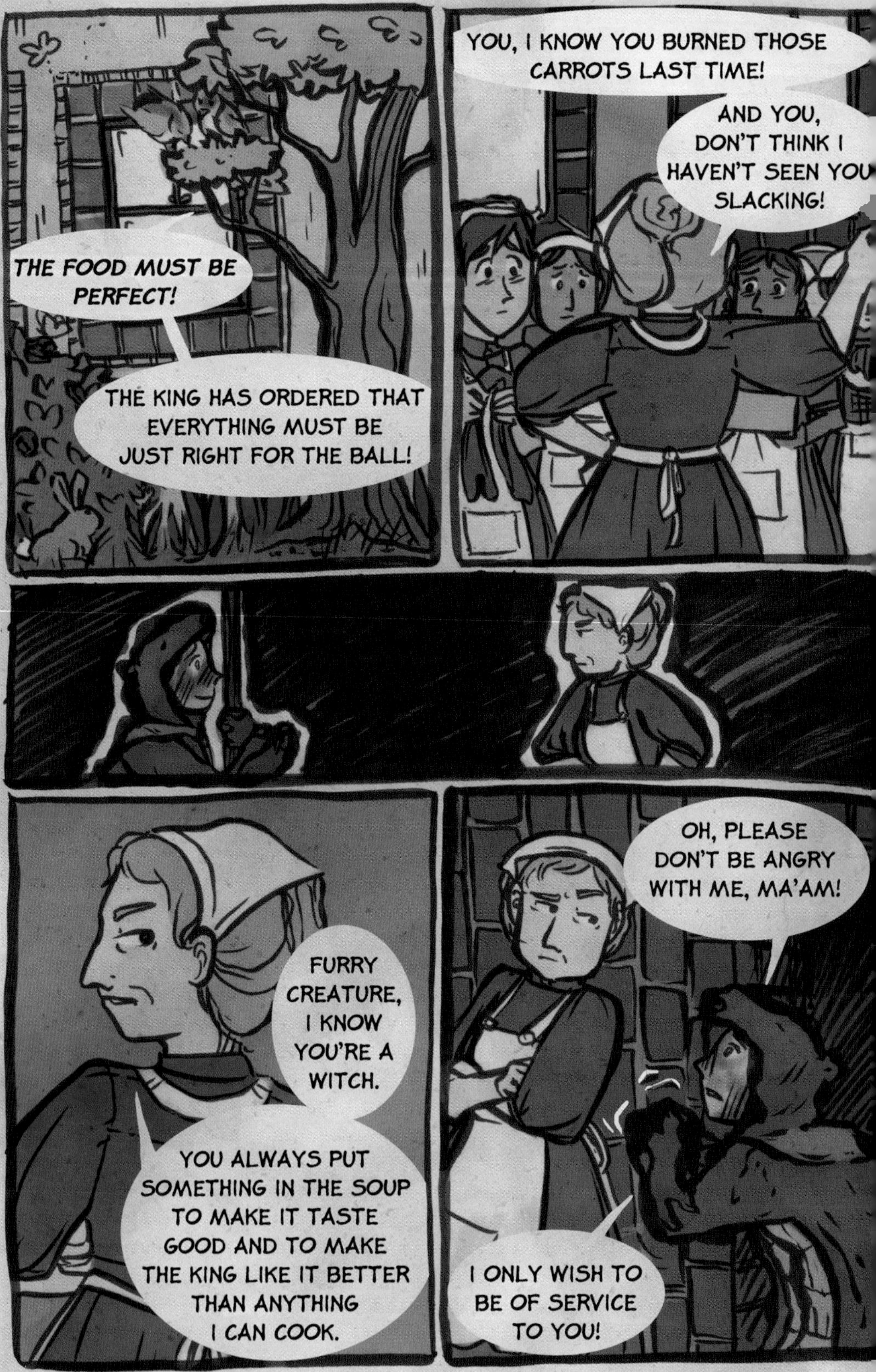
THE FOOD MUST BE PERFECT!
THE KING HAS ORDERED THAT EVERYTHING MUST BE JUST RIGHT FOR THE BALL!
YOU, I KNOW YOU BURNED THOSE CARROTS LAST TIME!
AND YOU, DON'T THINK I HAVEN'T SEEN YOU SLACKING!
FURRY CREATURE, I KNOW YOU'RE A WITCH.
YOU ALWAYS PUT SOMETHING IN THE SOUP TO MAKE IT TASTE GOOD AND TO MAKE THE KING LIKE IT BETTER THAN ANYTHING I CAN COOK.
OH, PLEASE DON'T BE ANGRY WITH ME, MA'AM!
I ONLY WISH TO BE OF SERVICE TO YOU!

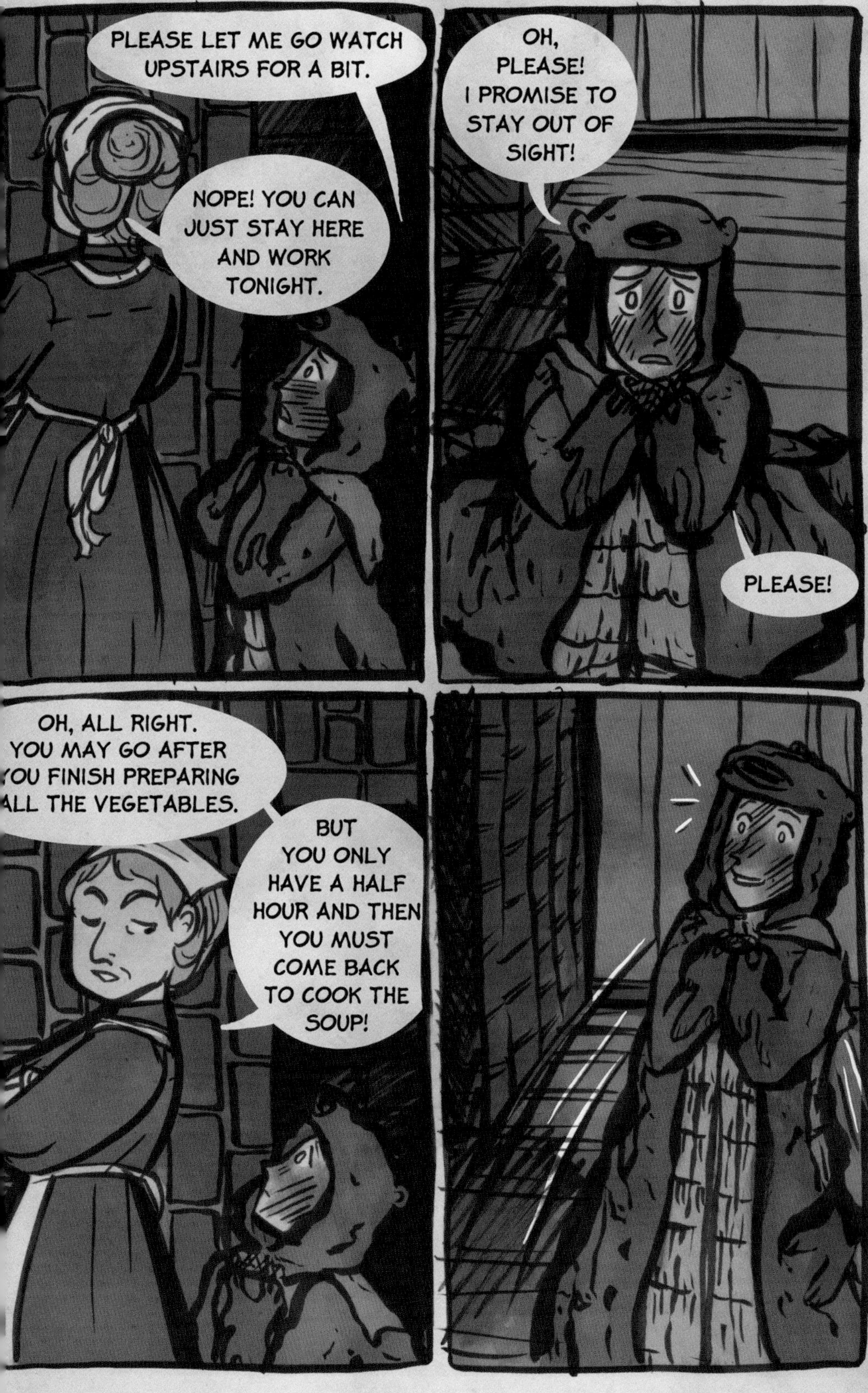
PLEASE LET ME GO WATCH UPSTAIRS FOR A BIT.
NOPE! YOU CAN JUST STAY HERE AND WORK TONIGHT.
OH, PLEASE! I PROMISE TO STAY OUT OF SIGHT!
PLEASE!
OH, ALL RIGHT. YOU MAY GO AFTER YOU FINISH PREPARING ALL THE VEGETABLES.
BUT YOU ONLY HAVE A HALF HOUR AND THEN YOU MUST COME BACK TO COOK THE SOUP!

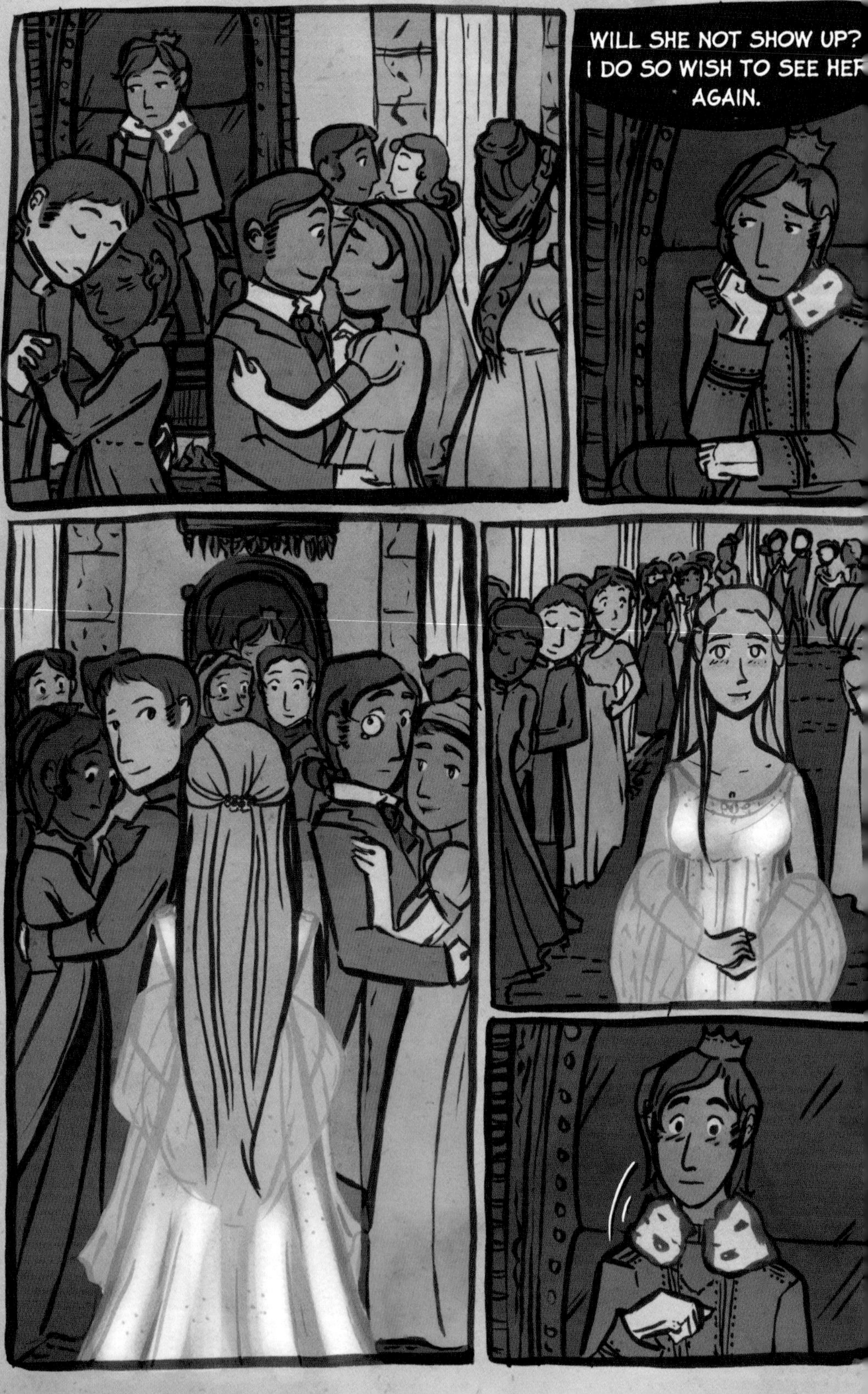
WILL SHE NOT SHOW UP? I DO SO WISH TO SEE HER AGAIN.

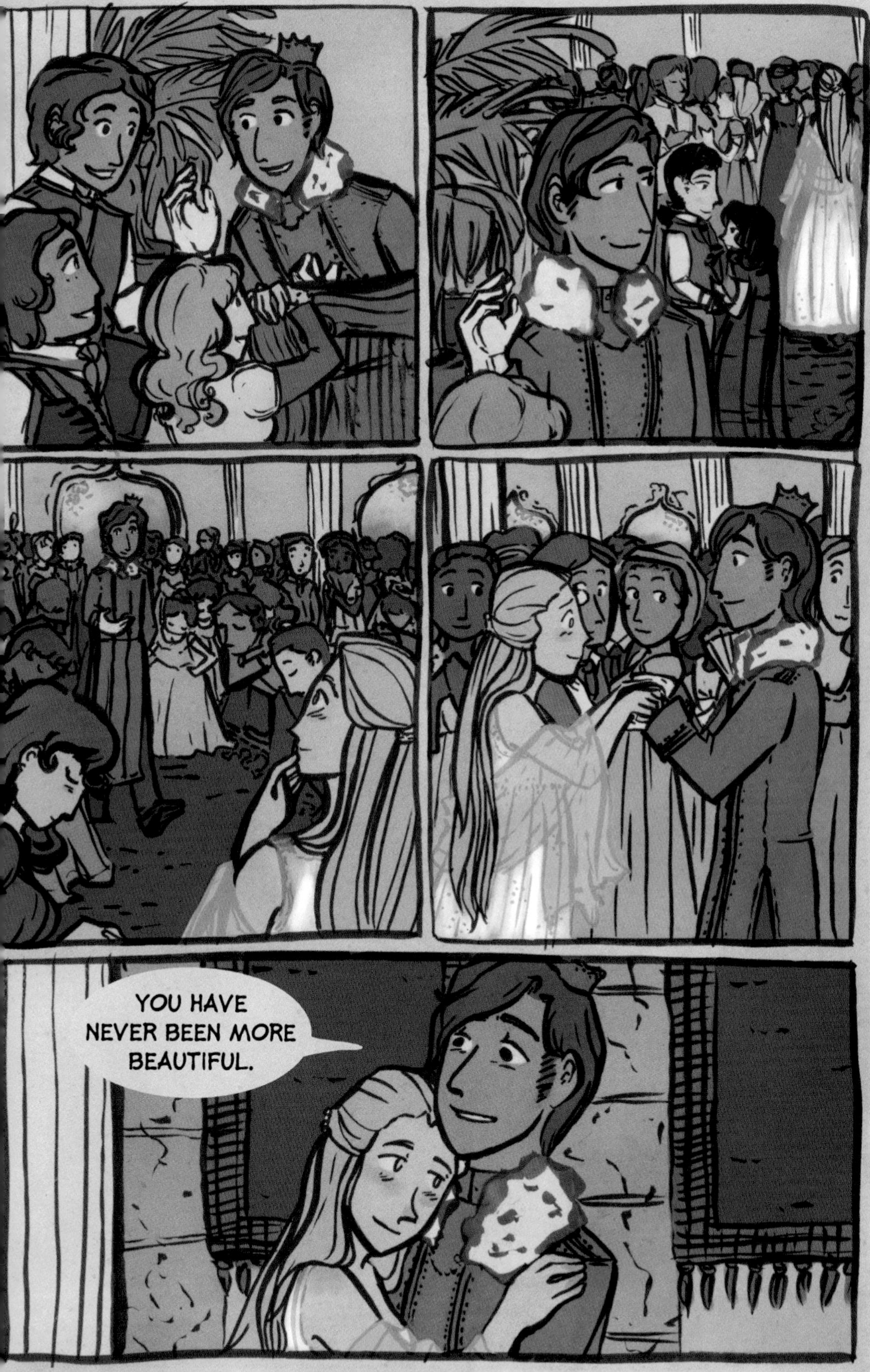
YOU HAVE NEVER BEEN MORE BEAUTIFUL.

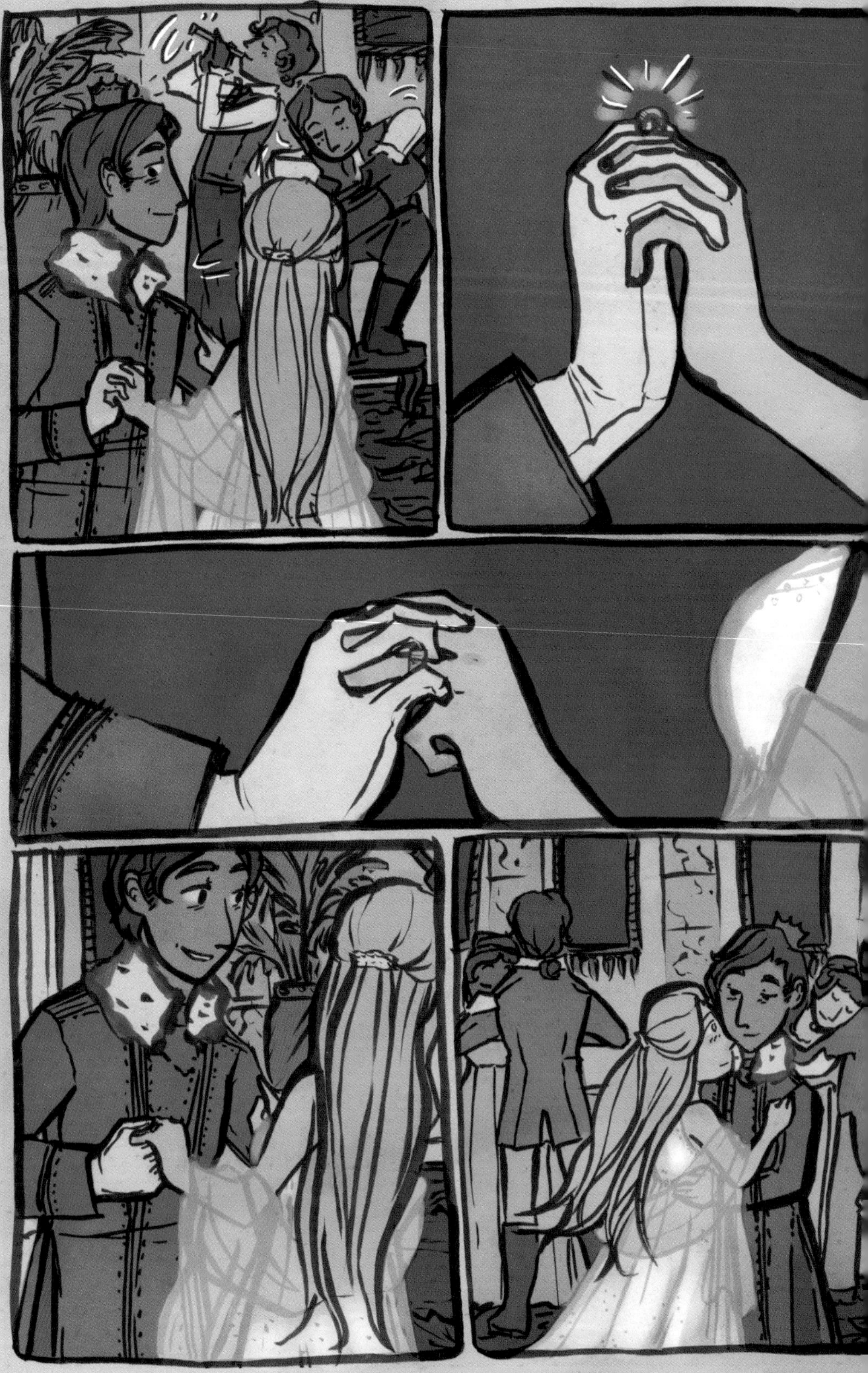

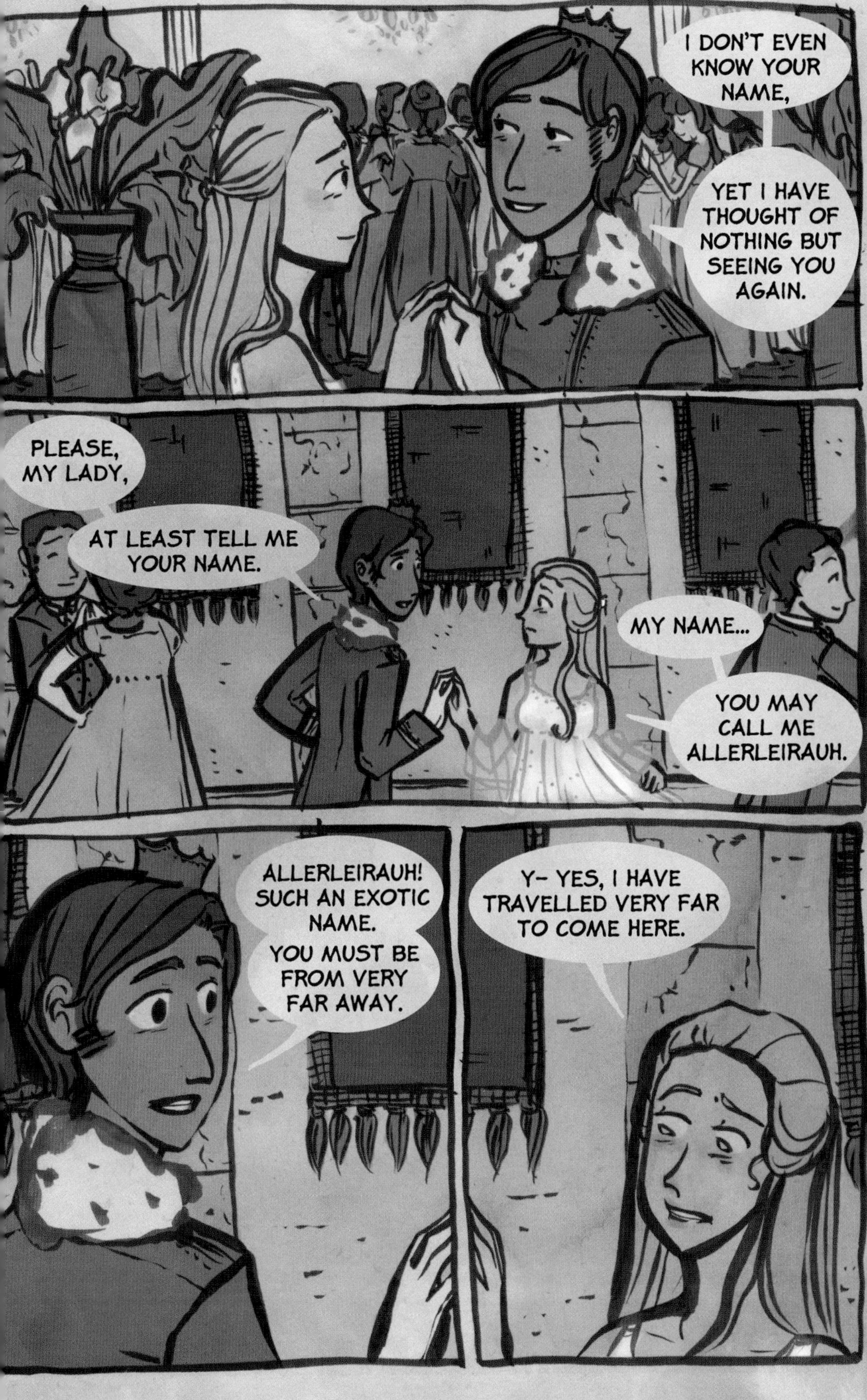
I DON'T EVEN KNOW YOUR NAME,
YET I HAVE THOUGHT OF NOTHING BUT SEEING YOU AGAIN.
PLEASE, MY LADY,
AT LEAST TELL ME YOUR NAME.
MY NAME...
YOU MAY CALL ME ALLERLEIRAUH.
ALLERLEIRAUH! SUCH AN EXOTIC NAME.
YOU MUST BE FROM VERY FAR AWAY.
Y- YES, I HAVE TRAVELLED VERY FAR TO COME HERE.

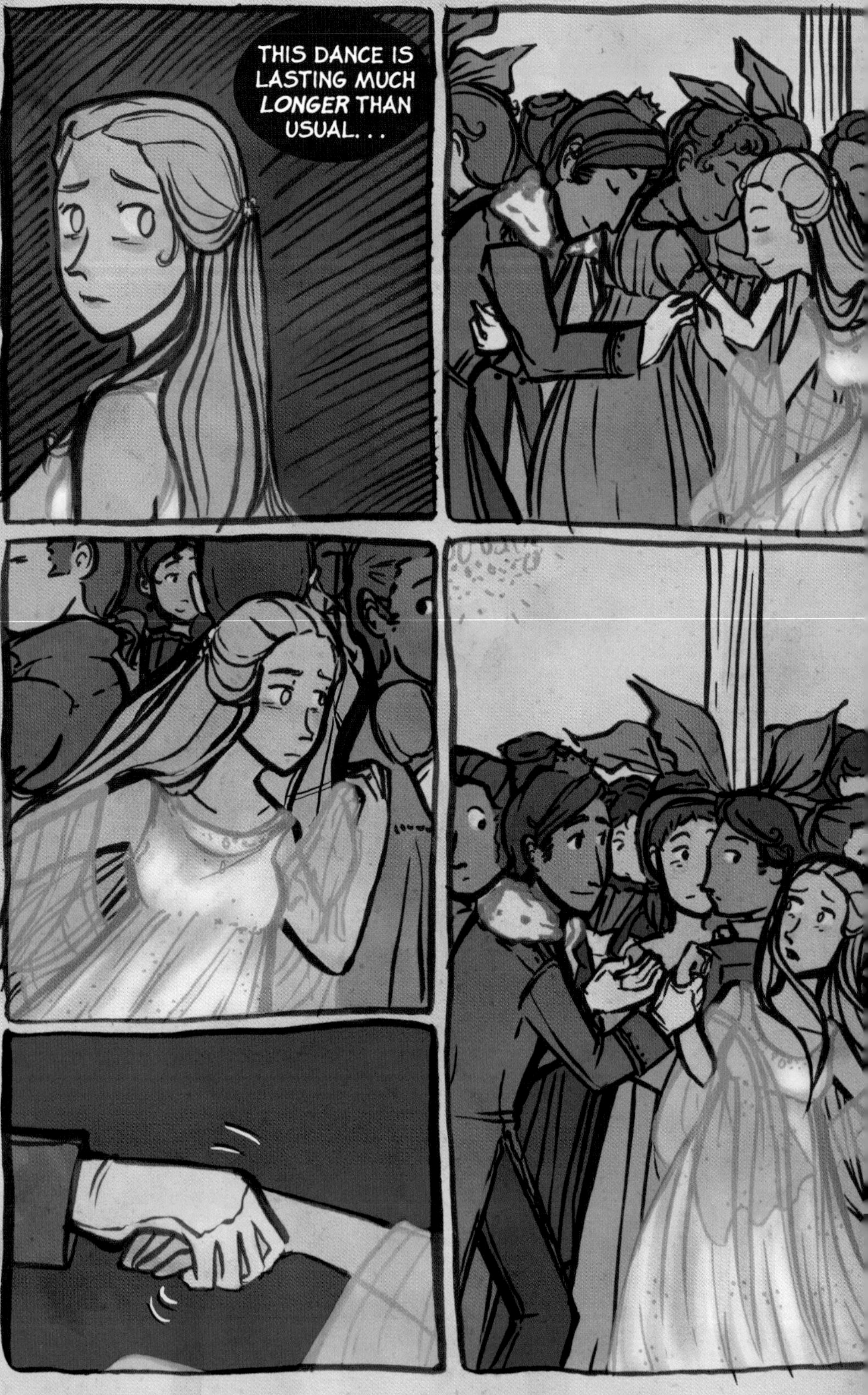
THIS DANCE IS LASTING MUCH LONGER THAN USUAL. . .

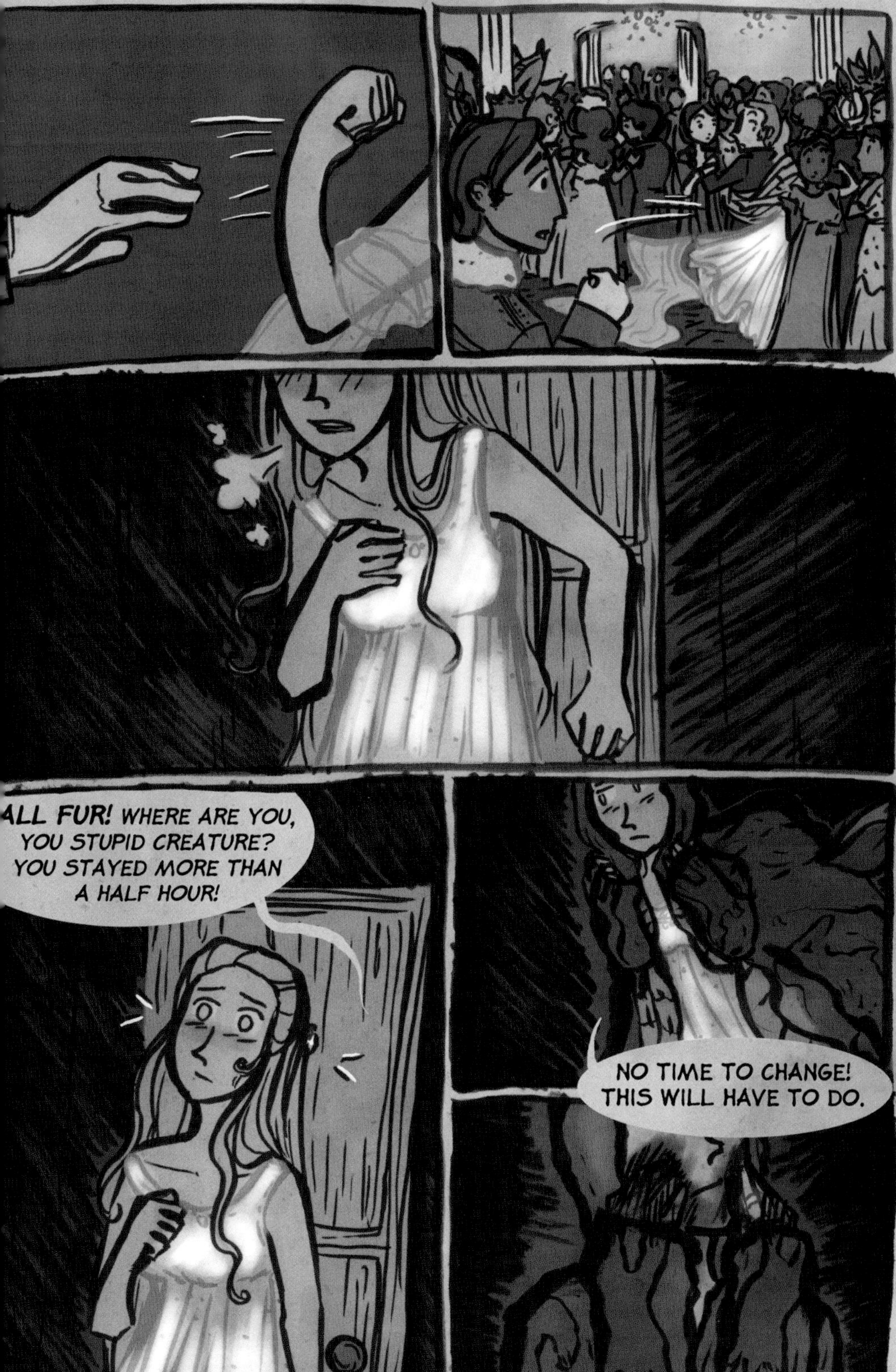
ALL FUR! WHERE ARE YOU, YOU STUPID CREATURE? YOU STAYED MORE THAN A HALF HOUR!
NO TIME TO CHANGE! THIS WILL HAVE TO DO.

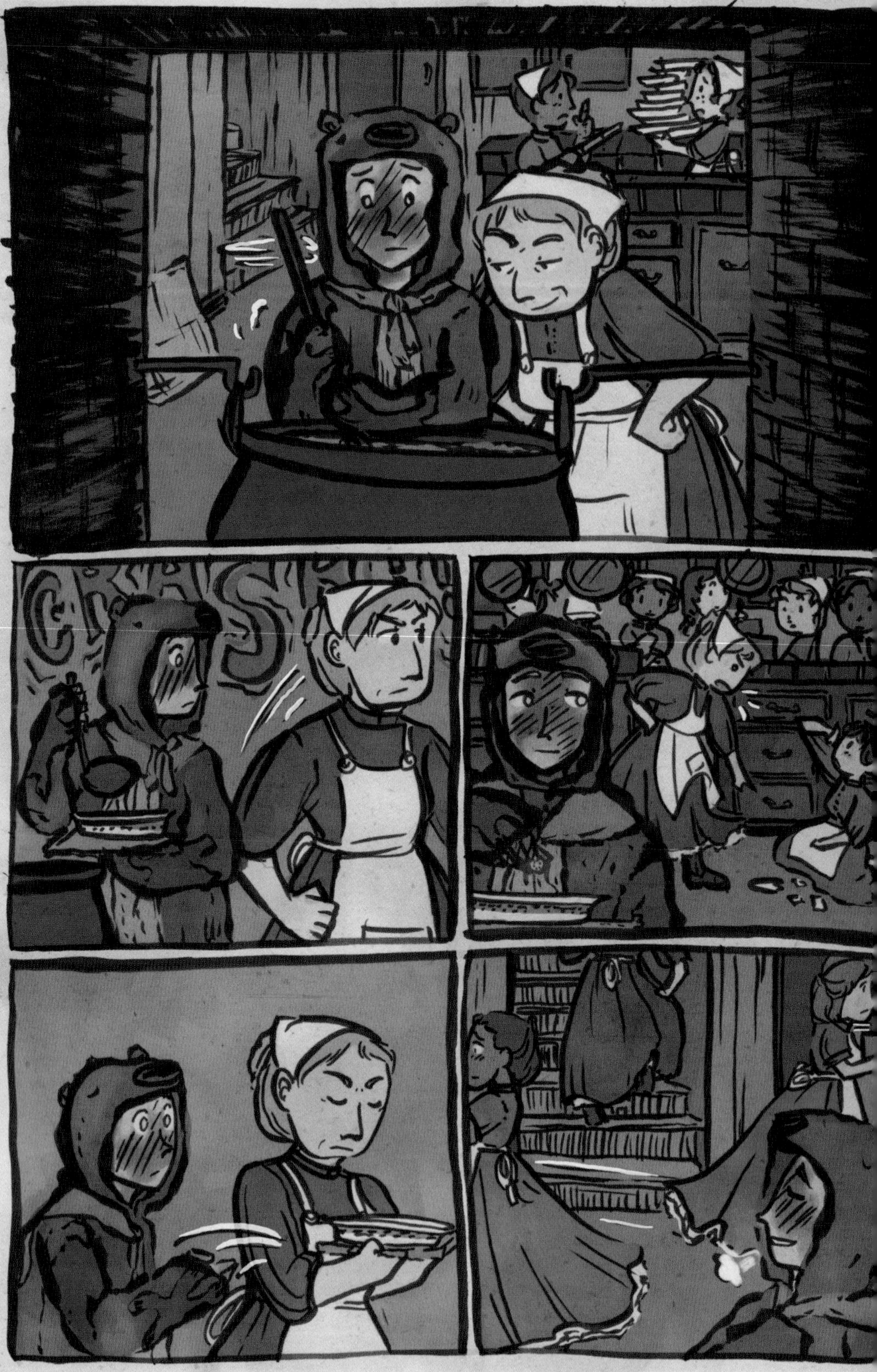

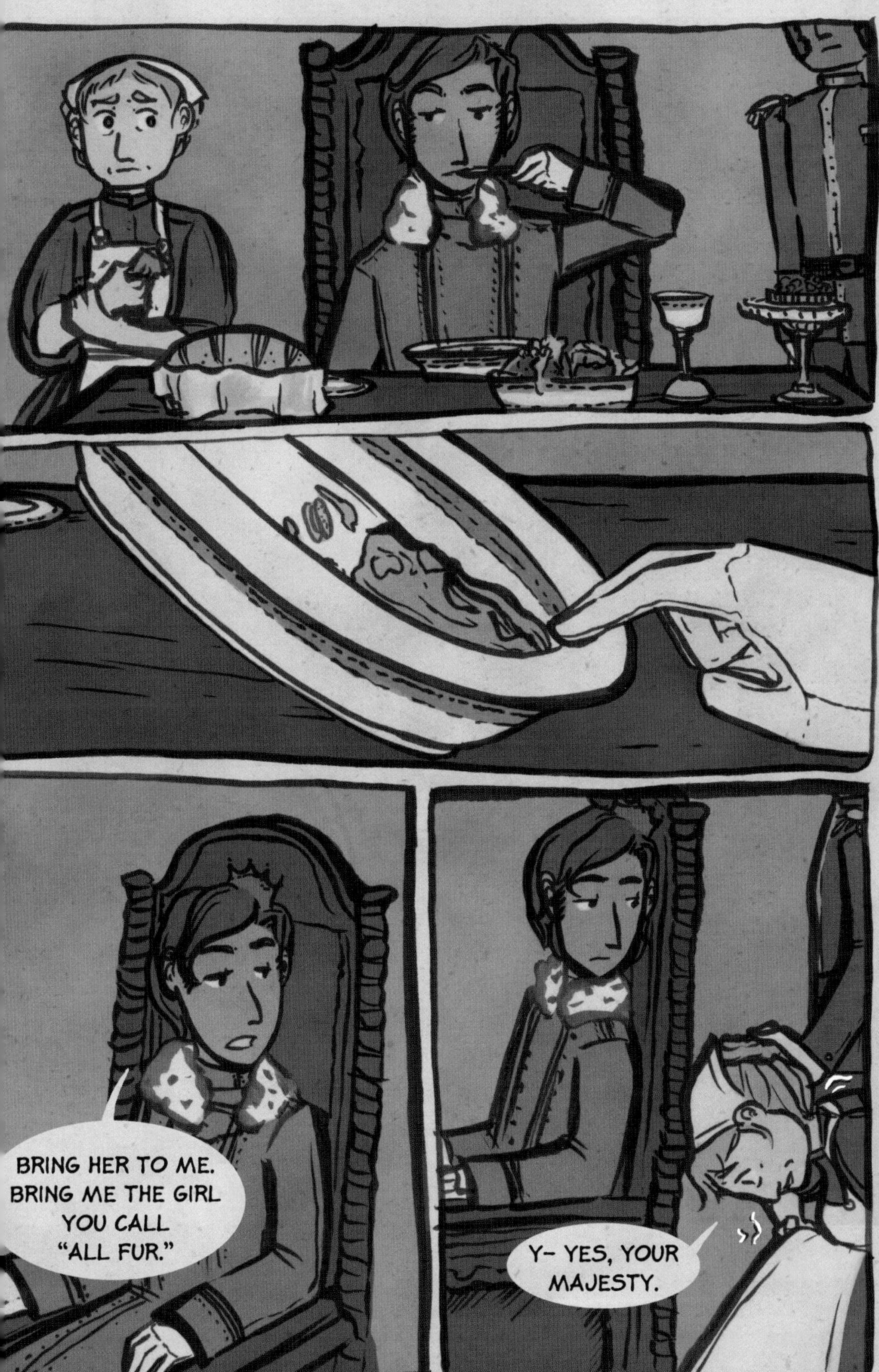
BRING HER TO ME. BRING ME THE GIRL YOU CALL "ALL FUR."
Y- YES, YOUR MAJESTY.

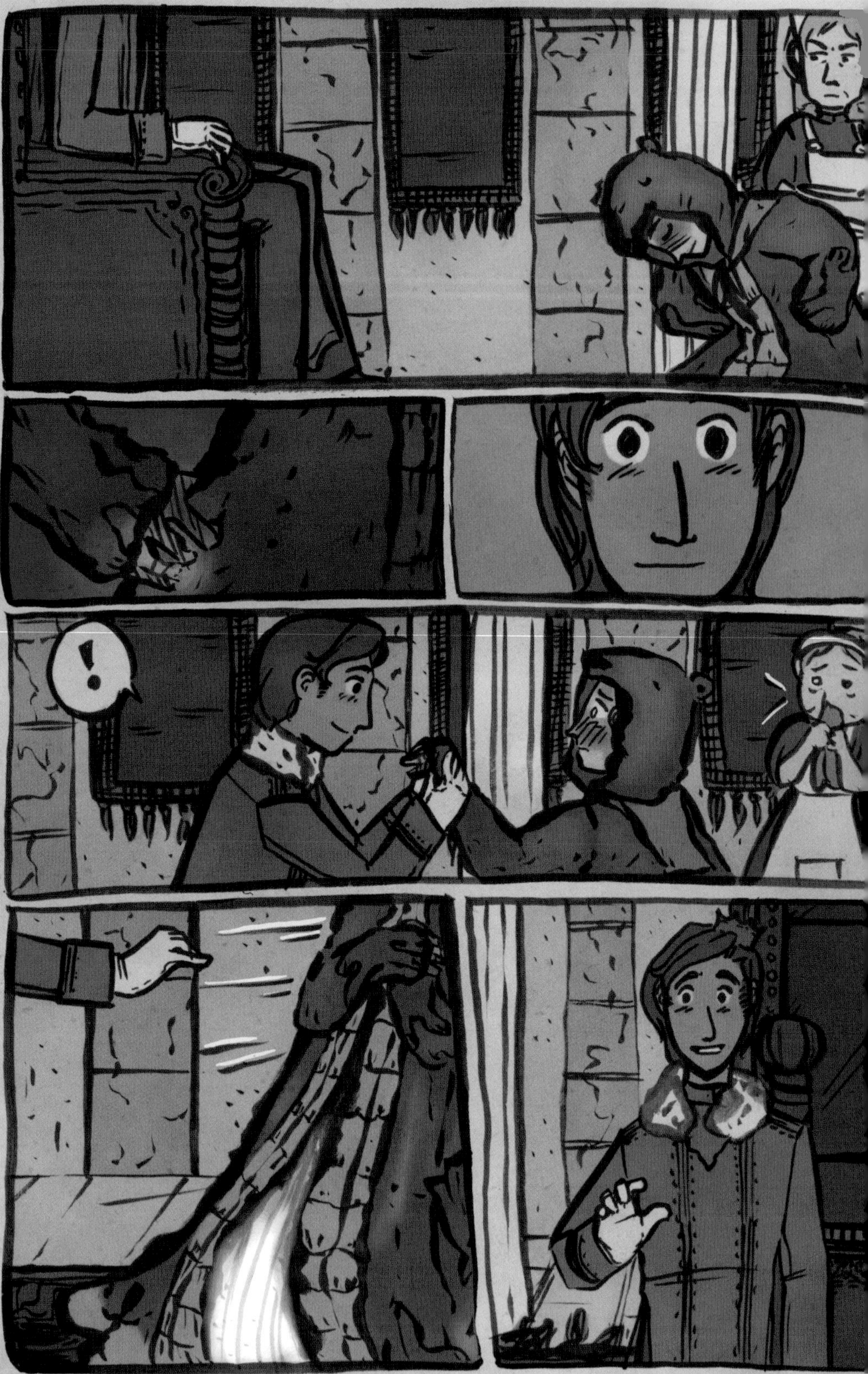
!

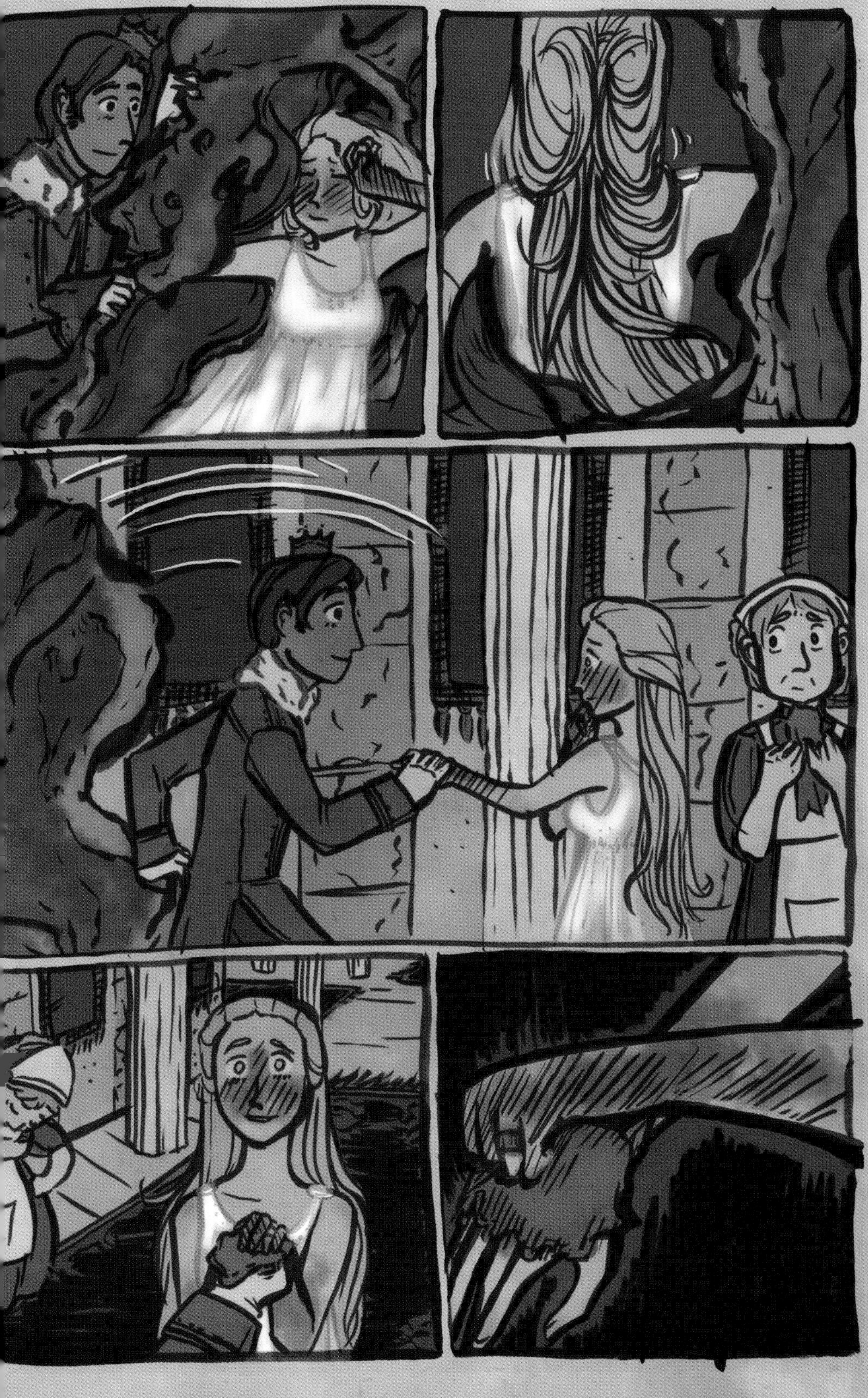

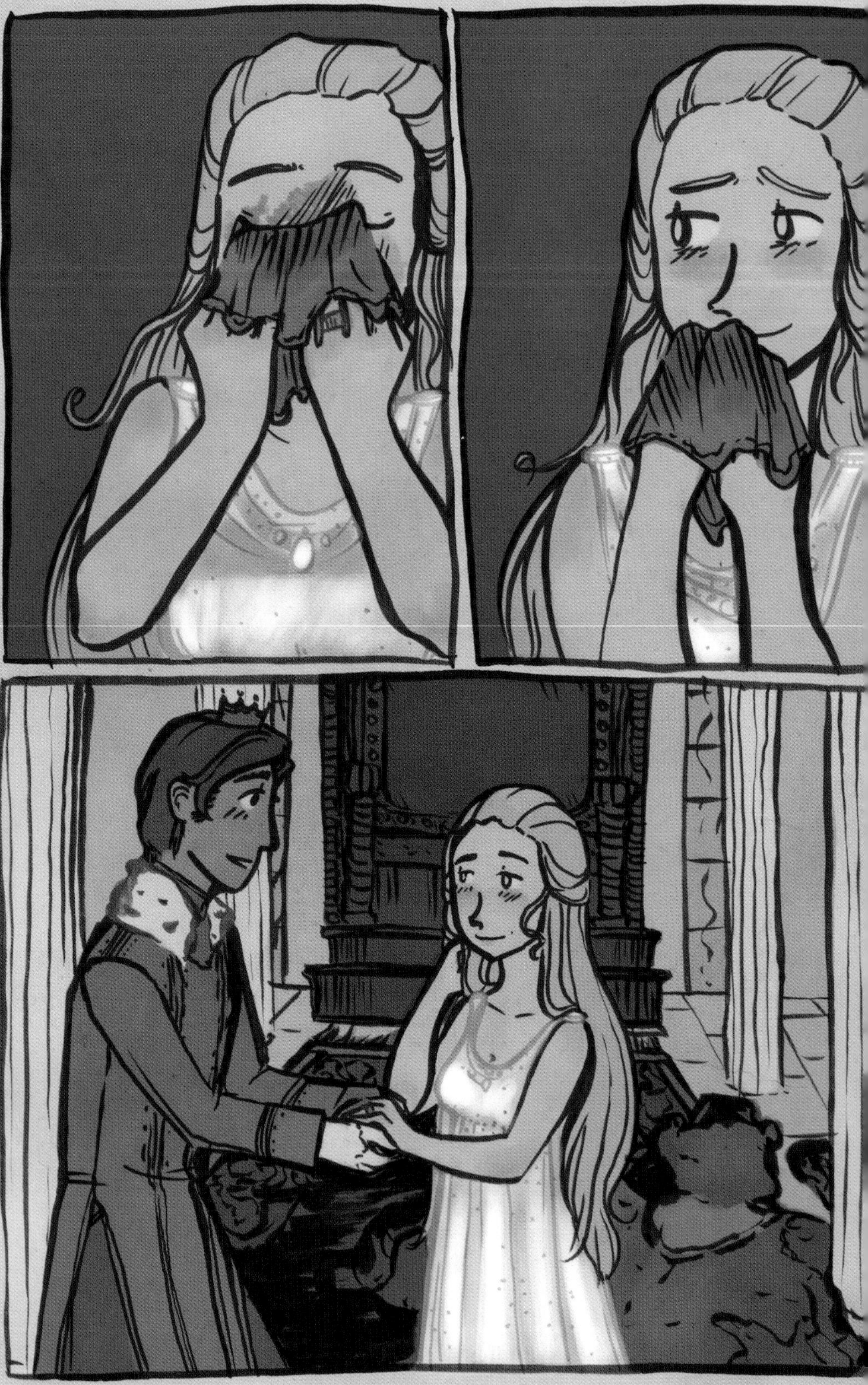

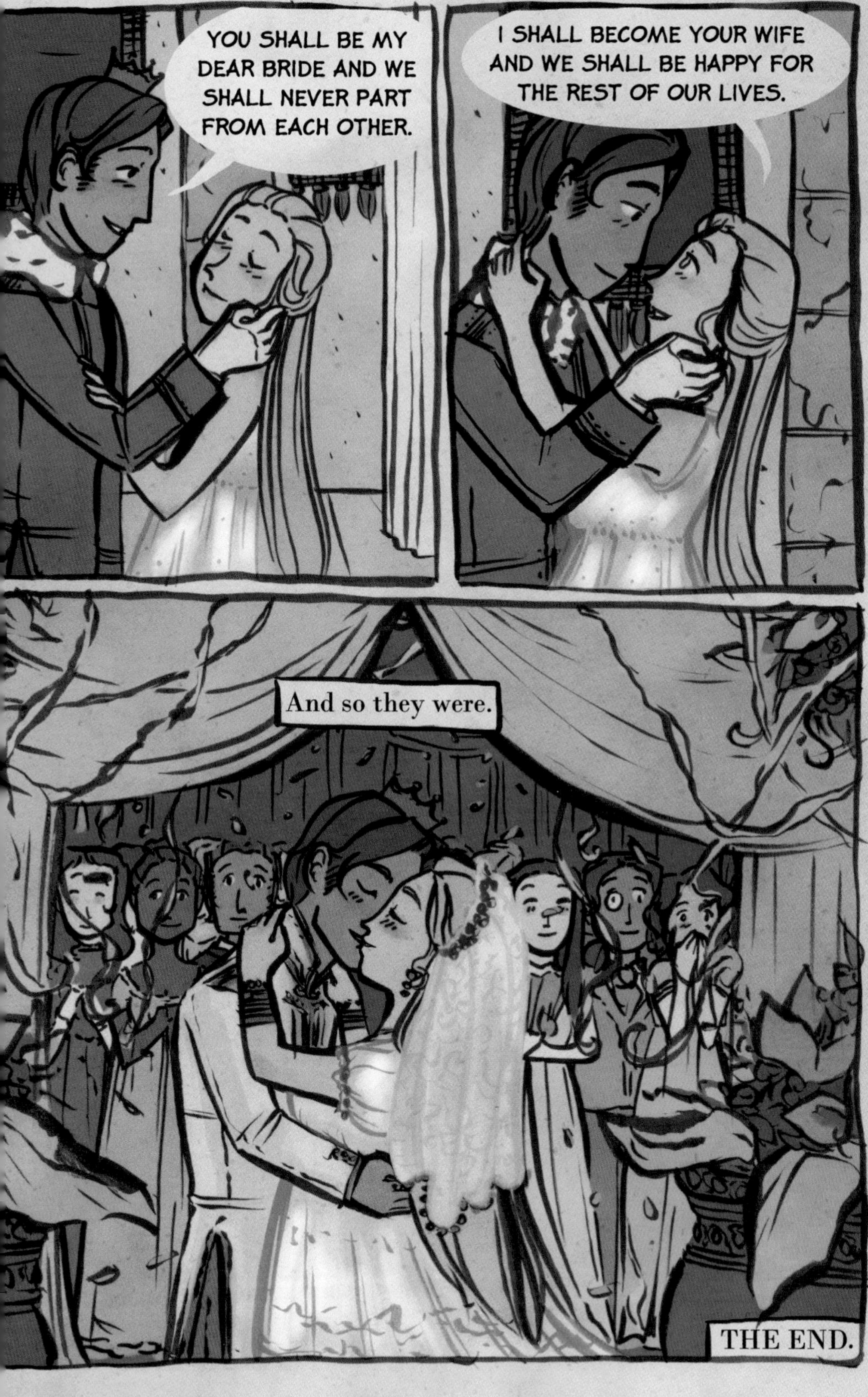
YOU SHALL BE MY DEAR BRIDE AND WE SHALL NEVER PART FROM EACH OTHER.
I SHALL BECOME YOUR WIFE AND WE SHALL BE HAPPY FOR THE REST OF OUR LIVES.
And so they were.
THE END.

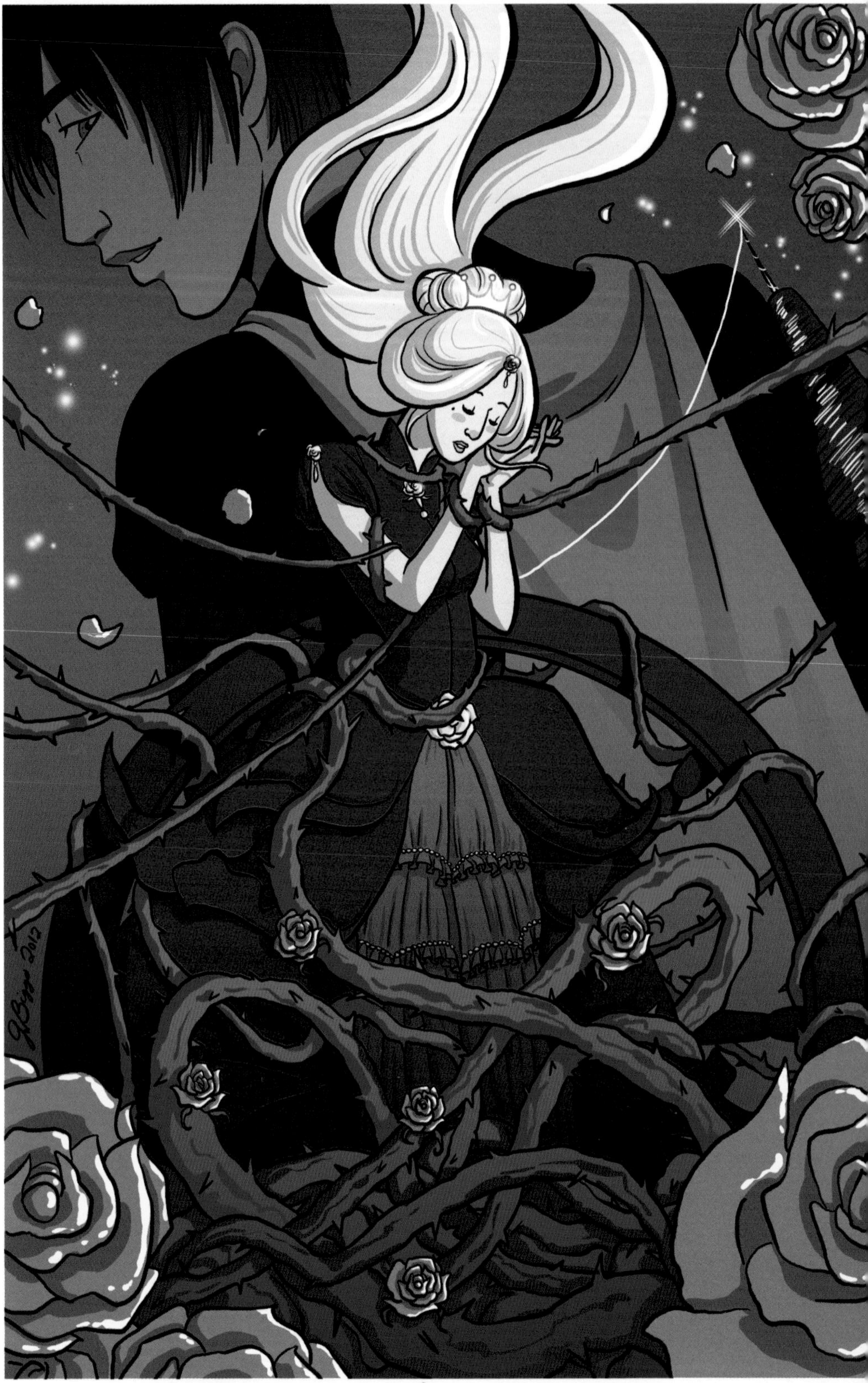

"Briar Rose" by Gina Biggs

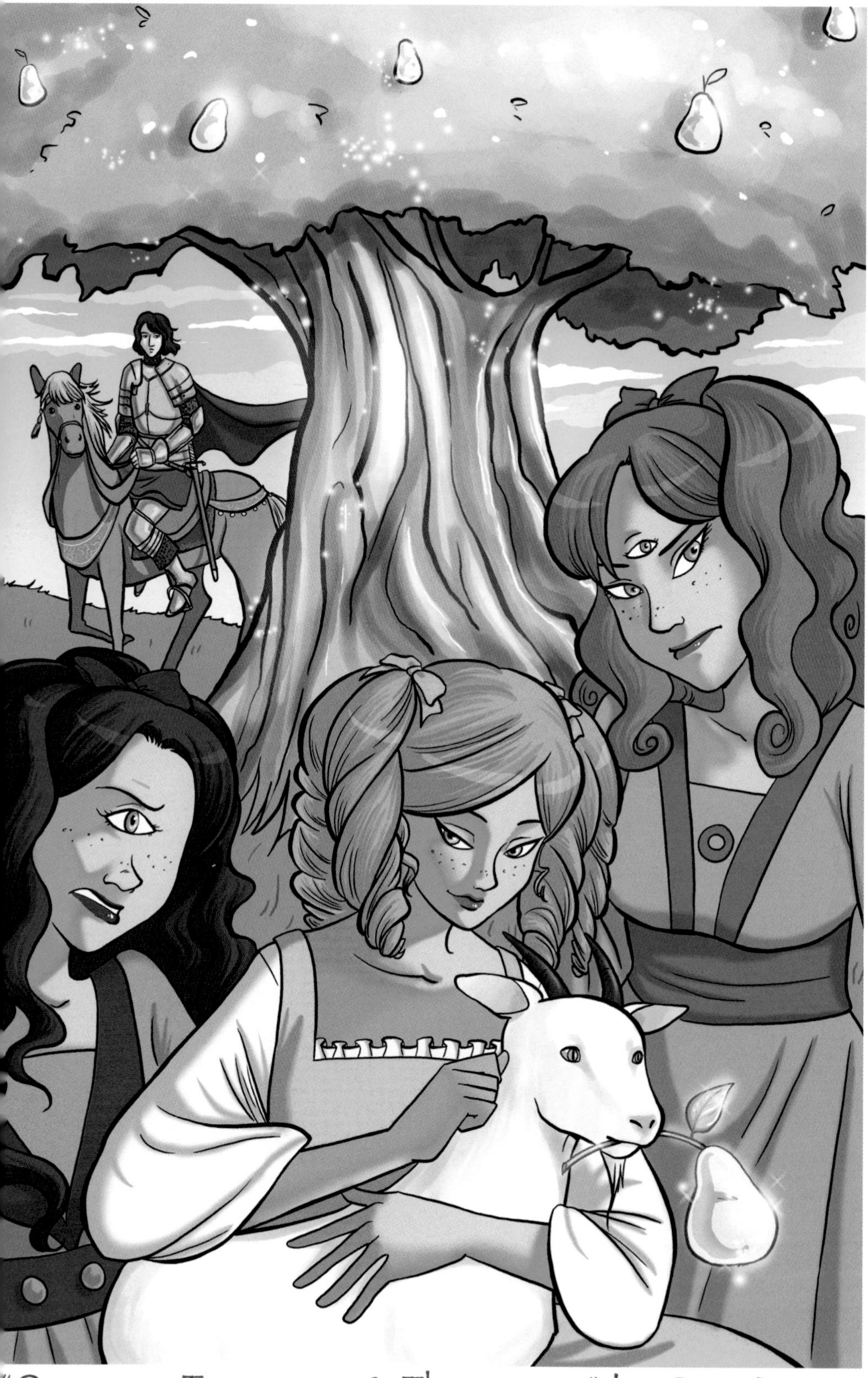

"One-eye, Two-eyes, & Three-eyes" by Gina Biggs

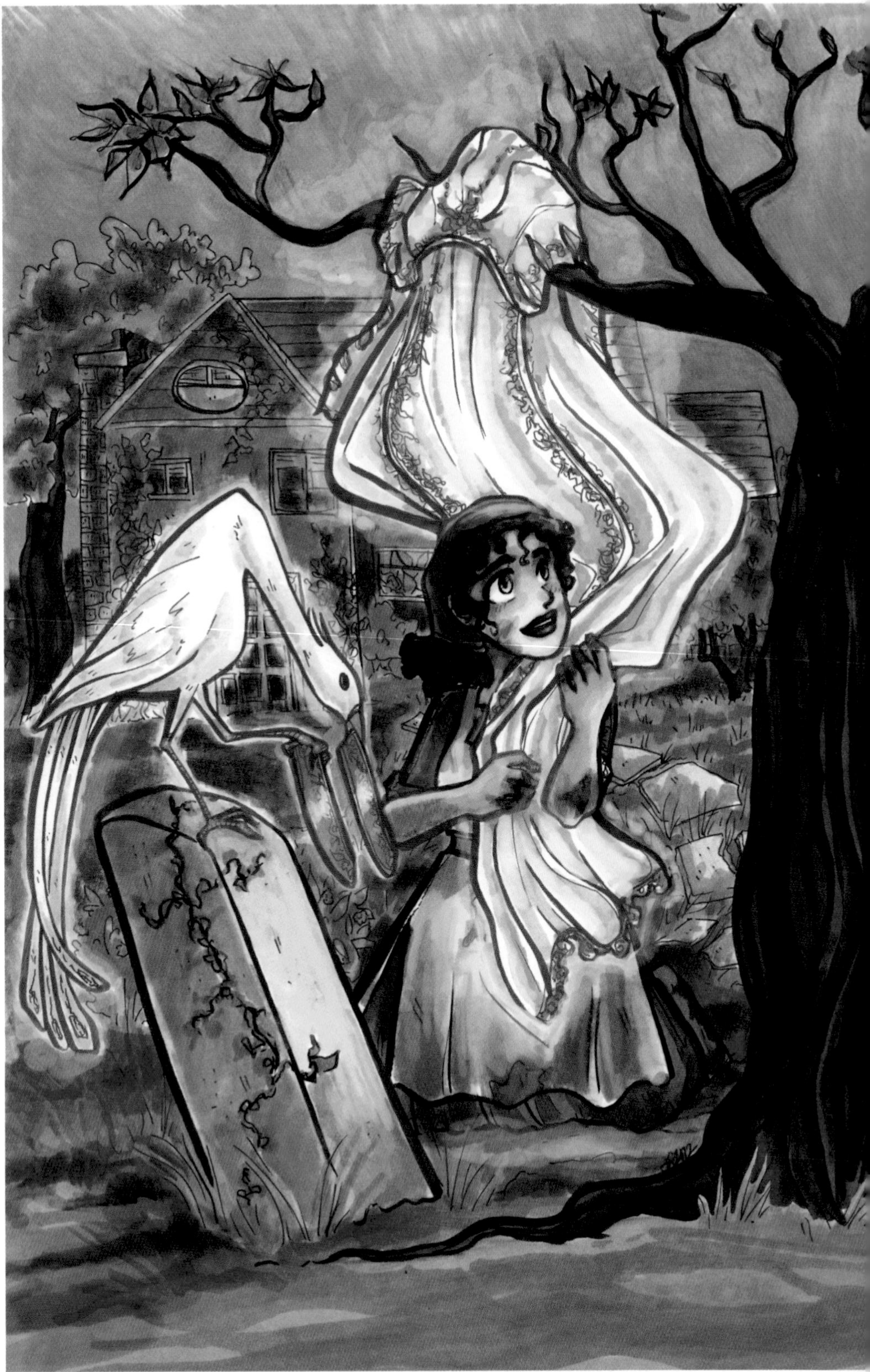

"Cinderella" by Elle Skinner

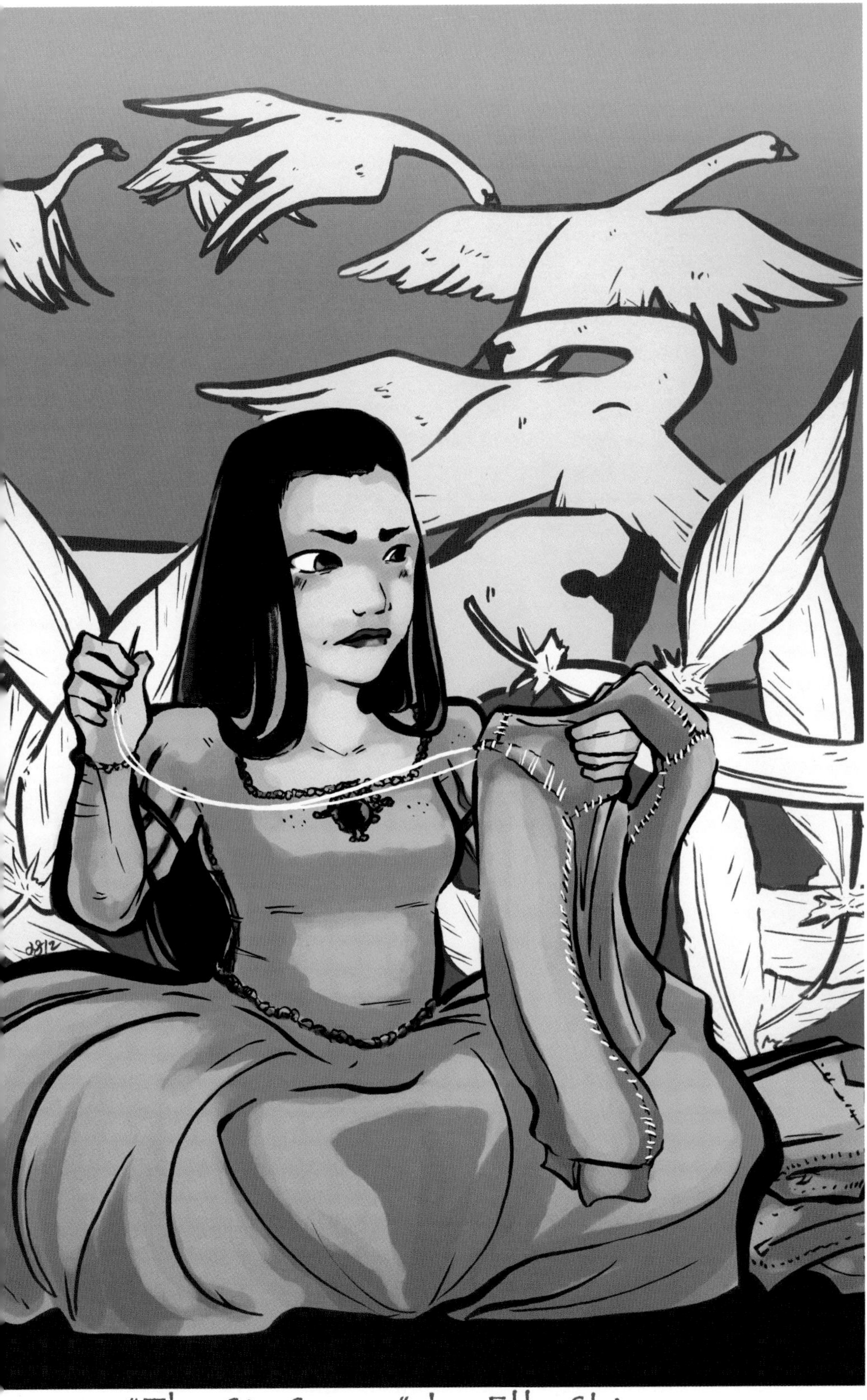

"The Six Swans" by Elle Skinner

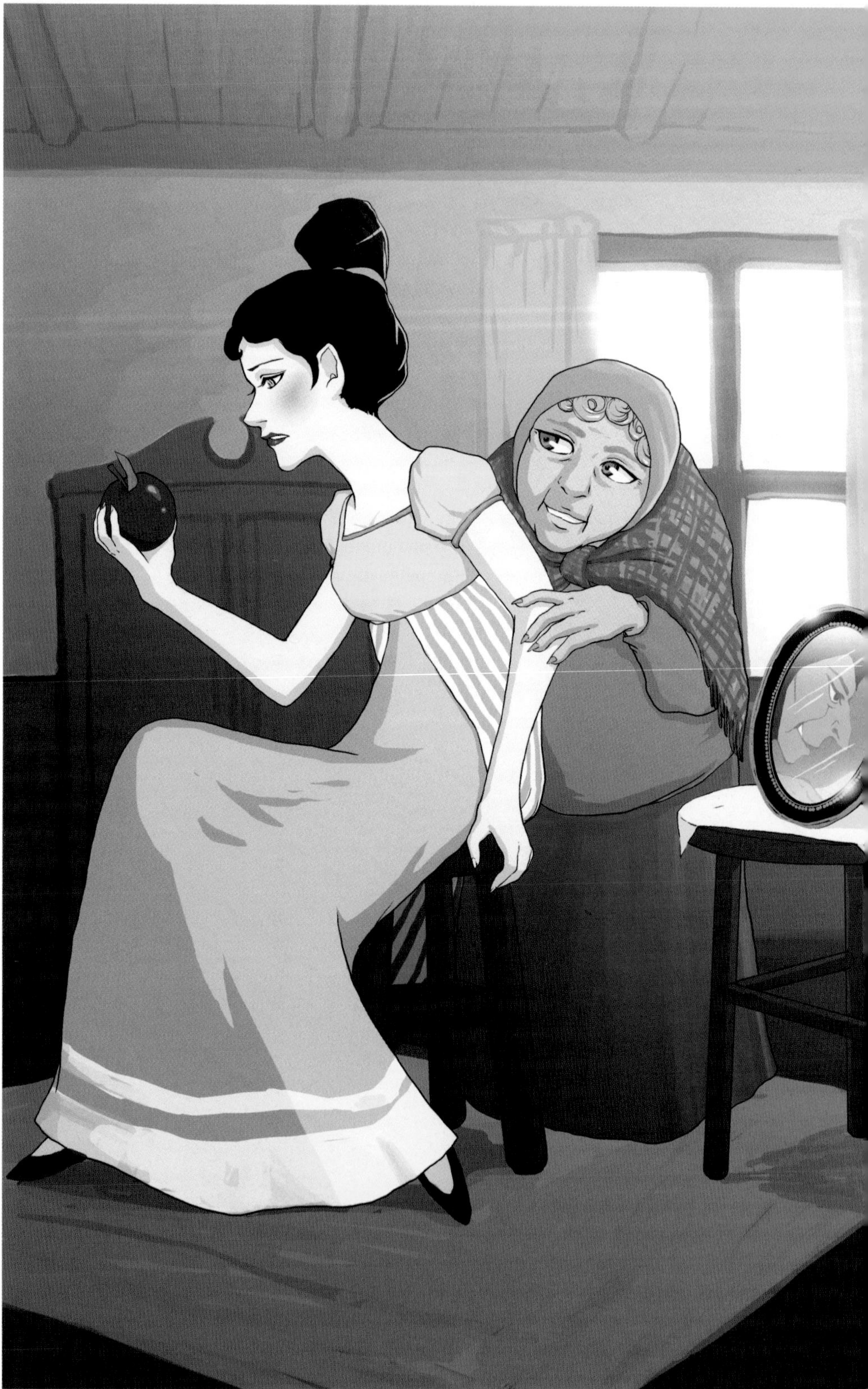

"Snow White" by Louisa Roy

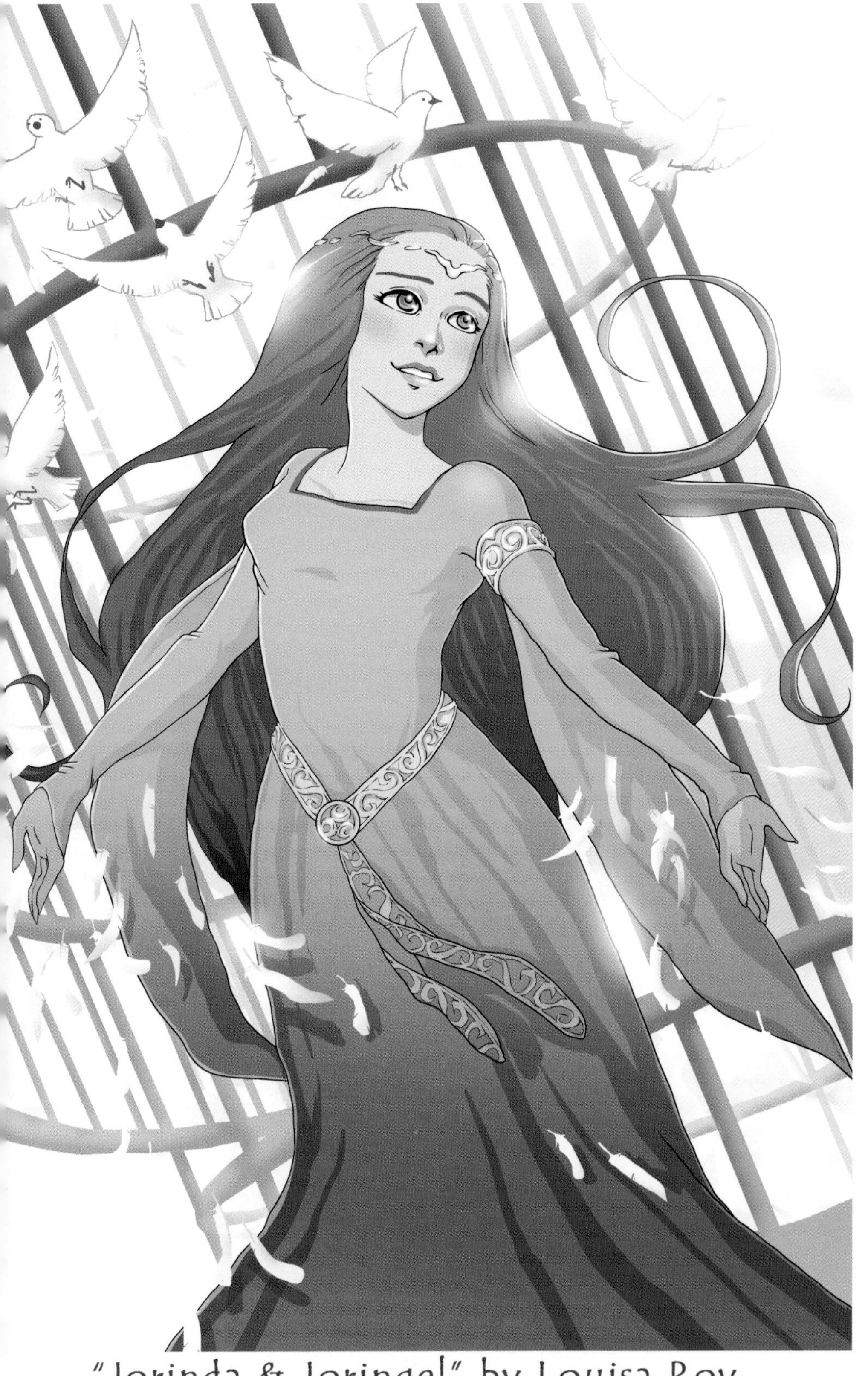

"Jorinda & Joringel" by Louisa Roy

Thank you for making this book possible

Hannah Karahkwenhawe Stacey, Cora Anderson
Kayleigh Calder, Ann Jun (Salanth),
Bob Aarhus, Chelsea Jahaliel, Amanda D Wolfe

Allan Money, Lindsay Watson, Joy Trujillo, Kelly Minckler
A Cedoz, Annie Amagai, Jessica Gant, Hans Olofsson,
Courtland Eppelsheimer, Elena Murphy, Angelia Pitman,
Hannah, Diane K. Flores, Heather Pitre, Cassandra Silvia,
Jason M Bissey, Princess Sarah of Miamisburg, C. Eldritch,
Marielle Messing, Mehmi, Donald and Sabrina Sutherland,
Vicki Hsu, Brandon Eaker, Matthew Bates, Ada Husten,
Margaret Colville, Nelson "LastAndroid" Beers, Dian Xin,
Alyssa Boettinger, Jennifer Edmondson, Bryce Armstrong,
Amy L. Miller, Doofy, Eric Agena, Lexie, John Merklinghaus
Emily Jane McDowell, Connemara, Mel Williams, cosleia,
Lindsey Parker, "D.J., Karen, Trae & Evan Cole", James C King
Katherine S, Nick R, M. Murase, Jennifer M. Thomas, Nina
Kathryn Carter, Sarah Rice, Ilana J Sprongl, Sarah Watson,
Brandon Oosterhoff, Joshua Marc Bement, Harald Demler
Tony Mattheis, Randy 'Mirokunite' Snow, Jessie Hoesing,
Barbie 'wench' Grover, Harri Smolander, Brittany Wilbert,
Gavran, Sol Rodriguez, Jennifer Denton, Sandra Wheeler,
Josh Fitzwater, Kristin Clark, Jason Green, Insaneydo, Rax,
Daniel Cook, Fiona E. DiGiandomenico, L. Karpoff,
Darth Vader, elizabeth catharine, Shana Dennis,
J L Molloy, Beth Revis, Trishia Carinio

...and so many more!